CertiPrep – CompTIA ITF+ (FC0-U61) Exam Prep Book 2025–2026

CertiPrep

Published by CertiPrep Publishing, 2025.

CERTIPREP – COMPTIA ITF+ (FC0-U61) EXAM PREP BOOK 2025–2026

First edition. November 11, 2025.

ISBN: 979-8232201876

Written by CertiPrep.

Table of Contents

Disclaimer

This book is an independent study resource created to help candidates prepare for the CompTIA IT Fundamentals (ITF+) exam (FC0-U61). It is not sponsored, endorsed, or approved by CompTIA, and it is not an official CompTIA training product.

CompTIA may update ITF+ exam objectives, policies, and testing procedures at any time. You are responsible for reviewing the most current exam details, exam objectives, and candidate policies on the official CompTIA website before you sit for the exam.

Every reasonable effort has been made to ensure accuracy at the time of writing, but we cannot guarantee that all information will remain current or error-free. Using this book does not guarantee a passing score. Your results will depend on your background, comfort with technology, hands-on practice, and study habits.

"CompTIA," "CompTIA IT Fundamentals," "CompTIA ITF+," "FC0-U61," and related marks are trademarks of CompTIA Properties, LLC. This book is independent of CompTIA and is not sponsored, endorsed, or affiliated with the organization.

About This Book

THIS CERTIPREP GUIDE is built to match the feel of your other exam prep books: conversational, practical, and tightly aligned to the official exam objectives instead of being a dry reference.

The CompTIA ITF+ (FC0-U61) exam covers six domains:

1. IT Concepts and Terminology – 17%
2. Infrastructure – 22%
3. Applications and Software – 18%
4. Software Development – 12%
5. Database Fundamentals – 11%
6. Security – 20%

This book follows that roadmap. Chapters are short and focused (10 mini-sections per chapter), designed so you can study effectively in 15–25 minute blocks. Each core chapter gives you:

- A quick, high-yield overview
- A small set of key bullets you *must* remember
- A straightforward explanation in plain English
- Practice questions (with rationales) at the end of the chapter

At the back of the book, you'll find a full-length practice exam built to feel like the real FC0-U61: 75 multiple-choice questions with mixed domains and realistic phrasing.

About the CompTIA ITF+ Certification

COMPTIA IT FUNDAMENTALS (ITF+) is CompTIA's "on-ramp" certification. It's meant to answer two big questions:

1. "Do I actually *like* IT?"
2. "Do I have the basic skills to move on to A+ and other IT certs?"

The FC0-U61 exam validates that you can:

- Understand core IT concepts (data, computing, troubleshooting basics)
- Recognize common hardware, devices, and networking basics
- Work with operating systems, applications, and web browsers
- Understand basic software development ideas
- Grasp database and data concepts at a beginner level
- Identify and avoid common security risks

Exam snapshot (FC0-U61)

- Number of questions: up to 75
- Question type: multiple choice
- Time limit: 60 minutes
- Passing score: 650 (on a scale of 900)
- Experience required: none officially, but basic computer familiarity helps

Who This Book Is For

THIS BOOK IS WRITTEN for:

- Students considering an IT or cyber career
- Career changers who want to test the waters in tech
- Non-IT professionals who need stronger "tech fluency"
- Absolute beginners who feel a bit intimidated by "all this computer stuff"

It assumes:

- You know how to use a mouse/trackpad and type (even if slowly)
- You may have used Windows, macOS, or a phone—but you might not know *how* they really work behind the scenes

You *do not* need:

- Prior programming experience
- Professional IT experience
- Any other certification

How to Use This Book

YOU CAN TREAT THIS as:

- A full study course over 4–8 weeks, **or**
- A structured review in the last 2–3 weeks before your exam

A simple plan:

1. **Read one chapter at a time.** Don't worry about memorizing every word—focus on the big ideas and bold terms.
2. **Do the practice questions immediately after the chapter.** Don't peek at answers.
3. **Check the answer key and read the explanations.** Mark any question you miss or guess on.
4. **Revisit those weak spots.** Reread the matching sections in the chapter and summarize them in your own words.

After you finish all content chapters, take the **full-length practice exam** under "real" conditions: 60 minutes, no notes, no pausing. Use that score to target your final review.

Book Overview

PART I – EXAM FOUNDATIONS & IT Mindset

1. **ITF+ Exam Overview and IT Fundamentals Mindset**
2. Tech Roles, Career Paths, and How ITF+ Fits In
3. Smart Study Plans, Labs, and Exam-Day Strategy

Part II – IT Concepts & Terminology (17%) (CompTIA CDN[1])
4. Data, Notation Systems, and Units (Binary, Hex, Storage, Speed)
5. Computing Basics and Troubleshooting Methodology
Part III – Infrastructure (22%)
6. Devices, Interfaces, and Peripherals
7. Inside the Computer: Components and Storage
8. Networks, Internet Services, and Wireless Basics
Part IV – Applications & Software (18%)
9. Operating Systems: What They Do and How They Differ
10. Productivity, Collaboration, and Business Software
11. Web Browsers, Cloud Apps, and Software Licensing

---

1. https://comptiacdn.azureedge.net/webcontent/docs/default-source/booksamples/itfplus_studyguide_fc0-u61_samplelesson.pdf?utm_source=chatgpt.com

Chapter 1

ITF+ Exam Overview and IT Fundamentals Mindset

This chapter introduces how the CompTIA ITF+ exam works and what it expects from you as a candidate. You'll see how the exam is structured, what domains it covers, and how to think like someone beginning an IT journey. The goal is to help you approach the rest of this book with the right expectations and mindset.

1.1 ITF+ Exam Snapshot

THE ITF+ (FC0-U61) exam is a beginner-friendly, multiple-choice test that measures your understanding of basic IT concepts. Before you start studying, you should know how long the exam is, how many questions you'll see, and how your score is calculated. Knowing the format reduces anxiety and lets you plan your test-taking strategy.

- **Number of questions and time limit**
- **Question types and difficulty level**
- **Passing score and scoring scale**

The ITF+ exam typically includes up to 75 multiple-choice questions and gives you 60 minutes to complete them. That means you have less than a minute per question on average, so pacing yourself is important. The questions are short, but you still need time to read carefully and avoid rushing. Even though the exam is designed for beginners, some questions will feel tricky or technical at first glance. Understanding the length and timing up front helps you practice under similar conditions and avoid surprises on exam day.

Most ITF+ questions are straightforward multiple-choice items. Some are simple definition questions, while others are short scenarios that describe a problem and ask what you should do. The exam does not expect expert-level troubleshooting or advanced math; instead, it focuses on common sense, basic IT literacy, and recognizing key terms. Distractors (wrong answers) may be partially correct to test whether you truly understand the concept. Because of this, reading every word in the question and every answer choice is crucial.

Your score is reported on a scale (for example, 100–900), and you must achieve at least the published passing score (such as 650) to pass. You won't see the raw number of questions you got right, but the scaled score reflects your overall performance across all domains. Not every question necessarily has the same weight, and some may be unscored pretest items. Treat every question as if it counts. Aiming comfortably above the minimum passing score in practice helps build a buffer for test-day nerves.

1.2 What ITF+ Actually Measures

ITF+ DOESN'T TRY TO turn you into a senior engineer or programmer. Instead, it measures whether you have a solid foundation in basic IT concepts that everyday users and entry-level professionals encounter. Think of it as proof that you can "speak tech" at a practical beginner level.

- **Breadth over depth of IT topics**
- **Practical, everyday tech tasks**
- **Conceptual understanding vs. memorization**

The exam covers a wide range of IT topics—hardware, software, networking, security, databases, and basic development—at a shallow depth. You don't need to know the intricate internals of every technology, but you should understand what each one is for and how it fits into the bigger picture. For example, you're not expected to design complex networks, but you should know what a router does. This broad exposure helps you see how different parts of IT connect and prepares you to specialize later.

A big focus of ITF+ is on everyday tasks people perform with technology. This includes installing common applications, connecting devices to Wi-Fi, managing files and folders, and recognizing basic security risks. The exam wants to know if you can operate and talk about technology the way someone in an office, classroom, or home environment would. These practical skills are valuable whether you pursue a formal IT career or not. They make you more self-sufficient and able to support others with simple tech issues.

While there are terms and definitions to remember, the exam is more interested in whether you truly understand what those terms mean in context. You might see a question that describes a situation without naming the concept directly, and you have to recognize what it is. Memorizing lists without understanding will only get you so far. When you study, focus on being able to explain concepts in your own words and picture how they show up in real life.

1.3 The Six Exam Domains

THE ITF+ EXAM IS DIVIDED into six domains, each representing a major area of IT knowledge. These domains guide what you need to study and how much each topic will matter on the test. Knowing their names and relative weight lets you build a smart study plan from the beginning.

- **IT Concepts & Terminology and Infrastructure**
- **Applications & Software and Software Development**
- **Database Fundamentals and Security**

The **IT Concepts & Terminology** domain covers things like data types, basic units (bits, bytes), binary vs. decimal, and general computer concepts. It ensures you can speak the basic language of IT. **Infrastructure** focuses on physical devices, their components, storage types, and how computers and other devices connect in networks. Together, these two domains make up a significant portion of the exam and give you a foundation for everything else.

The **Applications & Software** domain tests your understanding of operating systems, productivity tools (like word processors and spreadsheets), and how software is installed, managed, and updated. It also touches on web browsers and common settings users interact with. The **Software Development** domain introduces programming ideas at a very high level, such as what a programming language is, the purpose of logic and algorithms, and general development concepts. You'll see beginner-friendly questions rather than deep coding challenges.

The **Database Fundamentals** domain explains why databases exist, how data is organized into tables, records, and fields, and what basic queries do. It's about recognizing how data is stored and retrieved in structured ways. Finally, the **Security** domain focuses on common threats (like malware and social engineering), basic security principles, and practical safeguards for devices and data. Security has a relatively high weight on the exam, reflecting its importance in today's tech world. You'll need to recognize not only threats but also safe practices.

1.4 Who Takes ITF+ (and How It Fits Your Path)

ITF+ IS DESIGNED FOR people who are new to IT and want to confirm that they enjoy working with technology. It's also a good fit for non-technical roles that still interact with IT, such as customer support, office staff, and managers. Understanding the target audience helps you see why the exam looks the way it does.

- **Students and career explorers**
- **Non-IT professionals and home users**
- **A stepping stone to other certifications**

Many ITF+ candidates are students—high school, college, or vocational—who are curious about tech careers. They may not have any formal IT experience yet but want a structured way to test their interest. Passing ITF+ can boost confidence and show them they're on the right path. It can also help them stand out for internships or entry-level roles where general tech literacy is valuable. For career changers, ITF+ can serve as a gentle re-entry point into learning after years away from formal schooling.

Non-IT professionals also benefit from ITF+ because so many roles now intersect with technology. Salespeople, office managers, and team leads often need to communicate with IT staff or make basic technology decisions. Having ITF+ proves they can understand what's being discussed and make informed choices. Home users who want to be "the tech person" in their family can also use ITF+ as a structured learning goal, improving their ability to support relatives and friends.

In the bigger picture, ITF+ often sits at the start of a longer certification journey. After earning it, many candidates move on to **CompTIA A+**, which goes deeper into troubleshooting PCs, mobile devices, and operating systems. From there, paths branch into more specialized certifications like Network+ or Security+. You don't have to follow that route, but ITF+ gives you a solid foundation and a professional credential that confirms your basic skills.

1.5 How ITF+ Questions Are Built

ITF+ QUESTIONS ARE short, but the wording is intentional and precise. Understanding how questions are constructed helps you read them more effectively and avoid common traps. Words like "FIRST," "BEST," and "MOST likely" are signals that you should pay close attention to the details.

- **Short scenarios and direct questions**
- **Key words that change the meaning**
- **Distractors that test your understanding**

Most questions present a brief situation or statement and then ask you to choose the correct response from four options. A scenario might describe a user's problem, such as an inability to connect to Wi-Fi or open a file, and then ask what you should do next. Other questions may show a concept indirectly and ask what it represents. Since the scenarios are short, you must extract the important clues quickly. It's easy to skim and miss a critical phrase.

Certain words in the question stem dramatically change what the correct answer should be. When a question asks what you should do **FIRST**, it's usually looking for the initial, safest, and most logical step in a process—often something simple like checking connections or confirming settings. When it asks for the **BEST** option, more than one answer might be reasonable, and you must pick the one that is most practical and effective. "MOST likely" points you toward the most common explanation, not a rare edge case.

Distractors are wrong answers that may sound attractive or partially correct. They might be too advanced for the level of the exam, address a different problem than the one described, or simply be slightly inaccurate. The exam uses these distractors to see whether you truly understand the concept or are just guessing based on keywords. To handle them well, read every option all the way through before choosing. If two answers look similar, compare them carefully and ask which one actually matches the question's specific wording.

1.6 IT Fundamentals Thinking vs. "Random Clicking"

ITF+ IS NOT JUST ABOUT knowing facts; it's about applying a basic, logical approach to problems. CompTIA wants to see that you can think like someone who understands how to troubleshoot in a calm and structured way. Randomly clicking around is the opposite of what the exam rewards.

- **Structured troubleshooting approach**
- **Safe, minimal, and logical actions**
- **Verifying and learning from each fix**

A structured troubleshooting approach usually starts with clearly identifying the problem. That means understanding what the user is trying to do, what exactly is happening instead, and whether anything changed recently. From there, you form a simple theory about the cause and test that theory using a small, safe step. If the theory is wrong, you adjust your thinking and try again. This method is more efficient than wildly changing settings or reinstalling software without a plan.

Safe and minimal actions are important because beginners can easily make things worse by doing too much too quickly. Instead of wiping a hard drive, you might first check whether a cable is loose or whether Airplane mode is on. This kind of thinking shows that you respect the system and the user's data. The exam often rewards answers that involve simple checks and basic verification before more drastic steps. The idea is to fix the problem with as little disruption as possible.

After trying a fix, you should always verify whether it actually solved the original problem. If a user could not print before, you should confirm they can now print a test page. This verification step closes the loop and ensures that your actions had the intended effect. It also gives you a chance to learn from the experience—if your theory was right, you know what to try next time; if it was wrong, you understand more about what doesn't work. This reflective mindset is part of thinking like an IT professional, even at the fundamentals level.

1.7 Common Beginner Traps (and How to Avoid Them)

CERTAIN CONCEPTS CONSISTENTLY trip up beginners because they sound similar or seem related. The ITF+ exam likes to test these "trap pairs" to see whether you really know the difference. Learning to spot them now will save you points later.

- **RAM vs. storage devices**
- **Internet vs. World Wide Web**
- **Hardware vs. software**

RAM is the computer's short-term working memory, while storage devices like hard drives or SSDs provide long-term data storage. RAM holds active programs and data only while the computer is powered on; when the power goes off, RAM is cleared. Storage, on the other hand, keeps your files and installed programs even when the system is turned off. Questions may describe a user "running out of space" or wanting to "store more files," which relates to storage, not RAM. Understanding this distinction is a common test point.

The **Internet** and the **World Wide Web** are related but not identical. The Internet is a global network of networks that carries many kinds of traffic, including email, streaming, file transfers, and web pages. The World Wide Web (the web) is a collection of websites and web services that run on top of the Internet using protocols like HTTP and HTTPS. A question might ask which term describes the underlying global network versus the system of pages you view in a browser. Knowing the difference shows that you understand how these pieces fit together.

Hardware refers to the physical components you can touch—things like the keyboard, monitor, CPU, and cables. **Software** refers to programs and instructions, such as operating systems and applications, that run on that hardware. Some exam questions will test your ability to classify an item correctly or identify whether a problem is more likely software-related or hardware-related. Recognizing these categories helps you analyze issues logically and choose the right type of action.

1.8 Building a Realistic Study Plan Around the Domains

A GOOD STUDY PLAN RESPECTS your time, energy, and the structure of the exam. Rather than studying randomly, you should anchor your schedule to the six domains and their percentages. This helps you work steadily and feel in control of your progress.

- **Prioritizing high-weight domains**
- **Mixing reading, questions, and hands-on practice**
- **Using weekly and daily goals**

High-weight domains like Infrastructure and Security should naturally receive more of your time because they represent a larger portion of exam questions. That doesn't mean you ignore the smaller domains, but you might allocate more study sessions to those big areas. For example, you might plan extra practice questions and review sessions for networking basics and security best practices. When you build your calendar, you can visually block out more time for these topics to make sure they're not rushed.

Reading is important for building conceptual understanding, but it's not enough on its own. You should mix content reading with end-of-chapter questions and simple hands-on labs using real or virtual machines. Try things like browsing system settings, installing a basic application, or exploring network options on your own device. This combination of reading, seeing, and doing reinforces the same idea in multiple ways. It also makes studying feel less monotonous and more interactive.

Weekly and daily goals keep you moving without feeling overwhelmed. A weekly goal might be "Finish Chapters 1–3 and complete all practice questions," while a daily goal could be "Read one section and do 10 questions." Breaking your study into small, manageable chunks helps you stay consistent. Consistency is more powerful than occasional long cram sessions. By tracking your goals, you can quickly see where you're on track and where you might need an extra day of review.

1.9 Using Practice Questions the Right Way

PRACTICE QUESTIONS are one of your most powerful tools—if you use them correctly. They're not just about getting a score; they're about discovering what you understand and where you're still shaky. Treat each question as a mini lesson, whether you get it right or wrong.

- **Diagnosing strengths and weaknesses**
- **Reviewing explanations and linking back to content**
- **Simulating exam conditions over time**

When you answer practice questions, pay attention to how confident you feel, not just whether the answer turns out right. Mark questions as "Know," "Unsure," or "Guess" as you go. This helps you identify topics where you need deeper understanding, even if luck gave you a correct answer. Questions marked as "Unsure" or "Guess" are valuable clues about where to spend your next block of study time.

After grading, don't just glance at your score and move on. Read the explanations for each question, especially the ones you missed or guessed. Then link those explanations back to the relevant section of the chapter or exam objective. This double pass—question plus content review—locks the concept in more firmly. It also teaches you how exam writers think and what details they consider important.

As you get closer to exam day, it's helpful to occasionally simulate real test conditions. Set a timer, answer a block of questions without notes, and avoid pausing for distractions. This builds your mental stamina and familiarity with working under time pressure. Afterward, review your performance and adjust your study plan accordingly. Over time, you should see your scores and confidence rise together.

1.10 Putting It All Together Before You Go Deeper

THIS CHAPTER IS YOUR launchpad for the rest of the book. You now know how the exam is structured, what it measures, and how to think like a fundamentals-level IT problem solver. Before diving into the technical details, it's important to internalize these big ideas.

- **Clarity on exam purpose and structure**
- **Adopting an IT fundamentals mindset**
- **Preparing to move into domain-specific chapters**

Understanding the purpose and structure of ITF+ keeps you from feeling lost while you study. You know the number of questions, time limits, domains, and general level of difficulty. This knowledge helps you avoid over-preparing in niche areas and under-preparing in core ones. It also reduces test anxiety, because you're no longer facing an unknown challenge. Instead, you're working toward a clearly defined target.

An IT fundamentals mindset emphasizes logical thinking, careful reading, and safe, simple troubleshooting steps. You aren't expected to be a wizard, but you are expected to think through problems instead of guessing or randomly changing settings. This mindset will serve you well not only on the exam, but also in real-world situations where people rely on you for help. Approaching each problem with patience and structure is a crucial habit to build early.

With this foundation in place, you're ready to move into the domain-specific chapters that follow. Each chapter will use the same clear structure and end-of-section questions to build your knowledge step by step. As you work through them, remember the strategies you learned here: study by domain weight, use practice questions wisely, and aim for understanding rather than memorization. That combination will give you the best chance of success on the ITF+ exam.

Chapter 2

Tech Roles, Career Paths, and How ITF+ Fits In

This chapter helps you connect the ITF+ exam to real jobs and career paths. You'll see how different tech roles fit together, what skills they use day to day, and where ITF+ sits as an entry point. The goal is to help you study with a sense of direction, not just for a test score.

2.1 Why Understanding Tech Roles Matters

BEFORE YOU INVEST TIME and money into IT, it's useful to know what kinds of jobs actually exist. Many people think of "IT" as one giant role, but in reality there are many different specialties. Understanding the variety of roles helps you aim your learning toward the kind of work you might actually enjoy.

- **IT is a collection of specialties, not one job**
- **Better career decisions come from better information**
- **ITF+ gives you a safe way to explore**

IT as a field includes everything from people who fix laptops to people who design cloud systems and write software. Each role emphasizes different skills, such as troubleshooting, communication, security awareness, or coding. When you lump all of IT together, you might feel overwhelmed or assume you must be "good at everything." Recognizing that there are multiple paths lets you focus on discovering which mix of tasks actually appeals to you.

Better information leads to better decisions about your future. If you only see the stereotype of a lone programmer in a dark room, you might think IT isn't for you—when in reality there are people-focused roles, creative roles, and highly structured analytical roles. By learning what these jobs actually involve, you can rule out what doesn't fit and stay curious about what does. This keeps you from jumping into a path that doesn't match your strengths.

ITF+ fits in as a "low-risk experiment" to see how you respond to foundational concepts. As you study for the exam, you'll naturally discover which topics feel fun and which feel like a chore. Enjoying troubleshooting might point you toward support or help desk roles. Enjoying logic and problem design might point you toward development. ITF+ gives you a structured way to explore without committing to a full degree or advanced certification right away.

2.2 Major Categories of Tech Roles

TECH JOBS CAN BE GROUPED into a few broad categories, even though job titles vary between companies. Seeing these categories helps you mentally organize what you learn. It also gives you a way to talk about your interests with teachers, mentors, or potential employers.

- **Support and operations roles**
- **Build and development roles**
- **Security and governance roles**

Support and operations roles focus on keeping systems and users running day to day. These include help desk technicians, desktop support, system administrators, and operations center staff. Their work often involves answering user questions, fixing issues, monitoring systems, and performing routine maintenance. If you like solving puzzles for people and don't mind repetitive tasks with variation in the details, support and operations could be a strong fit.

Build and development roles focus on creating and improving systems or software. This category includes software developers, web developers, systems engineers, and cloud engineers. They spend a lot of time designing solutions, writing and testing code, and integrating different tools. These roles often require deeper technical knowledge and comfort with abstraction. If you enjoy building things from scratch and refining them over time, you may be drawn to this side of IT.

Security and governance roles focus on protecting systems, data, and users. Examples include security analysts, compliance specialists, and risk managers. Their work involves identifying vulnerabilities, monitoring for threats, designing controls, and ensuring policies are followed. These roles blend technical knowledge with awareness of laws, regulations, and human behavior. If you like thinking about "what could go wrong" and how to prevent it, security and governance might be appealing.

2.3 Entry-Level Roles You Can Aim For

YOU DON'T HAVE TO BECOME a senior engineer overnight. There are many entry-level roles designed for people with basic skills and a good attitude. Knowing what these roles look like gives you a target to aim for after ITF+ and related learning.

- **Help desk and technical support**
- **Junior or trainee roles in IT operations**
- **Tech-adjacent roles that benefit from ITF+**

Help desk and technical support positions are classic starting points in IT. In these roles, you respond to user issues via phone, chat, or in person. You might help users reset passwords, install basic software, troubleshoot connectivity issues, or explain how to use common applications. ITF+ prepares you by giving you the language and concepts behind these everyday problems. Over time, strong performers often move into more specialized or advanced positions.

Junior or trainee roles in IT operations include positions like junior system administrator assistant, data center technician, or IT intern. These jobs involve tasks such as racking and cabling equipment, monitoring alerts, applying basic updates, and documenting procedures. While they may sound intimidating, they often focus on repeating clear steps and learning from more experienced staff. ITF+ gives you the baseline understanding of hardware, networks, and security that makes on-the-job training much easier.

Tech-adjacent roles are jobs that are not purely "IT," but where IT knowledge is a big advantage. Examples include office administrator with IT duties, software sales associate, or customer success specialist for a tech product. In these roles, you might configure simple settings, explain technical concepts, or coordinate with IT teams. Having ITF+ on your resume helps you stand out by showing you understand more than just basic computer use.

2.4 What Support & Help Desk Roles Actually Do

SUPPORT AND HELP DESK roles are often the front line of IT. They see a wide variety of issues, ranging from simple "how do I...?" questions to more complex connectivity or configuration problems. Understanding what these roles do day to day helps you decide whether this kind of work fits your personality.

- **User-facing communication and problem solving**
- **Basic troubleshooting and documentation**
- **Soft skills: patience and clarity**

User-facing communication is a major part of help desk work. You're not just fixing computers; you're helping people who are frustrated, confused, or under time pressure. That means you need to listen carefully, ask clarifying questions, and restate the problem in your own words. Sometimes the issue isn't technical at all, but about expectations or misunderstandings. If you enjoy helping others and can stay calm when someone else is stressed, this environment may suit you.

Basic troubleshooting is at the core of support work. You'll check power, cables, network connections, logins, and software settings. You'll walk users through steps like rebooting, closing and reopening applications, or trying a different device. You'll also learn to use ticket systems to record the problem, the steps taken, and the result. ITF+ gives you the background on hardware, software, and networks so these tasks make sense instead of feeling like random magic.

Soft skills like patience and clarity are just as important as technical knowledge in a support role. Users may not describe problems in technical terms, and they may repeat themselves or leave out critical details. Your job is to stay patient, avoid blaming them, and explain solutions in a way they can follow. Practicing these skills early—during group projects, in class, or at home—can make you much more effective and happier in a help desk environment.

2.5 What System & Network Roles Actually Do

SYSTEM AND NETWORK roles focus on the behind-the-scenes technology that keeps organizations running. These jobs may be less visible to end users, but they are crucial for performance, reliability, and security. Understanding these roles can help you decide if you prefer working with systems more than with people directly.

- **System administrators and their responsibilities**
- **Network technicians and administrators**
- **The path from support to systems and networks**

System administrators manage servers, operating systems, and related services. They install and configure server software, manage user accounts and permissions, apply updates, and monitor system health. Their work ensures that shared resources like file servers, email, and business applications are available and functioning. While ITF+ doesn't make you a sysadmin, it introduces you to the concepts—like operating systems, storage, and security—that these roles rely on every day.

Network technicians and administrators focus on routers, switches, firewalls, and wireless access points. They ensure that data can move efficiently and securely between devices and locations. Tasks may include configuring IP addresses, managing VLANs, monitoring network traffic, and troubleshooting connectivity issues. If you enjoy thinking about how different pieces connect and communicate, networking might appeal to you. ITF+ gives you a basic vocabulary for understanding these systems so later certifications like Network+ are less intimidating.

Many professionals move from support roles into system or network positions over time. A common path is starting on the help desk, then gradually taking on more technical tasks under supervision—such as assisting with server updates or helping install new network equipment. As your experience and certifications grow, your responsibilities expand. ITF+ is an early stepping stone that signals you're serious about learning and gives you a context for on-the-job experiences.

2.6 What Software & Web Development Roles Actually Do

SOFTWARE AND WEB DEVELOPMENT roles focus on creating applications and services. While ITF+ is not a programming exam, it introduces basic development concepts that can spark your interest. Understanding what these roles actually involve can help you decide whether to explore coding more deeply.

- **Software developers and application builders**
- **Web developers and front-end/back-end work**
- **How ITF+ concepts support learning to code**

Software developers design, build, and maintain applications that run on computers, mobile devices, or servers. They spend much of their time writing code, debugging errors, testing features, and collaborating with other developers and stakeholders. Their work requires attention to detail and the ability to break problems into small, manageable pieces. While ITF+ won't teach you a full programming language, its focus on logic and basic development terminology makes your first steps into coding less confusing.

Web developers focus on websites and web applications. Front-end developers handle what users see and interact with—layouts, buttons, forms, and visual styles—using languages like HTML, CSS, and JavaScript. Back-end developers work on the server side, dealing with databases, APIs, and application logic. Some developers work across both areas, known as full-stack development. ITF+ helps by explaining concepts like clients and servers, data storage, and basic security concerns that web developers must understand.

ITF+ concepts such as algorithms, data, and security awareness provide a foundation for learning to code safely and effectively. Knowing what a database is or how data is structured will make database-related programming tasks more intuitive. Understanding basic security ideas helps you avoid common mistakes, like insecure handling of passwords or user input. If you find yourself enjoying the software development domain in ITF+, that's a good sign you might want to take a beginner programming course or try simple coding projects.

2.7 What Cybersecurity Roles Actually Do

CYBERSECURITY ROLES exist to protect systems, data, and people from digital threats. These jobs have become more visible in recent years due to high-profile breaches and increasing regulation. Even if you don't become a security specialist, having basic security awareness is essential in almost every IT role.

- **Security analysts and monitoring**
- **Security engineers and architects**
- **Security awareness in every role**

Security analysts often work in security operations centers (SOCs), where they monitor systems and logs for suspicious activity. They investigate alerts, determine whether they represent real threats, and escalate issues when needed. Their tasks can include analyzing malware behavior, checking access patterns, and responding to incidents according to documented procedures. ITF+ introduces core security terminology and concepts that make these tasks more approachable later on.

Security engineers and architects design and implement security controls at a system or network level. They may configure firewalls, set up intrusion detection systems, manage encryption standards, and work with development teams to build more secure applications. These roles require strong technical skills and a deep understanding of how attackers think. While ITF+ is only a starting point, it helps you understand why security must be integrated into everything, not added as an afterthought.

Security awareness is a shared responsibility, not just the job of the security team. Help desk staff must recognize phishing attempts, developers must protect user data, and system administrators must apply patches and configure permissions correctly. ITF+ emphasizes this by making security one of its main domains. No matter what path you choose, the security concepts you learn now will help you avoid risky behaviors and contribute to safer systems.

2.8 How ITF+ Connects to Other Certifications

ITF+ IS OFTEN THE FIRST step in a longer journey of certifications and learning. Understanding how it connects to other credentials helps you plan ahead even while you focus on the fundamentals. You don't need to decide your entire future right now, but seeing the bigger picture can be motivating.

- **ITF+ as a foundation for A+**
- **Branching into networking and security certs**
- **Non-CompTIA paths that benefit from ITF+**

CompTIA A+ is a common next step after ITF+. A+ dives deeper into hardware, operating systems, troubleshooting, and basic networking. Many entry-level IT support roles list A+ as a preferred or required certification. ITF+ gives you the baseline familiarity with these topics so that when you later see more detailed A+ material, it feels like expanding on what you already know instead of starting from zero.

From A+, many people move toward Network+ and Security+. Network+ focuses on networking concepts, protocols, and infrastructure, making it a natural fit for people who enjoy connectivity topics. Security+ focuses on a broad overview of security principles and practices, suitable for those interested in cybersecurity. ITF+ doesn't replace these certifications, but it primes you for them by building your comfort with key vocabulary and basic concepts in networks and security.

Beyond CompTIA, ITF+ is a good foundation for vendor-specific or cloud-focused paths. For example, understanding basic IT and security concepts helps when you tackle cloud certifications, software-specific admin exams, or even beginner-level programming credentials. Employers may not require ITF+ in every case, but it still shows that you've taken initiative to learn fundamentals. That can make you a more attractive candidate for training programs and entry-level opportunities.

2.9 Matching Your Interests and Personality to Roles

NOT EVERY IT JOB SUITS every personality, and that's okay. Part of exploring IT is figuring out what kinds of tasks and environments you enjoy. Matching your interests and personality to potential roles makes your career journey more sustainable and satisfying.

- **People-focused vs. system-focused work**
- **Structured vs. creative problem solving**
- **Pace, stress, and work environment preferences**

Some roles are very people-focused, such as help desk or customer-facing technical support. In these jobs, your day revolves around communication, empathy, and managing expectations. Other roles are more system-focused, such as back-end development or infrastructure engineering, where you may spend more time working with tools and code than with end users. Both types of roles are important, and ITF+ gives you exposure to both sides so you can see which feels more natural.

Different roles also emphasize different styles of problem solving. Some positions, like security analysis or operations, may require highly structured, procedure-driven approaches. Others, like web development or automation scripting, allow for more creative experimentation and design. As you study for ITF+, pay attention to whether you're more energized by clear processes or by open-ended challenges. That clue can guide you toward roles that fit your natural working style.

Pace, stress level, and work environment vary widely across IT roles. Some jobs involve frequent interruptions and changing priorities, such as frontline support. Others focus on longer projects with fewer daily surprises, such as certain development or project roles. Think about how you handle stress and whether you prefer stable routines or dynamic situations. Whatever your preference, there is likely an IT role that fits—but you'll be happier if you consciously aim for environments that match who you are.

2.10 Using ITF+ Study Time to Explore Career Options

STUDYING FOR ITF+ IS not just about passing an exam; it's also a chance to test-drive different parts of the IT world. By paying attention to which topics you enjoy most, you can gather real data about your interests. This chapter encourages you to treat your learning as both exam prep and career exploration.

- **Notice which domains you enjoy most**
- **Do small experiments outside the textbook**
- **Talk to people and adjust your path over time**

As you work through each domain in the ITF+ objectives, notice how you feel. If studying hardware and cabling energizes you, infrastructure roles might be appealing. If the software development section feels exciting, that's a hint you might enjoy coding. Similarly, if security scenarios fascinate you, you might explore cybersecurity later. Your reactions during study are powerful clues about what types of work could be satisfying long-term.

Small experiments outside the textbook can confirm or challenge your impressions. For example, if the development section seems interesting, try a free beginner coding tutorial. If networking grabs your attention, poke around your home router's interface (safely) or build a small lab in a virtual environment. These short experiments don't require a huge time commitment but give you a more realistic sense of the day-to-day tasks in a given area.

Finally, talking to people is one of the best ways to refine your path. Ask teachers, local IT staff, or online communities what their jobs are really like. Share what you're learning from ITF+ and which parts you enjoy. Over time, you'll get a clearer picture of which roles align with your interests and lifestyle. Remember that your path doesn't have to be perfect from day one; the key is to keep learning, adjusting, and using each step—including ITF+—as a building block.

Chapter 3

Smart Study Plans, Labs, and Exam-Day Strategy

This chapter focuses on how to study for ITF+ in a way that actually works, not just what to study. You'll learn how to build a realistic study plan, use labs and practice questions effectively, and handle exam day with confidence. The goal is to help you work smarter, not just harder, as you prepare.

3.1 Why Strategy Matters More Than Cramming

MANY TEST-TAKERS TRY to cram a huge amount of information at the last minute, hoping it will stick. Unfortunately, that approach usually leads to stress and shallow understanding. A simple, consistent strategy will almost always beat last-minute panic.

- **Consistent small sessions beat occasional marathons**
- **Understanding concepts outperforms pure memorization**
- **A plan reduces stress and decision fatigue**

Short, consistent study sessions give your brain time to process and store information. Spending 30–45 focused minutes several times a week is far more effective than a single six-hour cram the night before. This spacing effect allows you to revisit material just as you're about to forget it, strengthening your memory. It also makes studying less intimidating and easier to fit into your daily life. Over time, these small investments add up to a solid foundation.

Memorizing lists without understanding might work for very short-term recall, but it falls apart when questions are written in different words or presented as scenarios. When you understand the underlying concept, you can handle unfamiliar phrasing or situations more easily. ITF+ questions often test how well you grasp ideas in context, not whether you can recite a definition word for word. Focusing on the "why" behind each topic makes you more flexible and confident.

Having a plan reduces the mental energy spent deciding what to study each day. When you know that "today is Chapter 4, Section 4.3 plus 10 questions," you don't waste time debating your next move. This lowers stress and makes it easier to actually start. A simple written plan—on paper, in a planner, or in a digital tool—can keep you on track and help you see your progress at a glance.

3.2 Building a 4–8 Week Study Plan

YOU CAN PREPARE FOR ITF+ over different timelines, depending on how much time you have and how familiar you are with technology. A 4–8 week window is a common range for most candidates. Designing your plan around your life increases the odds that you'll stick with it.

- **Choosing a realistic timeframe**
- **Breaking the content into weekly goals**
- **Turning weekly goals into daily tasks**

Choosing a realistic timeframe starts with an honest look at your schedule and current knowledge. If you already use computers regularly and have some basic familiarity with IT concepts, four weeks of steady study might be enough. If you're newer to technology or have a busy life with work and family, six to eight weeks may be more comfortable. The key is to pick an end date that feels challenging but workable, not impossible.

Once you pick the timeframe, divide the book and exam objectives into weekly goals. For example, Week 1 might cover Chapters 1–3, Week 2 might cover Infrastructure topics, and so on. Each week should include reading and practice questions, not just one or the other. Try to keep the workload roughly balanced so you don't end up with an overwhelming final week. Having clear weekly targets gives you a sense of progress and keeps you from drifting.

Weekly goals become much more achievable when you convert them into small daily tasks. Instead of "do all of Infrastructure this week," you might say, "On Monday, read sections 6.1–6.3 and answer 10 questions; on Tuesday, read 6.4–6.5 and do 10 more questions," and so forth. Daily tasks should be small enough that you can check them off in 30–60 minutes. Small wins build momentum and make it easier to come back the next day.

3.3 Using the Exam Objectives as Your Map

THE OFFICIAL ITF+ EXAM objectives tell you exactly what topics can appear on the test. Treat them as your master checklist while you study. Aligning your book, labs, and practice questions with these objectives ensures you're not missing anything important.

- **Downloading and reviewing the objectives**
- **Checking off topics as you learn them**
- **Mapping book chapters to objective bullets**

Your first step should be to download the official exam objectives from CompTIA's website. This document lists domains, subdomains, and specific bullet points describing the skills and knowledge areas tested. Reading through it once, even if you don't understand everything yet, gives you a clear overview of what's ahead. It also shows you how broad the exam is and helps you avoid focusing too much on just one area.

As you study, use the objectives as a checklist. When you finish a section in the book, find the matching bullet points in the objectives and mark them as "seen" or "practiced." You might use checkmarks, color-coding, or brief notes like "review again" or "feels strong." This visual tracking lets you see which areas are covered well and which still need attention. It's especially helpful during final review weeks.

Many prep books, including this one, are designed to align closely with the exam objectives. Mapping chapters to the objective bullets helps you understand which parts of the book correspond to which exam sections. If you encounter a practice question that confuses you, you can trace it back to the relevant objective and then to the section that explains it. This back-and-forth strengthens your understanding and keeps your study efforts focused where they matter most.

3.4 Active Reading and Note-Taking Techniques

PASSIVE READING—JUST sliding your eyes over the page—doesn't lead to strong retention. Active reading means engaging with the material as you go. Simple note-taking techniques can turn reading time into learning time.

- **Highlighting sparingly and with purpose**
- **Writing short summaries in your own words**

- **Creating quick question-and-answer notes**

Highlighting can be useful, but only when used sparingly. If you highlight every sentence, nothing stands out. Instead, highlight just the key phrases or sentences that capture the main idea of a paragraph or concept. You might choose to mark definitions, key relationships (like "RAM is temporary"), or steps in a process. Later, when you review, these highlights can guide your focus instead of forcing you to reread everything.

Writing short summaries in your own words forces you to process and restate the ideas. After finishing a section, pause and write two or three sentences explaining what you just learned. You can do this in the margins, in a notebook, or in a digital note app. If you struggle to explain something simply, that's a sign you need to revisit the text. Over time, these summaries become a personalized mini-guide you can use for quick review.

Creating quick question-and-answer notes helps you prepare for exam-style thinking. For example, you might write: "Q: What is the main difference between RAM and storage? A: RAM is temporary working memory; storage is long-term." These mini flashcards—either on paper or in digital form—can be reviewed in spare moments. They encourage you to recall information actively instead of just recognizing it on the page.

3.5 The Right Way to Use Practice Questions

PRACTICE QUESTIONS are more than just a way to test yourself at the end. They're tools you can use throughout your study process to diagnose strengths and weaknesses. The way you approach these questions can dramatically affect how much you learn from them.

- **Answering honestly and tracking confidence**
- **Reviewing explanations, not just scores**
- **Turning missed questions into targeted review**

When you answer practice questions, be honest about how sure you are. You can quickly mark each question as "Know," "Unsure," or "Guess" before checking the answer. This lets you see where you are truly confident versus where you might have been lucky. Even if you get a question right, a "Guess" marking tells you that topic still needs more attention. Over time, you want to see more "Know" and fewer "Guess" marks.

After finishing a set of questions, avoid the temptation to just look at your score and move on. Spend time reading the explanations for both correct and incorrect answers. Ask yourself why the right answer is right and why the wrong options are wrong. This process helps you understand how questions are constructed and what clues to look for in the wording. It also teaches you exam-taking skills, not just content.

Missed questions are some of your best teachers. For each one, identify which topic or objective it relates to, then go back to that section in the book. Reread the explanation and, if possible, write a brief note about what you misunderstood. You might even create a mini flashcard based on that question. Treating mistakes as feedback rather than failures helps you improve quickly and makes studying feel more productive.

3.6 Simple Labs You Can Do at Home

HANDS-ON EXPERIENCE makes abstract concepts feel real. You don't need a full lab environment or expensive hardware to practice many ITF+ skills. With a basic computer and internet access, you can do simple labs that reinforce what you're learning.

- **Exploring operating system settings and tools**

- **Practicing basic networking and connectivity tasks**
- **Trying safe experiments with software installation and removal**

Exploring your computer's operating system is one of the easiest and most powerful labs. You can browse the Control Panel or Settings app, look at system information, and explore storage and network settings. Try opening Task Manager or a similar tool to see running processes and performance graphs. When you read about a concept in the book—like user accounts or updates—see if you can find and view those settings on your own system. Connecting the words on the page to real screens makes them easier to remember.

Basic networking and connectivity tasks are also simple to practice at home. You can disconnect and reconnect to Wi-Fi, check the properties of your network adapter, and observe what happens when you try to access the internet without a connection. If you have multiple devices, experiment with sharing files or using hotspot features, within safe and legal boundaries. These experiences make the networking domain less abstract and help you visualize how devices communicate.

Software installation and removal provide another set of useful labs. Download legitimate, safe software from trusted sources, then install and uninstall it while paying attention to the steps involved. Watch for prompts about permissions, installation locations, and shortcuts. Note how the software appears in your Start menu or applications list. These observations connect directly to exam topics about applications, updates, and system changes.

3.7 Managing Time and Avoiding Burnout

STUDYING FOR AN EXAM is a project that takes energy and attention. If you push yourself too hard without breaks or balance, you risk burnout. Managing your time and energy well keeps your study effort sustainable.

- **Using time blocks and breaks**
- **Balancing study with rest and other responsibilities**
- **Recognizing signs of overload and adjusting**

Time blocking means setting aside specific chunks of time for focused work, followed by short breaks. For example, you might study for 25 minutes, then take a 5-minute break, repeating this cycle a few times. During study blocks, silence distractions as much as possible—put your phone away, close unrelated tabs, and let others know you're focusing. Breaks should be real breaks: stand up, stretch, or grab water rather than scrolling social media endlessly. This rhythm keeps your brain more alert.

Balancing study with the rest of your life is crucial. If you have work, school, or family responsibilities, your plan needs to fit around those, not ignore them. It's better to commit to three realistic sessions per week and stick to them than to promise daily sessions and constantly fall short. Protecting sleep, exercise, and some downtime actually improves your ability to learn. Think of studying as part of a healthy routine, not something that completely replaces everything else.

Recognizing signs of overload—like constant fatigue, loss of motivation, or difficulty concentrating—is important. If you notice these, it may be time to dial back slightly, change your study method, or add variety with labs or different question formats. Sometimes a single day off to rest can reset your energy better than forcing yourself through another unproductive session. Being kind but honest with yourself helps you maintain steady progress over time.

3.8 Last-Week Review Plan

THE FINAL WEEK BEFORE your exam is not the time to learn everything from scratch. Instead, it's for reviewing, reinforcing, and sharpening your test-taking skills. A simple last-week plan can make a big difference in your confidence.

- **Focusing on weak areas first**
- **Doing a timed practice exam**
- **Scheduling light review the day before**

Start your last week by identifying your weakest areas using your notes, objective checklist, and past question performance. Spend the first few days reviewing those topics more intensively, rereading key sections, and doing focused practice questions. The goal is to pull your weakest domains up to a comfortable level, not to make them perfect. By targeting your gaps, you get more improvement for your time.

At least once in the last week, take a full or near-full practice exam under timed conditions. Simulate the real environment as much as you can: no notes, no pausing, and a fixed time limit. Afterward, review your results carefully, paying attention to both content mistakes and pacing issues. This gives you a realistic sense of how ready you are and whether you need to adjust anything in the remaining days.

The day before the exam should be a light review day, not a marathon cram session. Skim your summaries, objective checklist, and high-yield notes. Maybe do a small set of questions to stay warm, but avoid exhausting yourself. Try to relax, get good sleep, and prepare any logistics (like directions to the test center or checking your online testing setup). You want to walk into exam day as rested and calm as possible.

3.9 Exam-Day Logistics and Mindset

GOOD EXAM-DAY LOGISTICS and mindset can prevent avoidable problems and help you perform at your best. Even if you know the material, stress and disorganization can hurt your score. Planning ahead lets you focus your mental energy on the questions themselves.

- **Preparing logistics ahead of time**
- **Managing nerves during the exam**
- **Using the full exam time wisely**

Logistics include things like knowing where your test center is, what time you need to arrive, and what identification you must bring. If you're testing online, it means checking your system requirements, internet connection, and any proctoring rules in advance. Lay out what you need the night before so you're not scrambling in the morning. Removing these small uncertainties reduces stress and prevents last-minute panics.

Managing nerves during the exam is partly about mindset. Remind yourself that ITF+ is an entry-level exam and that you've prepared with a solid plan. If you encounter a difficult question, don't panic—mark it, guess if needed, and move on. You can come back later if you have time. Simple breathing techniques, like taking a slow deep breath before starting and periodically throughout the exam, help keep your mind clearer.

Using the full exam time wisely means pacing yourself and leaving a few minutes at the end to review. Keep an eye on the clock, but don't obsess over it. If you find yourself stuck on one question for too long, make your best choice and move forward so one item doesn't steal time from many others. In the last 5–10 minutes, revisit flagged questions and re-read the stems carefully, looking for key words like "FIRST" or "BEST" that might shift your answer.

3.10 Handling Mistakes and Learning from the Process

NO PREPARATION OR EXAM goes perfectly, and that's okay. How you handle mistakes—before, during, and after the test—can shape your growth. Treat this whole process as part of your long-term learning journey, not just a one-time event.

- **Accepting that some questions will be hard**
- **Learning from practice mistakes without beating yourself up**
- **Using your ITF+ experience to guide future growth**

Even with excellent preparation, you will encounter questions on the exam that feel difficult or unfamiliar. This is normal and built into the design of standardized tests. Instead of seeing a tough question as a sign that you're failing, treat it as a challenge to apply what you know as best you can. Eliminate obviously wrong answers, make a careful guess if needed, and move on. Remember that you don't need a perfect score to pass.

In your study process, mistakes are not evidence that you're "bad at IT"—they are pointers to what you need to review. When you miss a practice question, take a moment to understand exactly what went wrong. Did you misread a keyword? Confuse two concepts? Forget a definition? By identifying the specific cause, you can fix it, rather than feeling vaguely discouraged. This targeted reflection turns every error into an opportunity.

Whatever your final ITF+ result, the process of studying, practicing, and taking the exam teaches you valuable skills. You'll be better at organizing study plans, managing time, and reading technical material. If you pass, you have a credential and a foundation for further certifications. If you fall short, you have a clear starting point for another attempt with improved strategies. Either way, you are building habits that will help you over your entire career.

Chapter 4

IT Concepts and Terminology (Domain 1 Overview)

This chapter kicks off Domain 1: IT Concepts and Terminology. You'll explore how computers represent data, what basic terms like hardware and software really mean, and how to think about different device types. The goal is to give you a solid vocabulary so later chapters feel familiar instead of foreign.

4.1 Data, Information, and Files

COMPUTERS DEAL WITH data all day, but not all data is equally useful. ITF+ expects you to understand the difference between raw data, meaningful information, and how files store that information. This section sets the stage for later topics like storage, databases, and security.

- **Data vs. information**
- **Files and file types**
- **Metadata and why it matters**

Data is raw facts or figures, such as numbers, text strings, or timestamps, without context. **Information** is what you get when data is processed, organized, or interpreted in a way that makes it meaningful. For example, "72, 74, 71" is data; "these are today's temperatures" is information. IT professionals often think about how to collect, store, and turn data into information that helps people make decisions. Recognizing this distinction helps you understand why computers need both storage and processing.

A **file** is a named collection of data stored on a device. Files can represent documents, images, videos, programs, and more. Each file has a type—often indicated by an extension such as .docx, .jpg, or .mp4—that tells the operating system which application can open it. Understanding common file types helps you choose the right tool for a task and recognize which files might be risky (such as unknown executable files). It also helps you navigate and organize data more effectively.

Metadata is "data about data"—information that describes a file, such as its size, creation date, author, or permissions. When you right-click a file and view its properties, you're seeing metadata. This extra information helps systems and users search, sort, and manage files. In security and troubleshooting, metadata can also help identify who created or modified something and when it happened. Knowing that metadata exists explains why files can reveal more than just their visible contents.

4.2 Bits, Bytes, and Number Systems

COMPUTERS DON'T THINK in words; they think in ones and zeros. ITF+ expects you to understand basic digital units like bits and bytes, and to recognize that computers often use different number systems than humans do. You don't need to be a math genius, but you should be comfortable with the basics.

- **Bits and bytes as storage units**
- **Kilobytes, megabytes, gigabytes, and beyond**
- **Binary vs. decimal at a high level**

A **bit** is the smallest unit of digital information and can be either 0 or 1. A **byte** is typically 8 bits grouped together, and it's a common unit for measuring file sizes and memory. When you see a file that is 1,024 bytes or a device with 8 gigabytes of RAM, you're seeing these fundamental units in action. Knowing that a byte can represent a single character of text helps you connect human-readable information to the underlying digital representation.

Larger units like **kilobyte (KB)**, **megabyte (MB)**, **gigabyte (GB)**, and **terabyte (TB)** represent bigger and bigger amounts of data. In many contexts, 1 KB is roughly 1,000 bytes, 1 MB is about 1 million bytes, and so on, though exact definitions can vary. These units help you compare storage devices and understand file sizes in practical terms—like why a video takes up more space than a text document. Being able to roughly estimate these sizes helps you make sense of specifications and system requirements.

Humans usually use the **decimal** (base-10) number system, but computers use **binary** (base-2), which relies only on 0s and 1s. You don't have to convert large numbers by hand for ITF+, but you should know that binary underlies how computers store data and perform operations. Sometimes you'll also see **hexadecimal** (base-16), which is a more compact way of representing binary values. Recognizing that these alternate number systems exist explains some of the odd-looking values you might see in technical tools.

4.3 Hardware vs. Software vs. Firmware

ITF+ OFTEN TESTS WHETHER you can correctly categorize components and concepts. Three key terms—hardware, software, and firmware—describe different layers of a computing system. Understanding the differences helps you analyze problems more logically.

- **Hardware as physical components**
- **Software as programs and applications**
- **Firmware as embedded, low-level software**

Hardware refers to the physical parts of a computer system that you can touch and see. This includes items like the keyboard, monitor, motherboard, CPU, RAM sticks, and cables. When hardware fails, you might see symptoms like a device not powering on, strange noises, or visible damage. Hardware issues often require physical repair, replacement, or reconnection. Being able to identify hardware components by name is a core ITF+ skill.

Software includes operating systems, applications, utilities, and other programs that run on hardware. Examples are Windows, macOS, word processors, web browsers, and antivirus tools. Software problems often show up as error messages, crashes, or unexpected behavior within programs. Unlike hardware, software can usually be fixed by updating, reinstalling, reconfiguring, or changing settings. Understanding that software is instructions for the hardware helps you see why the same hardware can be used in different ways depending on what software you install.

Firmware is special software that is embedded into hardware devices, often stored on chips. It helps the hardware initialize and operate at a low level, sometimes before an operating system even loads. Examples include the BIOS/UEFI in a PC or the firmware inside a router or printer. Firmware can sometimes be updated to fix bugs or add features, but updates must be handled carefully because failures can make a device unusable. Recognizing firmware as the bridge between hardware and higher-level software helps you understand its importance.

4.4 Types of Computers and Devices

NOT ALL COMPUTING DEVICES are big desktop PCs. Today's world includes a wide range of form factors and device types, and ITF+ wants you to recognize the most common ones. Knowing which device is appropriate for which task is a practical skill in both home and business environments.

- **Desktops, laptops, and mobile devices**
- **Servers and thin clients**
- **IoT and embedded devices**

Desktops are stationary computers with separate monitors, keyboards, and towers or small form-factor cases. They're typically easier to upgrade and repair than portable devices. **Laptops** combine the screen, keyboard, and computer components into one portable unit, trading some upgradability for mobility. **Mobile devices** like smartphones and tablets are even more portable and often have touchscreens and cellular connections. Each type has strengths and trade-offs, and understanding them helps you recommend appropriate devices for different users.

Servers are powerful computers designed to provide resources or services to other devices on a network. They might host websites, file shares, applications, or databases. Unlike personal desktops, servers are often optimized for reliability, remote management, and continuous operation. **Thin clients** are simpler endpoint devices that rely heavily on servers for processing and storage; they mainly provide input and display. Recognizing how servers and thin clients work together is important for understanding many business environments.

IoT (Internet of Things) and embedded devices are specialized computing devices built into everyday objects. Examples include smart thermostats, fitness trackers, smart TVs, and industrial sensors. These devices often run simplified operating systems and may have limited interfaces. They connect to networks to send and receive data and can sometimes be controlled via apps. While convenient, they also introduce new security concerns because they may be poorly configured or rarely updated.

4.5 Input, Output, and Peripheral Devices

COMPUTER SYSTEMS INTERACT with the outside world through input and output. ITF+ expects you to recognize common input and output devices, along with peripheral devices that extend a system's capabilities. This helps you troubleshoot connectivity and usage issues.

- **Input devices (keyboard, mouse, scanners, etc.)**
- **Output devices (monitors, printers, speakers, etc.)**
- **Peripherals and connection types**

Input devices allow users to send data or commands into a computer. Common examples include keyboards, mice, touchpads, scanners, microphones, and webcams. On mobile devices, the touchscreen is a primary input method. When an input device fails, users may be unable to type, click, or otherwise interact with the system. Troubleshooting often includes checking physical connections, wireless pairing, settings, and drivers. Recognizing input devices is the first step toward helping users when they say "my computer isn't responding."

Output devices show or play information from the computer back to the user. Monitors, projectors, printers, and speakers are common examples. A monitor displays visual output, while speakers output audio and printers create physical copies of documents or images. If an output device doesn't work, the computer may still be functioning internally, but the user can't see or hear the results. Troubleshooting output involves checking cables, power, volume controls, display settings, or printer queues.

Peripherals are external devices that connect to a computer to provide input, output, or storage functions. They may connect via USB, HDMI, DisplayPort, audio jacks, or wireless technologies like Bluetooth. Examples include external hard drives, game controllers, and docking stations. Understanding the differences between connection types—like which ports carry video versus data—helps you plug things in correctly and diagnose issues when devices aren't recognized.

4.6 Operating Systems and Their Roles (High Level Preview)

YOU'LL SEE OPERATING systems in more detail later, but ITF+ expects a basic understanding early on. An operating system (OS) is essential for making hardware usable and for running applications. Knowing what an OS does at a high level sets you up for deeper learning.

- **What an operating system does**
- **Common operating systems on different devices**
- **User interfaces and system tools**

An **operating system** manages hardware resources and provides services to applications and users. It handles tasks like memory management, process scheduling, file systems, and device communication. Without an OS, most users would have no practical way to interact with the hardware. When you open a program, save a file, or print a document, the OS is coordinating those actions behind the scenes.

Different devices use different operating systems optimized for their form factors. Desktop and laptop computers often run Windows, macOS, or Linux distributions. Smartphones and tablets commonly run Android or iOS. Servers may use specialized editions of Windows Server or various Linux server distributions. Recognizing these OS names and knowing roughly where they are used helps you understand the landscape of computing environments.

User interfaces and system tools are how people interact with the OS. Graphical user interfaces (GUIs) provide windows, icons, menus, and pointers, while command-line interfaces (CLIs) use text commands. System tools include file managers, task managers, control panels, and settings apps. ITF+ won't require deep command-line skills, but you should know that these interfaces exist and that system tools are used to configure and troubleshoot systems.

4.7 The Basic Computing Process

AT A HIGH LEVEL, COMPUTERS follow a simple cycle: they receive input, process it, store data, and produce output. ITF+ expects you to understand this basic computing model. It's a mental framework you can apply to almost any digital device.

- **Input–Process–Output–Storage (IPOS) model**
- **CPU and memory in processing**
- **How storage fits into the cycle**

The **Input–Process–Output–Storage (IPOS)** model describes four core stages of computing. Input is data or commands entering the system; processing is what the computer does with that data; output is the result shown to the user; and storage is where data is kept for future use. For example, when you type a document: keyboard input becomes processed text, displayed as output on the screen, and saved into storage as a file. Seeing tasks through this lens helps you understand where a problem might be occurring.

The **CPU (Central Processing Unit)** and memory (especially RAM) are central to the processing step. The CPU executes instructions, performs calculations, and coordinates operations. RAM holds active data and instructions so the CPU can access them quickly. If the CPU or RAM is overloaded or malfunctioning, processing slows down or fails, leading to freezes or crashes. Recognizing these roles helps you interpret performance issues and system specifications.

Storage—such as hard drives, SSDs, or cloud storage—allows data to persist after power is turned off. It's where operating systems, applications, and user files live. In the IPOS model, storage is the long-term memory that supports repeated use of data and programs. When storage fills up or becomes corrupted, it can disrupt the entire cycle. Understanding storage's place in the process prepares you for later chapters on file systems and backup strategies.

4.8 Common Computing Terminology (Client, Server, Cloud, Virtualization)

ITF+ WANTS YOU TO BE comfortable with some key terms you'll see across many IT topics. Words like client, server, cloud, and virtualization describe how modern systems are organized. Grasping them early will make network, application, and security discussions easier to follow later.

- **Client and server concepts**
- **Cloud computing basics**
- **Virtualization at a beginner level**

A **client** is a device or program that requests services or resources from another system. A **server** is the system that provides those resources, such as files, web pages, or applications. For example, your web browser is a client requesting pages from a web server. This client–server model is fundamental to how most networked applications work. Understanding it helps explain why some resources are centralized and others are local.

Cloud computing refers to delivering computing services—like servers, storage, databases, and applications—over the internet. Instead of running everything on local hardware you own, you access resources hosted in data centers managed by providers. Users benefit from scalability and reduced need for physical infrastructure. At the ITF+ level, you should recognize that "the cloud" is just someone else's servers and infrastructure, accessed remotely.

Virtualization allows one physical machine to run multiple virtual machines, each with its own operating system and applications. This is done using software called a hypervisor. Virtualization improves resource utilization and flexibility because you can create, modify, or delete virtual machines without changing the underlying hardware. For ITF+, you don't need to configure virtualization, but you should understand that it's a way to simulate separate computers on a single physical host.

4.9 Basic Troubleshooting and Help-Seeking Terminology

EVEN AT THE FUNDAMENTALS level, you're expected to understand some common troubleshooting language. Knowing how to describe problems, steps, and tools clearly is important when working with users or other IT staff. This section introduces basic terms you'll see throughout the exam.

- **Symptoms vs. causes**
- **Workarounds vs. permanent fixes**
- **Escalation and documentation**

Symptoms are what you can observe: error messages, slow performance, or devices not responding. **Causes** are the underlying reasons those symptoms appear, such as a faulty cable, misconfiguration, or malware. IT work often involves starting from symptoms and reasoning toward likely causes. Confusing the two can lead to mistaken assumptions—for example, treating a symptom ("can't print") as if it were the cause itself. ITF+ questions may describe symptoms and ask what you should check next.

A **workaround** is a temporary solution that allows the user to keep working without fully resolving the root cause. For example, printing from a different computer because the usual one has a driver issue. A **permanent fix** addresses the underlying problem, such as reinstalling the correct driver. Workarounds are sometimes necessary to keep business moving, but they should not be mistaken for true resolution. Understanding this difference helps you choose the best answer when the exam asks for a "BEST" long-term step.

Escalation means handing a problem off to someone with more expertise or authority when it's beyond your scope. **Documentation** involves recording the problem, steps taken, and outcome in a ticketing system or log. These practices ensure continuity and help others understand what's been tried. Even at an entry level, you're expected to know when to escalate and to keep notes that can be referenced later. This language often appears in troubleshooting scenario questions.

4.10 Pulling the Concepts Together

THIS SECTION TIES THE terminology and basic concepts together into a coherent picture. You've learned about data, hardware, software, devices, and high-level computing models. The goal now is to see how these pieces fit into real-world thinking.

- **Using correct terminology in context**
- **Connecting basic concepts to later domains**
- **Building confidence with the "language of IT"**

Using correct terminology helps you communicate clearly with both users and IT professionals. When you can accurately distinguish between hardware and software, input and output, or client and server, conversations become more efficient and less confusing. On the exam, precise wording can be the difference between a right and wrong answer. In real life, it can mean the difference between a quick fix and a messy misunderstanding.

The concepts in this chapter connect directly to later domains like Infrastructure, Applications, and Security. For example, understanding file types and metadata helps when you learn about storage and backup. Knowing client–server and cloud basics makes later networking and security topics less abstract. Treat this chapter as a foundation you'll keep building on, not as isolated trivia. Each new domain will reuse this vocabulary and these ideas.

As you grow comfortable with these basic terms, your confidence in reading and talking about IT will increase. Instead of feeling lost when you see technical language, you'll recognize familiar patterns. This shift—from feeling intimidated to feeling curious—is one of the biggest benefits of mastering IT concepts and terminology early. It primes you to tackle the rest of the exam content with less fear and more focus.

Practice Questions – Chapter 4 (25 Questions)

1. Which statement best describes the difference between data and information?

A. Data is always useful; information is never useful

B. Data is raw values, while information is processed data that has meaning

C. Data and information are identical terms

D. Data refers only to images; information refers only to text

2. A file with the extension ".jpg" is most likely which type of file?

A. Text document

B. Spreadsheet

C. Image

D. Executable program

3. Which of the following is an example of metadata for a file?

A. The main text inside a document

B. The image displayed on the monitor

C. The file's size and creation date

D. The user's spoken description of the file

4. How many bits are in a typical byte?

A. 4

B. 8

C. 16

D. 32

5. Which unit usually represents a much larger amount of data than a kilobyte (KB)?

A. Bit

B. Byte

C. Megabyte (MB)

D. Nibble

6. Which term refers to the physical components of a computer system?

A. Hardware

B. Software

C. Firmware

D. Shareware

7. What is firmware best described as?

A. A type of removable storage

B. Embedded low-level software stored on a device

C. A cloud-based application

D. A replacement for hardware

8. A user wants a computer that is easy to move between home and school and has an integrated screen and keyboard. Which device type is MOST appropriate?

A. Desktop tower only

B. Rack-mounted server

C. Laptop

D. Thin client without a monitor

9. Which device is specifically designed to provide resources or services to other devices on a network?

A. Smartphone

B. Server

C. Printer

D. Webcam

10. A keyboard and mouse are examples of which type of devices?

A. Output devices

B. Storage devices

C. Input devices

D. Network devices

11. Which of the following is an output device?

A. Microphone

B. Scanner

C. Monitor

D. Keyboard

12. External devices such as printers, external drives, and game controllers that connect to a computer are commonly called:

A. Servers

B. Peripherals

C. Firewalls

D. Kernels

13. Which statement best describes an operating system?

A. A device used only for storing data

B. A program that manages hardware and provides services to applications

C. A hardware component that cools the CPU

D. A special type of peripheral

14. Which operating system is MOST commonly associated with smartphones and tablets?

A. Windows Server

B. macOS only

C. Android and iOS

D. MS-DOS

15. In the IPOS model, which stage involves showing processed data back to the user?

A. Input

B. Process

C. Output

D. Storage

16. Which components are MOST involved in processing tasks within a computer?

A. CPU and RAM

B. Keyboard and mouse
C. Monitor and speakers
D. Printer and scanner
17. What is the primary function of long-term storage devices like hard drives or SSDs?
A. To process instructions for the CPU
B. To temporarily hold data while power is on
C. To permanently store data and programs even when power is off
D. To display information on the screen
18. In a client–server model, which device or program typically requests services?
A. Server
B. Client
C. Firewall
D. Switch
19. Cloud computing is best described as:
A. Running all applications from a USB drive
B. Delivering computing services over the internet from remote data centers
C. Using only local storage on a desktop
D. A special type of physical server used at home
20. What does virtualization allow you to do?
A. Run a single operating system on many physical machines
B. Run multiple virtual machines on one physical host
C. Eliminate the need for an operating system
D. Replace RAM with cloud storage
21. In troubleshooting, which term refers to what the user can directly observe, such as an error message or slow performance?
A. Cause
B. Symptom
C. Escalation
D. Workaround
22. A workaround is best described as:
A. A permanent solution that removes the root cause of a problem
B. A temporary way to keep working despite an unresolved issue
C. A method of avoiding all documentation
D. A technique for overclocking the CPU
23. What does escalation usually involve in an IT support context?
A. Ignoring difficult problems
B. Turning off the device and walking away
C. Handing the problem to someone with more expertise or authority
D. Always reinstalling the operating system
24. Which of the following is an example of documentation?
A. A user complaining verbally
B. A technician's written record of the problem and steps taken in a ticketing system
C. A printed company logo
D. A social media post about the exam

25. Why is using correct terminology (like hardware vs. software) important for ITF+ candidates?
A. It impresses friends but has no real use
B. It makes exam questions longer
C. It improves communication, reduces confusion, and helps identify correct answers
D. It is only required for programming tasks

Answer Key – Chapter 4 (with Explanations)

1. B – DATA IS RAW values, while information is processed data that has meaning

Data becomes information when it is organized or interpreted in a way that makes it useful. Saying they're identical or restricting them to certain media (like images vs. text) misunderstands the concepts.

2. C – Image

The .jpg extension is commonly used for image files. Text documents often use extensions like .txt or .docx, spreadsheets use .xlsx, and executables use .exe or similar.

3. C – The file's size and creation date

Metadata includes descriptive details about the file, such as size, dates, and sometimes author. The main text or displayed content is the file's actual data, not metadata.

4. B – 8

A byte typically contains 8 bits. This is a fundamental digital unit used throughout computing for memory and storage measurements.

5. C – Megabyte (MB)

A megabyte is significantly larger than a kilobyte. Bits and bytes are smaller units, while an MB represents roughly a million bytes in many contexts.

6. A – Hardware

Hardware refers to the physical components of a computer system. Software, firmware, and shareware are all types of programs or licensing classifications, not physical parts.

7. B – Embedded low-level software stored on a device

Firmware is software stored on hardware (like chips) that helps control the device at a low level. It's not removable storage, a cloud app, or a replacement for hardware.

8. C – Laptop

A laptop integrates the screen and keyboard in a portable form factor, ideal for moving between locations. Desktops and servers are less portable, and a thin client without a monitor wouldn't meet the user's needs alone.

9. B – Server

Servers provide resources or services—such as files, web pages, or applications—to other devices on a network. Smartphones, printers, and webcams can be clients or peripherals but aren't primarily designed as servers.

10. C – Input devices

Keyboards and mice are classic input devices that allow users to send data and commands into a computer. Output devices show or play information; storage and network devices serve other roles.

11. C – Monitor

A monitor displays visual output from the computer, making it an output device. Microphones and scanners are input devices, while keyboards are also input.

12. B – Peripherals

Peripherals are external devices connected to the computer to extend its capabilities, such as printers, external drives, and controllers. Servers, firewalls, and kernels serve different purposes.

13. B – A program that manages hardware and provides services to applications

An operating system coordinates hardware, runs applications, and provides user interfaces and system tools. It is software, not storage or a physical cooling component.

14. C – Android and iOS

Android and iOS are the dominant operating systems on smartphones and many tablets. Windows Server and macOS have different primary use cases, and MS-DOS is an older OS not typically used on modern mobile devices.

15. C – Output

Output is the stage where processed data is presented back to the user, such as on a screen or through a printer. Input is data coming in, processing is what the CPU does, and storage keeps data long-term.

16. A – CPU and RAM

The CPU performs calculations and executes instructions, while RAM holds active data and programs for quick access. Input and output devices are important but are not primarily responsible for processing.

17. C – To permanently store data and programs even when power is off

Long-term storage devices retain data when the system is shut down. RAM is volatile and loses contents when power is removed; CPU, display, and other components serve different roles.

18. B – Client

In a client–server model, the client requests services or resources from the server. The server responds to these requests, while devices like firewalls and switches have supporting roles.

19. B – Delivering computing services over the internet from remote data centers

Cloud computing provides access to computing resources hosted in remote data centers via the internet. It's not about USB-only use or strictly local setups.

20. B – Run multiple virtual machines on one physical host

Virtualization uses software (hypervisors) to create multiple virtual machines on a single physical system. This improves flexibility and hardware utilization.

21. B – Symptom

Symptoms are the observable effects of a problem, like error messages or slowness. The cause is the underlying issue producing those symptoms.

22. B – A temporary way to keep working despite an unresolved issue

A workaround helps maintain productivity without fully fixing the root cause. Permanent fixes address the underlying problem; workarounds are usually short-term.

23. C – Handing the problem to someone with more expertise or authority

Escalation involves passing an issue to a higher tier of support or a specialist when it's beyond your scope. Ignoring the problem or always reinstalling the OS is not professional escalation.

24. B – A technician's written record of the problem and steps taken in a ticketing system

Documentation captures what happened and what was done in a way others can review. Complaints, logos, or random posts are not proper technical documentation.

25. C – It improves communication, reduces confusion, and helps identify correct answers

Accurate terminology ensures clear communication between users and IT staff and helps you interpret exam questions correctly. It's a practical skill, not just something to "sound smart."

Chapter 5

Computing Basics and Troubleshooting Methodology

This chapter deepens your understanding of how computers work day to day and how IT people approach problems in a structured way. You'll look at common system performance concepts, the basic boot and shutdown process, and CompTIA's troubleshooting steps. The goal is to help you think like an entry-level troubleshooter, not just a button-clicker.

5.1 What "Performance" Really Means

WHEN USERS SAY, "MY computer is slow," they can mean many different things. ITF+ expects you to understand basic performance concepts so you can interpret what's actually going on. This section gives you a simple mental model for "performance."

- **Performance as response time and throughput**
- **Common user symptoms of "slowness"**
- **The difference between perceived and actual performance**

Response time is how long it takes the system to react to a given action, like opening an app or loading a web page. **Throughput** is how much work a system can do in a given period, such as the number of pages printed per minute. When performance is poor, either response time has increased (things feel laggy) or throughput has dropped (less gets done in the same amount of time). Understanding these ideas helps you ask better questions when users complain about slowness.

Common symptoms of "slowness" include applications taking longer to open, websites loading slowly, files saving sluggishly, or the mouse pointer lagging. Sometimes the entire system feels unresponsive; other times, only specific tasks are affected. Users might not describe these symptoms precisely, so you'll need to listen carefully and ask follow-up questions. Recognizing patterns—like browser-only slowness versus everything being slow—points you toward different potential causes.

Perceived performance isn't always the same as actual system capability. For example, a fast computer on a very slow internet connection will still "feel" slow while browsing. Likewise, a system might be powerful but overloaded with too many background programs. Small improvements like closing unnecessary apps or cleaning up browser tabs can make a noticeable difference. Understanding the gap between perception and underlying causes is a core part of troubleshooting.

5.2 CPU, RAM, and Storage in Everyday Use

THREE CORE COMPONENTS—CPU, RAM, and storage—play major roles in how a system feels to the user. ITF+ wants you to understand how these parts interact in everyday tasks. When something goes wrong, you'll often think in terms of one or more of these being constrained.

- **CPU as the "brain" doing the work**
- **RAM as short-term working memory**

- **Storage as long-term data holding**

The **CPU (Central Processing Unit)** executes instructions and performs calculations. When many demanding tasks run at once—like video editing, gaming, or multiple heavy apps—the CPU can become a bottleneck. High CPU usage can cause delays, stuttering, or temporary freezes. Task managers and system monitors help you see CPU usage in real time, which is useful when diagnosing performance complaints.

RAM holds active programs and data that the CPU is currently working with. If you don't have enough RAM for the tasks you're doing, the system may start using slower storage as "virtual memory," which can cause heavy slowdown. Symptoms include apps taking a long time to switch between or frequent pauses while the disk light is active. Closing unnecessary programs or adding more RAM are common solutions to memory-related performance issues.

Storage—whether a hard disk drive (HDD) or solid-state drive (SSD)—holds the operating system, applications, and user files. Traditional HDDs are slower because they involve moving mechanical parts, while SSDs are much faster. If storage is very full, fragmented (on HDDs), or failing, you may experience slow boot times, long file operations, or errors. Understanding how storage affects daily use helps you decide whether a performance issue might be hardware, configuration, or even a failing drive.

5.3 The Basic Boot and Shutdown Process

EVERY TIME A COMPUTER turns on or off, it goes through a series of steps. While ITF+ doesn't demand deep technical detail, you should understand the general flow. This helps you recognize where problems might be occurring during startup or shutdown.

- **Power-on and firmware initialization**
- **Loading the operating system**
- **Proper shutdown vs. forced power-off**

When you power on a computer, the firmware (such as BIOS or UEFI) starts first. It performs basic hardware checks, initializes components, and finds a bootable device—like a hard drive, SSD, or network boot option. This stage is sometimes called POST (Power-On Self-Test). If there are serious hardware issues, you may see error messages or hear beep codes at this point.

After firmware initialization, control passes to the bootloader, which begins loading the operating system from storage into memory. You'll usually see a splash screen or logo while this happens. The OS then starts its own services, drivers, and background processes, and eventually displays the login screen or desktop. If problems occur during this phase, you might see boot loops, blue or black screens, or very long startup times.

Proper shutdown uses the OS's built-in process to close applications, stop services, and safely write data to storage. This reduces the risk of data corruption and file system errors. A forced power-off—holding down the power button—should be reserved for situations where the system is completely frozen and unresponsive. Repeated improper shutdowns can contribute to data loss or system instability, which is why users should be encouraged to shut down correctly.

5.4 The CompTIA Troubleshooting Methodology (Overview)

COMPTIA PROMOTES A structured troubleshooting methodology that appears across many of its certifications. ITF+ expects you to know this process at a high level. Following these steps keeps you from guessing randomly and helps you resolve problems more systematically.

- **Identifying the problem**
- **Establishing and testing a theory**
- **Implementing, verifying, and documenting the solution**

Identifying the problem comes first. That means talking to the user, observing symptoms, and gathering relevant information, like error messages or recent changes. You might ask, "What were you doing when this happened?" or "Has this ever worked correctly?" Skipping this step leads to wasted effort and incorrect assumptions. Clear problem identification often reveals simple solutions.

Once you understand the problem, you **establish a theory** of what might be causing it. Start with the most likely and simplest possibilities—like loose cables, misconfigured settings, or a full storage drive. Then you **test** your theory using safe, minimal steps. If the theory is wrong, you develop a new one based on what you learned. This cycle of hypothesis and test is more efficient than trying random changes.

When a theory is confirmed, you **implement** the appropriate fix, such as changing a setting or replacing a component. Next, you **verify** that the solution actually resolved the original problem—don't just assume success. Finally, you **document** what happened and the steps taken, so others can learn from the incident and you have a record for future reference. This full cycle represents the professional way to troubleshoot.

5.5 Step 1: Identify the Problem

THE FIRST TROUBLESHOOTING step might seem obvious, but it's often rushed or skipped. Identifying the problem means understanding what the issue really is from both the user's and system's perspective. Doing this well can save a lot of time later.

- **Asking good questions and listening**
- **Reproducing the issue when possible**
- **Checking the obvious basics**

Asking good questions helps clarify vague complaints like "it's broken." You can ask what the user was doing, what they expected to happen, and what actually occurred. It's also useful to ask if anything changed recently—for example, new software installations, updates, or hardware changes. Listening carefully without interrupting builds trust and ensures you don't miss important details. Sometimes users reveal the cause without realizing it.

Reproducing the issue, when safe and possible, lets you see the problem firsthand. You might ask the user to walk you through the steps that lead to the error. If you can't reproduce it, note the conditions under which it happens: time of day, specific applications, or network connections. Intermittent issues can be trickier, but any reproducible pattern provides a strong starting point.

Checking the obvious basics can quickly resolve many problems. This includes verifying that devices are plugged in and powered on, network cables are seated, Wi-Fi is enabled, and volume or brightness settings are correct. ITF+

questions often reward answers that start with these simple checks instead of jumping immediately to complex or destructive actions. It's surprising how often basic issues are the root of the problem.

5.6 Step 2: Establish and Test a Theory

ONCE YOU KNOW WHAT the problem looks like, it's time to form a theory about why it's happening. This is where your knowledge of systems and common issues comes into play. Testing your theory means trying small, low-risk steps to see if you're on the right track.

- **Starting with the most likely causes**
- **Keeping theories simple and focused**
- **Testing with minimal, reversible changes**

Starting with the most likely causes means considering common issues first. For a "no internet" complaint, you might think about the router, Wi-Fi connection, or service provider before assuming a rare hardware failure. Your experience, plus patterns you've seen in practice questions, will guide these choices. ITF+ expects you to prioritize reasonable theories instead of jumping to exotic explanations.

Keeping theories simple and focused helps you avoid confusion. A good theory is specific, such as "The user's device is not connected to the correct Wi-Fi network," rather than "The network is doomed." Simple theories are easier to test and either confirm or reject. If a theory tries to explain everything at once, it's harder to know what evidence would support or contradict it.

Testing your theory with minimal, reversible changes protects the user's data and system. For example, you might try reconnecting to a network, closing and reopening an application, or temporarily disabling a non-critical add-on. These actions are easy to undo and unlikely to create new problems. Avoid drastic steps—like reinstalling the OS—until you've exhausted simpler options and have strong evidence they're needed.

5.7 Step 3–5: Implement, Verify, and Document

AFTER A THEORY IS CONFIRMED, you move into action. The last troubleshooting steps focus on applying the fix, making sure it really worked, and recording what happened. Skipping these steps can lead to recurring problems and confusion later.

- **Implementing the chosen solution**
- **Verifying full system functionality**
- **Documenting the problem and resolution**

Implementing the chosen solution means performing the specific change you've decided on, such as updating a driver, modifying a setting, or replacing a cable. It's often best to inform the user what you plan to do before making changes, especially if it might temporarily interrupt their work. Take care to avoid affecting unrelated systems or settings while you work. The goal is to fix the problem as cleanly as possible.

Verifying full system functionality goes beyond just checking that the original symptom is gone. Ask the user to repeat their normal workflow to ensure everything behaves as expected. If the issue involved printing, for instance, have them print a test document. Verification also includes checking that no new problems were introduced by the fix. This confirmation provides closure for both you and the user.

Documenting the problem and resolution in a ticketing system or log ensures that the knowledge is not lost. Include symptoms, suspected cause, steps taken, and final outcome. This documentation helps other technicians handle similar issues more efficiently. It also creates a record you can reference if the problem returns, saving time and frustration.

5.8 Safety, ESD, and Basic Physical Precautions

EVEN AT THE FUNDAMENTALS level, ITF+ expects awareness of basic safety principles when working with hardware. Mistakes can damage components or harm people. This section covers simple precautions you should keep in mind.

- **Power and electrical safety basics**
- **Electrostatic discharge (ESD) awareness**
- **Physical handling of devices**

Power safety begins with turning devices off and unplugging them before opening cases or working inside them, unless a specific procedure requires otherwise and you are trained for it. Avoid working on equipment with wet hands or in damp environments. Be cautious around power supplies and exposed wires; these can carry dangerous voltages. Using properly grounded outlets and surge protectors helps protect devices and people.

Electrostatic discharge (ESD) occurs when built-up static electricity suddenly transfers from your body to a component. Sensitive parts like RAM sticks and CPUs can be damaged even by small, invisible discharges. To reduce risk, technicians may use anti-static wrist straps, mats, or grounding techniques. At a minimum, you should avoid touching metal contacts and handle components by their edges. Awareness of ESD is a key part of safe hardware work.

Physical handling of devices also matters. Laptops, monitors, and other devices should be lifted carefully and not placed in unstable positions. Cables should be routed to prevent tripping hazards and strain on ports. When inserting or removing connectors, apply gentle, even pressure instead of forcing them. Careful handling extends the life of equipment and reduces the likelihood of physical damage being mistaken for mysterious "technical problems."

5.9 When (and How) to Escalate

NOT EVERY PROBLEM CAN or should be solved at the first level of support. Knowing when to escalate an issue is an important skill. ITF+ wants you to recognize that escalation is professional, not a sign of failure.

- **Recognizing problems beyond your scope**
- **Following escalation procedures**
- **Handing off with clear information**

Recognizing problems beyond your scope means being honest about your knowledge and permissions. If an issue involves complex networking, sensitive data, or systems you're not authorized to modify, escalation may be required. Continuing to experiment in these cases can make things worse. It's better to say, "This needs a higher level of support," than to risk data loss or extended downtime.

Following escalation procedures means using whatever process your organization has in place—usually creating or updating a ticket and assigning it to the correct team or person. Some environments have clear tiers (Level 1, Level 2, etc.), while others route by specialty (network, security, application). The key is to use the proper channel so the issue reaches someone with the right expertise. Skipping or ignoring procedure can delay resolution.

Handing off with clear information increases the chance of a fast, successful resolution. Include details about the symptoms, troubleshooting steps already taken, and any error messages observed. This prevents the next technician from repeating work and gives them a head start. Good handoff notes also show professionalism and respect for your colleagues' time.

5.10 Building a Troubleshooter's Mindset

THIS SECTION TIES TOGETHER computing basics and structured troubleshooting into a mindset you can carry forward. ITF+ rewards candidates who think logically, communicate clearly, and avoid impulsive actions. Developing this mindset now will serve you in all future IT roles.

- **Staying calm and methodical**
- **Balancing curiosity with caution**
- **Learning from each issue you encounter**

Staying calm and methodical is crucial when systems misbehave, especially if users are stressed or impatient. Panicking leads to rushed decisions and missed details. Taking a breath, following your troubleshooting steps, and communicating clearly can defuse tense situations. A calm presence reassures users that you're in control, even when you're still figuring things out.

Balancing curiosity with caution means being interested in how systems work and eager to learn, while still protecting data and respecting boundaries. It's great to explore settings and tools in lab environments, but production systems demand care. The troubleshooting process is your safety net: gather info, test small changes, and avoid risky actions without justification. This balance helps you grow without causing unnecessary harm.

Learning from each issue you encounter turns everyday problems into valuable lessons. After resolving a problem, take a moment to reflect: What caused it? How could it have been prevented? What clues will you watch for next time? Over months and years, this habit builds a deep library of experience in your mind. That's what eventually separates a beginner from a seasoned troubleshooter.

Practice Questions – Chapter 5 (25 Questions)

1. When a user says, "My computer is slow," which of the following is the BEST initial response?

A. Immediately replace the computer
B. Ask follow-up questions to clarify what "slow" means in their situation
C. Tell the user it must be a virus
D. Reinstall the operating system right away

2. Which component is MOST responsible for executing instructions and performing calculations?

A. Hard drive
B. CPU

C. Monitor
D. Keyboard
3. If a system has too little RAM for the tasks it is running, which symptom is MOST likely?
A. The screen turns off permanently
B. The system frequently slows down and uses storage as virtual memory
C. The mouse stops working but everything else is fine
D. The printer prints blank pages
4. Compared to a traditional hard disk drive (HDD), a solid-state drive (SSD) typically:
A. Is slower and has moving parts
B. Is faster and has no moving parts
C. Only works on laptops
D. Cannot store an operating system
5. During the power-on process, which component typically runs first to check hardware and locate a boot device?
A. Operating system
B. Application software
C. Firmware (BIOS/UEFI)
D. Printer driver
6. Proper shutdown of a computer is important primarily because it:
A. Makes the screen brighter
B. Reduces the risk of data corruption and file system errors
C. Improves the color quality of images
D. Increases Wi-Fi speed
7. Which of the following is the FIRST step in CompTIA's troubleshooting methodology?
A. Establish a theory of probable cause
B. Identify the problem
C. Document the findings
D. Implement the solution
8. Asking a user, "What were you doing when the problem started?" is part of which troubleshooting activity?
A. Implementing a fix
B. Identifying the problem
C. Documenting the solution
D. Escalating the ticket
9. Which of the following is the BEST example of "checking the obvious first"?
A. Replacing the motherboard without testing
B. Confirming the monitor's power cable is plugged in
C. Reinstalling all applications
D. Resetting every network device at once
10. After forming a theory about a problem, what should you do next according to the troubleshooting process?
A. Immediately escalate the issue
B. Test the theory with safe, minimal changes
C. Document the theory and stop
D. Reboot the device repeatedly
11. Why is it important to use minimal, reversible changes when testing a theory?

A. To ensure the user cannot see what you are doing
B. To avoid making the problem worse and to keep changes easy to undo
C. To finish as quickly as possible without thinking
D. To avoid telling anyone what you changed
12. After implementing a solution, what is the NEXT step?
A. Immediately move on to another ticket without checking
B. Verify that the system is functioning properly
C. Undo the solution to test it again
D. Close the ticket with no notes
13. Documenting the problem and solution is helpful because it:
A. Is only for managers to read
B. Provides a record that can help with future similar issues
C. Replaces the need to talk to users
D. Guarantees a promotion
14. Which action is MOST appropriate before opening a computer case to work inside?
A. Increase the room's humidity
B. Unplug the power cable and turn the device off
C. Plug in as many devices as possible
D. Shake the computer to test for loose parts
15. Electrostatic discharge (ESD) is best described as:
A. A type of network cable
B. A sudden transfer of static electricity that can damage components
C. A cooling system for CPUs
D. A special type of software update
16. How should you handle internal components like RAM modules to minimize ESD risk?
A. Hold them by their metal contacts
B. Toss them onto a carpeted floor
C. Handle them by the edges and avoid touching contacts
D. Store them in a glass of water
17. Which situation BEST indicates that escalation is appropriate?
A. The user is polite and patient
B. The issue involves a system you are not authorized to configure
C. The problem was solved in two minutes
D. You have plenty of free time
18. When escalating an issue, which of the following is MOST helpful to include?
A. A detailed description of your lunch
B. Only the user's name
C. Symptoms, steps already taken, and any error messages
D. Your opinion of the user's attitude
19. Which behavior demonstrates a good troubleshooter's mindset?
A. Panicking when something unexpected happens
B. Guessing randomly until the problem disappears
C. Staying calm, following a method, and learning from each issue
D. Refusing to talk to users

20. Which example is a workaround rather than a permanent fix?
A. Replacing a faulty network cable
B. Reinstalling a corrupted driver
C. Printing from a different computer while the main PC's issue is investigated
D. Applying a vendor patch that resolves a known bug

21. A user's PC freezes frequently. You find that the system has very little RAM and many heavy applications open at once. Which theory is MOST reasonable?
A. The monitor is broken
B. The system is running out of memory under load
C. The keyboard layout is incorrect
D. The printer ink is low

22. A system starts, shows the manufacturer logo, then repeatedly restarts before reaching the desktop. This problem MOST likely occurs during which phase?
A. Proper shutdown
B. Firmware/boot and OS loading
C. Network printing
D. Application installation

23. Which of the following is a sign of a failing hard drive?
A. Crisp, clear display
B. Frequent clicking noises and long file access times
C. Faster-than-normal boot times
D. Improved audio quality

24. During the exam, you notice you are spending too long on one difficult question. What is the BEST action?
A. Stay on the question until time runs out
B. Choose your best answer, mark it if possible, and move on
C. Leave it blank permanently
D. Restart the entire exam

25. Why is it important to verify that a solution resolved the original problem before closing a case?
A. To impress the user with extra steps
B. To ensure the root issue is truly fixed and no new issues were introduced
C. To make the ticket longer to read
D. To avoid documenting anything

Answer Key – Chapter 5 (with Explanations)

1. B – ASK FOLLOW-UP questions to clarify what "slow" means in their situation

"Slow" can refer to many issues (startup, internet, apps, etc.). Clarifying the symptoms is part of identifying the problem and prevents you from jumping to drastic, unnecessary actions.

2. B – CPU

The CPU executes instructions and performs calculations, acting as the "brain" of the computer. Hard drives store data, monitors display output, and keyboards provide input.

3. B – The system frequently slows down and uses storage as virtual memory

When RAM is insufficient, the system uses slower storage as virtual memory, causing noticeable slowdowns. The other symptoms are not typical results of low RAM alone.

4. B – Is faster and has no moving parts

SSDs use flash memory and have no moving mechanical parts, making them faster and often more reliable than traditional HDDs. They can absolutely store operating systems and work on many device types.

5. C – Firmware (BIOS/UEFI)

Firmware initializes hardware and performs POST before handing control to the bootloader and operating system. Applications and drivers load later in the process.

6. B – Reduces the risk of data corruption and file system errors

Proper shutdown ensures data is written safely and processes are stopped correctly. Forced power-offs increase the chance of corruption and instability.

7. B – Identify the problem

The first step in CompTIA's troubleshooting methodology is to identify the problem by gathering information and understanding the symptoms. The other steps come after.

8. B – Identifying the problem

Asking what the user was doing when the issue began helps clarify and define the problem. This is part of the information-gathering phase.

9. B – Confirming the monitor's power cable is plugged in

Checking simple, obvious things like power and connections can quickly resolve many issues. Replacing major components or resetting everything without testing is wasteful and risky.

10. B – Test the theory with safe, minimal changes

After forming a theory, you should test it with small, controlled actions. Immediate escalation or random reboots skip the structured process.

11. B – To avoid making the problem worse and to keep changes easy to undo

Minimal, reversible changes limit the risk of causing new issues and allow you to backtrack if needed. This is especially important when you're not yet certain of the cause.

12. B – Verify that the system is functioning properly

Verification ensures that the original problem is truly resolved and that no new problems have appeared. Skipping this step can lead to unresolved issues and user frustration.

13. B – Provides a record that can help with future similar issues

Documentation is useful for technicians and organizations because it records what happened, what was tried, and what worked. It supports faster resolution of similar problems in the future.

14. B – Unplug the power cable and turn the device off

Powering down and disconnecting power reduces the risk of electrical shock and damage when working inside a computer. Increasing humidity or shaking the device are unsafe and unnecessary.

15. B – A sudden transfer of static electricity that can damage components

ESD can damage sensitive internal components even when you don't feel it. It is not a type of cable, cooling system, or software.

16. C – Handle them by the edges and avoid touching contacts

Holding components by the edges and avoiding contacts reduces ESD risk and physical damage. Dropping them on carpet or putting them in water would be disastrous.

17. B – The issue involves a system you are not authorized to configure

Working on systems beyond your authorization or expertise is a key reason to escalate. Being polite or having free time has nothing to do with escalation decisions.

18. C – Symptoms, steps already taken, and any error messages

Clear, concise information helps the next-level technician continue where you left off without repeating work. Personal details or irrelevant commentary are unhelpful.

19. C – Staying calm, following a method, and learning from each issue

A strong troubleshooter's mindset includes calmness, structured methods, and reflection. Panic, random guessing, or refusal to communicate undermine effective support.

20. C – Printing from a different computer while the main PC's issue is investigated

This workaround allows work to continue without fixing the root cause. Replacing cables, reinstalling drivers, or applying patches are aimed at permanent resolution.

21. B – The system is running out of memory under load

Frequent freezes with many heavy applications and little RAM strongly suggest memory pressure. Monitor, keyboard, or printer issues don't match the described symptoms.

22. B – Firmware/boot and OS loading

The repeated restart after the logo suggests a problem during or just after the boot process. It's happening before the desktop and application phase, not during shutdown or printing.

23. B – Frequent clicking noises and long file access times

Clicking sounds and slow file operations are classic signs of a failing HDD. Improved performance or display quality would not indicate failure.

24. B – Choose your best answer, mark it if possible, and move on

Managing time is crucial on the exam. Marking the question and moving on allows you to answer more questions instead of getting stuck.

25. B – To ensure the root issue is truly fixed and no new issues were introduced

Verification confirms that your solution actually solved the original problem and didn't create side effects. It's a critical part of professional troubleshooting before closing a case.

Chapter 6

Devices, Interfaces, and Peripherals (Infrastructure – Part 1)

This chapter begins the Infrastructure domain by focusing on devices you can see and touch. You'll learn how common device types connect and communicate, and how to recognize the ports and interfaces you'll see most often. The goal is to make the physical side of IT feel familiar instead of mysterious.

6.1 System Unit and Core External Components

A TYPICAL DESKTOP SETUP has several visible parts that work together as one system. ITF+ expects you to identify the main external components and understand their basic roles. This section gives you the "tour" of a standard workstation.

- **System unit (tower or case)**
- **Display, keyboard, and pointing device**
- **Basic cable connections to the system unit**

The **system unit** (often called the tower or case) contains the main internal components: motherboard, CPU, RAM, storage, power supply, and expansion cards. Even though most users interact with the monitor or keyboard, the system unit is where the actual computing work happens. You'll typically find ports on the front and back for connecting peripherals, along with power buttons and indicator lights. Recognizing the system unit as the central hub helps you understand where most cables ultimately connect.

The **display (monitor)**, **keyboard**, and **pointing device** (such as a mouse or touchpad) form the core user interface. The monitor provides visual output, while the keyboard and pointing device provide input. If any of these devices fail, the user's ability to interact with the system is severely limited. IT support often involves checking whether these components are properly connected, powered, and configured. Knowing their roles makes it easier to interpret user complaints like "my computer won't type" or "the screen is blank."

Basic cable connections link the system unit with external devices. The monitor might connect via HDMI, DisplayPort, DVI, or older VGA connectors. Keyboards and mice usually connect via USB or, on older systems, PS/2 ports. Power cables connect the system unit and monitor to electrical outlets or power strips. Being able to identify which cable belongs to which device is essential when setting up or troubleshooting a workstation.

6.2 Internal Components (High-Level Awareness)

ALTHOUGH ITF+ DOESN'T require you to build a PC from scratch, you should know the major internal components at a high level. This helps you understand what you're looking at if you open a case or see a diagram. It also provides a foundation for later hardware topics.

- **Motherboard and expansion slots**
- **CPU, RAM, and storage drives**
- **Power supply and cooling**

The **motherboard** is the main circuit board that connects all internal components. It contains slots and connectors for the CPU, RAM, storage devices, expansion cards, and external ports. Expansion slots (such as PCIe) allow additional cards like graphics adapters or network cards to be installed. When you see references to "onboard" components, they are often built into the motherboard. Understanding that everything connects through the motherboard helps explain why swapping it is a major repair.

The **CPU**, **RAM**, and **storage drives** are key players in performance and capacity. The CPU plugs into a special socket on the motherboard, RAM modules fit into memory slots, and storage devices connect via interfaces like SATA or NVMe. Hard disk drives (HDDs) and solid-state drives (SSDs) may be mounted in bays or directly on the board, depending on form factor. Recognizing these components by name and general location helps you follow hardware discussions and diagrams.

The **power supply unit (PSU)** converts wall power into the lower voltages required by internal components. It distributes power through cables to the motherboard, drives, and sometimes graphics cards. Cooling components, such as fans and heatsinks, help remove heat generated by the CPU, GPU, and other parts. Overheating can cause instability, crashes, or hardware damage. Awareness of power and cooling as part of the system explains why airflow and proper installation matter.

6.3 USB and Other Common Peripheral Interfaces

MODERN PERIPHERALS connect through a variety of interfaces, with USB dominating general-purpose use. ITF+ expects you to recognize common connection types and their basic characteristics. This section focuses on the most frequently encountered ports.

- **USB (Types A, B, C, and mini/micro)**
- **Legacy interfaces (PS/2, VGA, serial, parallel)**
- **Audio ports and card readers**

USB (Universal Serial Bus) is a versatile interface used for keyboards, mice, flash drives, printers, and many other peripherals. **USB Type-A** is the classic rectangular connector; **Type-B** is often seen on printers; **mini-USB** and **micro-USB** appeared on older phones and devices; and **USB Type-C** is a newer, reversible connector used on modern phones, laptops, and accessories. Knowing these shapes and names helps you identify which cables and ports you're dealing with on real systems.

Legacy interfaces still appear on older hardware. **PS/2** ports (round, usually purple for keyboard and green for mouse) were once common for input devices. **VGA** is an older blue 15-pin connector used for analog video output. **Serial** and **parallel** ports were used for early mice, modems, and printers. While USB and newer video standards have largely replaced them, ITF+ may still reference these legacy ports, and you might see them in older business environments.

Audio ports and card readers serve specialized purposes. Common audio jacks include a green port for speakers or headphones and a pink one for microphones, though color coding can vary. Some systems also have optical audio ports. **Card readers** accept memory cards, such as SD cards from cameras or phones, allowing data transfer. Recognizing these ports helps you assist users with tasks like plugging in headphones or transferring photos.

6.4 Display Interfaces and Basic Display Concepts

DISPLAYS CONNECT TO graphics outputs using specific standards. ITF+ expects you to recognize common display interfaces and understand basic display ideas. This helps you troubleshoot "no picture" complaints and choose appropriate connections.

- **HDMI, DisplayPort, and DVI**
- **VGA as an older analog standard**
- **Basic display settings (resolution and refresh rate)**

HDMI (High-Definition Multimedia Interface) is widely used for both computers and consumer devices like TVs and game consoles. It carries digital video and audio over a single cable. **DisplayPort** is common on modern PCs and monitors, especially in office and professional environments, and also carries audio plus high-resolution video. **DVI** is an older digital standard that can carry video but typically not audio. Recognizing these connectors on the back of a PC or monitor is essential for proper setup.

VGA is an older, analog-only display interface with a blue 15-pin connector. Because it's analog, it can produce fuzzier images, especially at higher resolutions. While many new devices no longer include VGA, you may still encounter it in legacy equipment or older projectors. Adapters sometimes allow conversion between VGA and digital interfaces, but the quality and capabilities may be limited. ITF+ may refer to VGA as an example of an older video standard.

Basic display settings like **resolution** and **refresh rate** affect clarity and smoothness. Resolution refers to how many pixels are displayed (for example, 1920×1080), while refresh rate (measured in hertz) indicates how many times per second the image is updated. If resolution is set too low, the image may look blocky; if set too high for a particular monitor, you may see issues or blank screens. Understanding these settings is useful when helping users adjust their displays.

6.5 Storage Devices and External Storage

STORAGE IS NOT JUST inside the computer; many devices connect externally to provide additional capacity or portability. ITF+ expects you to recognize common storage types and how they attach to systems. This section focuses on the variety you'll encounter in everyday work.

- **Internal HDDs and SSDs (quick recap)**
- **External drives and flash storage**
- **Optical drives and their uses**

Internal **HDDs (hard disk drives)** and **SSDs (solid-state drives)** store the operating system, applications, and user data. HDDs use spinning platters and read/write heads, while SSDs use flash memory with no moving parts, offering better speed and durability. These drives typically connect to the motherboard through interfaces like SATA or NVMe. Understanding these basics makes external storage devices easier to conceptualize, since they often use similar technologies in a portable form.

External drives and flash storage provide additional or portable space. **External HDDs and SSDs** usually connect via USB and are used for backups, extra storage, or moving large files between systems. **USB flash drives** (thumb drives) are small, portable devices ideal for transferring smaller amounts of data quickly. These external options are handy but must be handled safely—especially when unplugging—to avoid data corruption. Recognizing external storage devices is key when users talk about "plugging in a drive" or "using a thumb drive."

Optical drives read and sometimes write discs such as CDs, DVDs, or Blu-ray discs. While less common in modern laptops, they still appear in some desktops and external drive units. Optical media can be used for software installation, movies, music, or long-term archiving. However, many software distributions have moved to downloads or USB, so optical drives are less central than they once were. ITF+ still expects you to know they exist and their basic purpose.

6.6 Printers, Multifunction Devices, and Scanners

PRINTERS AND RELATED devices are a frequent source of help desk requests. ITF+ expects you to recognize common printer types and the basics of how they connect and operate. Understanding the fundamentals can make seemingly annoying printer issues much easier to manage.

- **Common printer types (inkjet, laser)**
- **Multifunction devices (print/scan/copy/fax)**
- **Printer connectivity options (USB, network, wireless)**

Inkjet printers spray tiny droplets of ink onto paper to form images and text. They are common in homes and small offices, often because they are inexpensive upfront and can handle color well. **Laser printers** use toner powder and a laser-based process to create sharp text and graphics, often at higher speeds and lower cost per page. Knowing the basic differences helps you understand why some environments prefer one type over the other and what typical maintenance (like replacing ink or toner) looks like.

Multifunction devices combine several functions into one unit—usually printing, scanning, copying, and sometimes faxing. These devices save space and can be more convenient than separate machines. However, a problem with the device can affect multiple functions at once. When troubleshooting, it's important to know whether only one feature (like scanning) is affected or all of them. This distinction helps you focus on either device-specific issues or broader connectivity problems.

Printers can connect to systems via **USB**, **network (Ethernet)**, or **wireless (Wi-Fi)**. USB connections typically link a single computer directly to the printer. Network printers connect to a router or switch, making them accessible to many users on the same network. Wireless printers join a Wi-Fi network, offering flexibility in placement. Understanding these connectivity options helps you interpret error messages and user descriptions like "I can print from one computer but not another."

6.7 Mobile Devices and Their Accessories

MOBILE DEVICES ARE core parts of modern infrastructure, even if they don't look like traditional computers. ITF+ expects you to recognize common mobile devices and the accessories they rely on. This section covers how these devices fit into the broader device landscape.

- **Smartphones and tablets**
- **Wearables and other mobile form factors**

- **Common mobile accessories (chargers, docks, headsets)**

Smartphones and **tablets** run mobile operating systems (like Android or iOS) and combine computing, communication, and multimedia functions in portable form. They access the internet via Wi-Fi and cellular networks and run apps for email, browsing, productivity, and entertainment. Even though they look different from PCs, they're still computers with CPUs, memory, storage, and operating systems. IT support increasingly involves helping users with mobile issues such as app installation and connectivity.

Wearables like smartwatches and fitness trackers are smaller devices that often pair with smartphones. They collect data (such as steps or heart rate) and display notifications or limited app functions. Other mobile form factors include e-readers, handheld gaming devices, and ruggedized tablets used in industrial environments. Recognizing these as part of the IT ecosystem helps you understand why infrastructure now includes more than just desktops and laptops.

Common mobile accessories include chargers and power adapters, docks or docking stations, and audio devices like wired or Bluetooth headsets. Docks may provide additional ports, external display connections, or integrated power delivery. When users have problems with mobile devices, issues may involve not only the device itself but also these accessories—for example, faulty cables or misconfigured Bluetooth pairings. Knowing what accessories exist helps you ask the right questions.

6.8 Basic Network and Internet-Connected Devices

INFRASTRUCTURE IS NOT just end-user devices; it also includes the equipment that connects them. ITF+ expects you to recognize the basic devices that make up small networks and enable internet access. This section introduces the most common network hardware you'll see.

- **Modems and routers**
- **Switches and access points**
- **Network-attached storage (NAS) basics**

A **modem** connects a local network to an internet service provider over technologies like cable, DSL, or fiber. It translates signals between your provider's network and your home or office network. A **router** directs traffic between devices on your local network and the wider internet, assigning IP addresses and enforcing basic rules. Many home devices combine modem and router functions in a single box, which can confuse users but simplifies wiring.

Switches are devices that connect multiple wired devices on the same local network, such as desktops, printers, and servers. They forward data only to the port that needs it, improving efficiency compared to older hubs. **Wireless access points (APs)** provide Wi-Fi connectivity, allowing devices to join the network without cables. Some routers have built-in switch and wireless capabilities, especially in small networks, but large environments often use separate dedicated devices.

Network-attached storage (NAS) devices are dedicated storage units connected to the network, providing shared file access to multiple users. They often support features like user accounts, shared folders, and backup tasks. NAS units are useful for small offices or home labs where central storage is needed but a full server would be overkill. Recognizing NAS devices helps you understand where shared files might be located and why they are accessible from multiple systems.

6.9 Ports, Cables, and Labeling Best Practices

WITH SO MANY DEVICES and interfaces, it's easy to get lost in a tangle of cables. ITF+ expects you to know common port and cable types and to appreciate basic labeling practices. Good cable management reduces errors and speeds up troubleshooting.

- **Identifying common ports and cable ends**
- **Using color coding and labels**
- **Avoiding cable damage and confusion**

Identifying common ports and cable ends involves learning the shapes and symbols of USB, HDMI, Ethernet (RJ-45), audio jacks, and power connectors. Over time, you'll recognize these on sight and instinctively know what each one is for. This skill is essential when setting up new devices or helping users plug things in correctly. Even at the fundamentals level, being able to say "this is an HDMI port" versus "this is an Ethernet port" is very useful.

Color coding and labels help you keep track of which cable goes where, especially in more complex setups. For example, you might use colored cables for different networks or label cables with tags indicating their destination (like "Printer 1" or "Monitor 2"). On the back of a crowded system unit or in a network closet, these labels save time by reducing guesswork. Users and other technicians will appreciate clear, readable labels when making changes or performing maintenance.

Avoiding cable damage and confusion means routing cables neatly, not bending them sharply, and ensuring they're not pinched under furniture or doors. Strain on connectors can damage ports and cause intermittent problems that are hard to diagnose. Tidy cable management also reduces tripping hazards and makes systems easier to service. These good habits make your work more professional and reduce support headaches.

6.10 Putting Device and Interface Knowledge to Use

THIS FINAL SECTION ties together your understanding of devices, interfaces, and peripherals into practical thinking. ITF+ wants you not only to recognize parts by name, but also to apply that knowledge to basic setup and troubleshooting scenarios. The more familiar these components feel, the easier later Infrastructure topics will be.

- **Translating user descriptions into device terms**
- **Choosing appropriate devices and connections**
- **Using physical checks as part of troubleshooting**

Users describe problems in everyday language, not technical jargon. They might say "the box under my desk" instead of "system unit" or "the blue cable" instead of "VGA." Your job is to translate these descriptions into device terms so you know what to look at. As you learn the official names and functions, try to mentally map them to the casual phrases you hear in real life. This skill bridges the gap between user talk and IT terminology.

Choosing appropriate devices and connections is part of basic infrastructure planning. For example, you might recommend a laptop over a desktop for a traveling employee, or suggest an SSD upgrade for someone doing heavy work on large files. You might decide to use HDMI instead of VGA for clearer monitor output. ITF+ will test whether you recognize which device or interface is best suited to a simple scenario, so practice thinking about trade-offs.

Using physical checks—like verifying cables, ports, and power—is an essential part of troubleshooting. Many issues have simple physical causes, such as loose connections or unplugged devices. Because you now know what common ports and devices look like, you can quickly scan a setup and spot obvious problems. Combining this visual inspection with the troubleshooting methodology from earlier chapters makes you a far more effective beginner-level technician.

Practice Questions – Chapter 6 (25 Questions)

1. Which component typically contains the CPU, RAM, storage, and power supply in a desktop setup?

A. Monitor
B. System unit (tower/case)
C. Keyboard
D. Printer

2. The monitor, keyboard, and mouse are BEST described as:

A. Internal components
B. Operating system tools
C. Core external input/output devices
D. Network devices

3. The motherboard's main purpose is to:

A. Provide power to the building
B. Connect and allow communication between internal components
C. Store user data long term
D. Display images on the monitor

4. Which internal component is responsible for converting wall power into the voltages required by computer components?

A. RAM
B. CPU
C. Power supply unit (PSU)
D. Hard drive

5. Which connector type is a common, rectangular general-purpose port used for keyboards, mice, and flash drives?

A. RJ-45
B. HDMI
C. USB Type-A
D. VGA

6. PS/2 ports were historically used for which type of devices?

A. Network switches and routers
B. Keyboards and mice
C. Printers and scanners
D. Monitors and projectors

7. Which display interface carries digital audio and video over a single cable and is common on TVs and computers?

A. VGA
B. HDMI

C. Parallel

D. PS/2

8. VGA is best described as:

A. A modern digital interface with audio

B. An older analog-only video connector

C. A storage device

D. A type of USB plug

9. Which term refers to a small, portable device that plugs into a USB port and is commonly used to transfer files between computers?

A. NAS

B. USB flash drive

C. Internal SSD

D. Inkjet cartridge

10. Which device type uses spinning platters and read/write heads to store data?

A. SSD

B. HDD

C. CPU

D. RAM module

11. Multifunction devices typically combine which of the following functions?

A. Print, scan, copy, and sometimes fax

B. CPU, RAM, and storage in one chip

C. Modem, router, and switch

D. Operating system and applications

12. Which printer type most commonly uses toner and is known for fast, sharp text output?

A. Inkjet

B. Laser

C. Dot matrix

D. Thermal receipt printer

13. A printer is connected to a Wi-Fi network and can be accessed by multiple PCs without cables. This is an example of which connectivity type?

A. Direct USB-only

B. Networked wireless printing

C. Parallel-only printing

D. Local serial connection

14. Which device is MOST commonly used to connect a local network to an internet service provider's network?

A. Switch

B. Access point

C. Modem

D. NAS

15. Which device connects multiple wired computers on the same local network and forwards data only to the appropriate port?

A. Router

B. Switch

C. Printer

D. Webcam

16. A wireless access point (AP) is primarily used to:

A. Provide electricity to desktop computers

B. Offer Wi-Fi connectivity to wireless devices

C. Print documents over Bluetooth

D. Store long-term backups

17. A NAS device is BEST described as:

A. A device that provides network-based shared storage to multiple users

B. A type of mobile phone

C. A replacement for all switches and routers

D. A portable flash drive

18. Which cable is MOST likely used for a wired Ethernet connection in a typical office?

A. HDMI

B. USB-C

C. RJ-45 cable

D. Audio 3.5mm cable

19. Why is labeling cables and ports a good practice?

A. It is required for devices to power on

B. It makes systems look more colorful

C. It helps identify connections quickly and reduces troubleshooting time

D. It stops all network attacks

20. A user describes "the box under my desk with all the wires coming out of it." Which component are they MOST likely referring to?

A. Monitor

B. System unit (tower/case)

C. Keyboard

D. Router

21. A smartphone and tablet are both examples of:

A. Servers

B. Mobile computing devices

C. NAS devices

D. Thin clients

22. A user can't hear audio through their wired headphones. Which physical check is MOST appropriate to try first?

A. Reinstall the operating system

B. Verify the headphones are plugged into the correct audio jack

C. Replace the CPU

D. Change the monitor's refresh rate

23. A home device provided by an ISP combines both modem and router functions. What is one potential source of confusion this might cause?

A. Users may think it is a printer

B. Users might not realize both internet and local network issues relate to the same box

C. The device cannot provide Wi-Fi

D. The device cannot connect to any computers

24. A user wants the clearest possible image on a modern monitor and currently uses a VGA cable. Which is the BEST recommendation?

A. Continue using VGA; it is always best quality

B. Switch to HDMI or DisplayPort if available on both devices

C. Use only audio cables

D. Disconnect the cable entirely

25. Why is neat routing of cables (instead of leaving them tangled) a good practice?

A. It prevents operating system crashes

B. It eliminates the need for documentation

C. It reduces strain on connectors, lowers trip hazards, and makes maintenance easier

D. It increases CPU speed

Answer Key – Chapter 6 (with Explanations)

1. B – SYSTEM UNIT (tower/case)

The system unit houses core internal components like the CPU, RAM, storage, and power supply. Monitors, keyboards, and printers are external devices connected to it.

2. C – Core external input/output devices

The monitor outputs visual information, while the keyboard and mouse provide input. They are primary external I/O devices that users interact with regularly.

3. B – Connect and allow communication between internal components

The motherboard acts as the central circuit board connecting CPU, RAM, storage, and expansion cards. It does not power the building, store data long-term, or display images.

4. C – Power supply unit (PSU)

The PSU converts AC power from the wall into lower DC voltages used by internal components. RAM, CPU, and drives consume this power but do not perform the conversion.

5. C – USB Type-A

USB Type-A is the common rectangular port used for many peripherals like keyboards, mice, and flash drives. RJ-45 is used for Ethernet, HDMI for audio/video, and VGA for analog video.

6. B – Keyboards and mice

PS/2 ports, colored purple and green, were historically used for keyboards and mice. Printers and scanners used other interfaces like parallel or USB; monitors used VGA or similar.

7. B – HDMI

HDMI is a digital interface that can carry both high-definition video and audio over one cable. VGA is analog-only; parallel and PS/2 are legacy interfaces for other purposes.

8. B – An older analog-only video connector

VGA is an analog video standard with a 15-pin blue connector. It does not carry digital audio and is being replaced by newer digital standards.

9. B – USB flash drive

A USB flash drive is small, portable, and commonly used to move files between systems via USB ports. NAS units, internal SSDs, and ink cartridges serve different roles.

10. B – HDD

Hard disk drives use spinning platters and mechanical heads to store data. SSDs use flash memory with no moving parts, while CPU and RAM are processing and memory components, not primary long-term storage.

11. A – Print, scan, copy, and sometimes fax

Multifunction devices combine several document functions into one unit. CPU/RAM/storage combinations are different components, and modem/router/switch combos are networking devices, not printers.

12. B – Laser

Laser printers use toner and a laser-based process to produce sharp text, often at high speed. Inkjets use liquid ink; dot matrix and thermal printers are different, more specialized technologies.

13. B – Networked wireless printing

A Wi-Fi–connected printer accessible by multiple PCs exemplifies networked wireless printing. Direct USB connections usually serve one PC at a time; parallel and serial connections are older, wired options.

14. C – Modem

A modem provides the connection to the ISP's network and translates signals between your local network and the provider. Switches and access points operate inside the local network; NAS provides storage.

15. B – Switch

Switches connect multiple wired devices on the same network and intelligently forward traffic only where needed. Routers connect networks together (like local to internet), while printers and webcams are endpoints.

16. B – Offer Wi-Fi connectivity to wireless devices

Wireless access points allow devices like laptops and smartphones to connect to a wired network wirelessly. They do not supply power, handle printing, or act as backup storage.

17. A – A device that provides network-based shared storage to multiple users

NAS devices are dedicated storage units on the network, accessible by many clients. They are not phones, network infrastructure replacements, or portable flash drives.

18. C – RJ-45 cable

Ethernet cables using RJ-45 connectors are standard for wired network connections. HDMI carries video/audio, USB-C is multi-purpose but not primarily network-only, and 3.5mm is used for audio.

19. C – It helps identify connections quickly and reduces troubleshooting time

Labeling cables and ports speeds up setup and problem-solving by reducing confusion. It does not directly power devices or prevent all security issues.

20. B – System unit (tower/case)

The description of a box with many wires under the desk matches the system unit. Monitors and keyboards are usually on the desk; routers are often smaller and may be elsewhere.

21. B – Mobile computing devices

Smartphones and tablets are mobile computing devices with their own OS, apps, and connectivity. They are not servers, NAS units, or thin clients by default.

22. B – Verify the headphones are plugged into the correct audio jack

Checking the physical connection is a simple, appropriate first step. Reinstalling the OS or replacing the CPU is excessive for a likely misplugged or muted audio issue.

23. B – Users might not realize both internet and local network issues relate to the same box

When modem and router functions are combined, users may not understand that one device affects both internet access and local routing. This can complicate troubleshooting conversations.

24. B – Switch to HDMI or DisplayPort if available on both devices

Digital connections like HDMI or DisplayPort generally provide clearer images than analog VGA, especially at higher resolutions. Audio cables and disconnecting the cable do not improve picture quality.

25. C – It reduces strain on connectors, lowers trip hazards, and makes maintenance easier

Neatly routed cables are less likely to be damaged, pulled out, or tripped over. This doesn't directly change CPU speed but does contribute to reliability and easier support.

Chapter 7

Inside the Computer – Components and Storage (Infrastructure – Part 2)

This chapter dives deeper into what's *inside* the system unit and how storage really works. You'll learn what each major component does, how they connect, and how different storage types affect performance and reliability. The goal is to make you comfortable with the "guts" of a computer so later infrastructure topics feel natural.

7.1 The Motherboard: The System's Backbone

THE MOTHERBOARD IS the central platform that ties all the internal components together. ITF+ wants you to recognize its role and the key things that attach to it. Understanding this backbone makes the layout of a computer much less mysterious.

- **Motherboard as the main circuit board**
- **Common onboard components and headers**
- **Expansion slots for add-on cards**

The **motherboard** is the main printed circuit board (PCB) inside the system. It provides electrical paths (traces) that allow the CPU, RAM, storage, and other components to communicate. It also hosts firmware chips and connectors for power, ports, and front-panel buttons. When a motherboard fails, many or all system functions are affected, which is why replacing it is a major repair. Recognizing it as the central hub helps explain why everything plugs into it.

Motherboards include **onboard components** like integrated audio, network controllers, and USB controllers. They also have **headers**—small pin connectors—for front-panel ports, power/reset buttons, and case LEDs. You'll see connectors for fans, SATA ports for drives, and slots for RAM and the CPU socket. Even if you never build a PC, knowing these exist helps you understand diagrams and why some issues (like a broken front USB port) may be traced back to motherboard connections.

Expansion slots, such as PCI Express (PCIe), allow you to add capabilities via cards. Common add-on cards include dedicated graphics cards, extra network adapters, or storage controllers. These cards plug into specific slots and are secured with screws or clips. Expansion gives systems flexibility to handle specialized tasks, and knowing that this is possible explains why business workstations may look similar outside but be configured very differently inside.

7.2 The CPU: Central Processing Unit Basics

THE CPU IS OFTEN CALLED the "brain" of the computer, but ITF+ only needs you to understand it at a high level. You don't have to know the internal architecture, just what it generally does and what affects its performance. This section focuses on the essentials.

- **CPU's role in executing instructions**
- **Clock speed and cores (basic idea)**
- **Cooling considerations for the CPU**

The **CPU (Central Processing Unit)** executes instructions from programs and the operating system. It performs calculations, makes logical decisions, and coordinates other hardware operations. Every time you open an application, run a command, or load a page, the CPU is involved. Faster or more capable CPUs can handle more instructions per second, which affects responsiveness, especially for demanding tasks.

Clock speed (measured in gigahertz) indicates how many cycles per second the CPU can perform, while **cores** refer to how many processing units exist within the chip. More cores allow a CPU to work on multiple tasks in parallel, which can improve performance for multitasking or multi-threaded applications. ITF+ doesn't require you to compare detailed benchmarks; you just need to know that higher clock speeds and more cores generally mean more processing capability, within limits.

CPUs generate significant heat, which must be managed with **cooling solutions** like heatsinks and fans. If cooling is inadequate—due to dust buildup, fan failure, or poor installation—the CPU may throttle its speed to avoid damage or the system may shut down unexpectedly. This is why airflow and proper fan operation matter. Awareness of CPU cooling helps you interpret symptoms like sudden shutdowns under heavy load.

7.3 RAM: System Memory and Its Function

RANDOM ACCESS MEMORY (RAM) plays a crucial role in system performance. ITF+ wants you to know what RAM does, how it differs from storage, and what happens when there isn't enough of it. This section sharpens that distinction.

- **RAM as temporary working memory**
- **Volatile vs. non-volatile storage**
- **Symptoms of insufficient RAM**

RAM holds data and instructions that the CPU is actively using. Because RAM is much faster than long-term storage, it allows quick access to running programs and open files. When you launch an application, parts of it are loaded into RAM so the CPU can work with it efficiently. RAM capacity is one of the key specs that influences how many applications can run smoothly at once.

Volatile storage, like RAM, loses its contents when power is turned off. **Non-volatile** storage, like HDDs and SSDs, retains data even when the system is shut down. This is a fundamental difference: RAM is for short-term work; storage is for long-term data. ITF+ will test whether you can correctly identify which is which and what they're used for. Confusing them is a common beginner mistake.

When there isn't enough RAM, the system may rely heavily on virtual memory—using slower storage space as an extension of RAM. Symptoms include frequent pauses, prolonged app switching, and constant drive activity. Programs may crash or refuse to open if memory is too constrained. Closing unused applications or upgrading RAM capacity are typical responses to these issues.

7.4 Storage Technologies: HDD vs. SSD vs. Hybrid

STORAGE DEVICES ARE where your OS, applications, and files live long-term. ITF+ expects you to understand the basic differences between main storage technologies. This section compares HDDs, SSDs, and hybrid options.

- **HDD (Hard Disk Drive) characteristics**
- **SSD (Solid-State Drive) characteristics**

- **Hybrid drives and common use cases**

HDDs store data on spinning magnetic platters with a moving read/write head. They offer relatively large capacities at low cost per gigabyte. However, because they involve mechanical movement, they are slower to access data and can be more vulnerable to physical shock. HDDs are still widely used for bulk storage and backups where speed is less critical. Recognizing an HDD's strengths and limitations helps explain why systems feel slower when using them as primary drives.

SSDs use flash memory with no moving parts, providing much faster access times and lower latency. This results in quicker boot times, faster application launches, and more responsive systems. SSDs are also more resistant to drops and vibration, making them ideal for laptops and portable devices. Their main drawback is typically higher cost per gigabyte compared to HDDs, though prices continue to decrease over time.

Hybrid drives combine elements of HDDs and SSDs, often by including a small amount of solid-state storage as a cache for frequently accessed data. The goal is to provide better performance than a pure HDD while keeping costs lower than a large SSD. For ITF+, you just need to know that hybrid drives try to balance speed and capacity. They can be a good compromise in systems where budget and performance must both be considered.

7.5 Storage Interfaces and Form Factors

STORAGE DEVICES DON'T just differ in technology; they also connect in different ways and come in different shapes. ITF+ covers the basics of common interfaces and form factors. Understanding these helps you recognize how drives fit and connect inside systems.

- **SATA vs. NVMe (high-level)**
- **2.5" vs. 3.5" drives and M.2 form factor**
- **Internal vs. external storage connections**

SATA (Serial ATA) is a common interface used by many HDDs and some SSDs. It offers decent performance and uses familiar flat data cables plus power connectors. **NVMe** drives, on the other hand, connect via PCIe and provide much faster data transfer, especially for SSDs. NVMe drives often come in the M.2 form factor and plug directly into the motherboard. ITF+ doesn't require you to know speeds, just that NVMe is a faster, modern option compared to SATA.

Physical **form factors** include 3.5" and 2.5" drives, as well as M.2 modules. Traditional desktop HDDs often use the larger 3.5" form factor, while laptop drives and many SSDs use 2.5". **M.2** is a slim, stick-like module that mounts flat on the motherboard, commonly used for NVMe SSDs. Knowing these form factors helps you understand why some drives fit in certain bays and not others.

Internal storage connects directly inside the system via SATA, NVMe, or similar interfaces. **External storage** uses connections like USB or Thunderbolt to attach from outside the case. External drives are convenient for backups or portable storage, but they usually aren't as fast or integrated as internal drives. Recognizing the difference helps you interpret user descriptions like "the external drive I plug in" versus "the main drive inside my PC."

7.6 File Systems and Basic Folder Structure

ONCE DATA IS ON A DRIVE, it needs to be organized so the operating system can find it. File systems and folders provide this structure. ITF+ expects basic awareness of file systems and how files and directories are arranged.

- **What a file system does**
- **Common folder paths and user data locations**
- **Why file organization and naming matter**

A **file system** defines how data is stored and retrieved on a storage device. It manages structures like directories (folders), file names, and metadata, and keeps track of where each file's data is physically located. Examples include NTFS on Windows or ext4 on many Linux systems. While ITF+ doesn't require deep knowledge of each type, you should know that the file system is what makes a raw drive usable for storing files.

Common folder paths help users and technicians find important data. On Windows, user documents are often stored under C:\Users\<username>\Documents, while downloads go to a Downloads folder. On other operating systems, similar user home directories exist. Knowing these default locations helps you locate files, back up user data, and understand where applications might save settings.

Good file organization and naming make it easier to find things and reduce confusion. Using descriptive names and logical folder structures (like organizing by project or date) helps both users and support staff. Poor organization leads to lost files, accidental deletion, and wasted time searching. ITF+ may test your understanding of basic file navigation and the importance of organizing data sensibly.

7.7 Storage Capacity, Free Space, and Performance

STORAGE CAPACITY ISN'T just about whether files fit; it also affects performance and reliability. ITF+ expects you to understand the impact of full or nearly full drives. This section explains why free space matters.

- **Capacity vs. used and free space**
- **Impact of low free space on performance**
- **Monitoring and managing storage usage**

Every drive has a **total capacity**, part of which is **used space** (data already stored) and part **free space** (available for new data). Operating systems show these values in properties dialogs or disk management tools. Understanding these metrics helps you answer questions like "Do I have room to install this program?" or "Why am I getting low disk space warnings?" Knowing that a drive can't be overfilled without consequences is key.

Low free space can slow systems down, especially on the drive that hosts the operating system. The OS needs room for temporary files, virtual memory, updates, and logs. When a drive is nearly full, the system struggles to allocate space efficiently, which can cause delays, failed updates, or crashes. On HDDs, fragmentation can also worsen performance, though SSDs handle this differently.

Monitoring and managing storage means periodically checking free space and cleaning up unnecessary files. Tools like disk cleanup utilities, uninstalling unused programs, and moving large media files to external or network storage are common strategies. ITF+ may present scenarios where freeing space is the best answer to performance or error problems. Recognizing when storage is the bottleneck is a useful troubleshooting skill.

7.8 Backups and Data Protection Basics

DATA STORED ON A DRIVE is vulnerable to many risks, including hardware failure, accidental deletion, and malware. ITF+ expects you to understand the basic idea of backups and why they are critical. This section lays out core backup concepts.

- **Why backups are essential**
- **Backup types (full vs. incremental – high level)**
- **Local vs. cloud backup options**

Backups are **copies of data** kept in separate locations so that information can be restored if something goes wrong. Hardware can fail without warning, users can delete files by accident, and ransomware can encrypt important data. Without a backup, recovery may be impossible or very expensive. Understanding this risk helps you see why backup strategies are a fundamental part of IT planning.

Backup types include **full backups**, which copy all selected data, and **incremental** or **differential** backups, which copy only changes since the last backup of a certain type. Full backups are simple to understand but consume more time and storage. Incremental approaches are more efficient but require careful management to restore. ITF+ only requires that you understand the concept that backups can be done in different ways, not the full technical details.

Local backups use external drives, NAS devices, or other on-site storage. **Cloud backups** send data over the internet to remote servers managed by providers. Local backups can be faster to restore but are vulnerable to physical disasters at the same location. Cloud backups add off-site protection but depend on network connectivity and provider reliability. Many organizations use a combination of both for resilience.

7.9 Optical Media, Removable Storage, and Their Uses

NOT ALL STORAGE IS fixed or always connected. Optical discs and removable storage media still have roles in some environments. ITF+ expects you to recognize these alternatives and what they're good for.

- **Optical media (CD, DVD, Blu-ray)**
- **Removable flash-based media (USB, SD cards)**
- **Use cases and limitations of removable storage**

Optical media like CDs, DVDs, and Blu-ray discs store data using laser-readable patterns on a disc surface. They can be read-only (pressed media) or recordable/re-writable. Historically, they were used for software distribution, movies, music, and backups. While many modern systems ship without optical drives, they still show up in legacy systems and some media workflows. ITF+ may reference them as examples of removable, non-magnetic storage.

Removable flash-based media includes **USB flash drives** and **memory cards** like SD, microSD, and CompactFlash. These devices are solid-state, small, and easily portable. They are widely used to transfer data between systems, expand storage in cameras and phones, or boot lightweight operating systems and recovery tools. Their convenience makes them very common in both home and office settings.

Removable storage has benefits and limitations. On the plus side, it's portable, easy to share, and often inexpensive. On the downside, it can be lost, stolen, or damaged, and some media are relatively easy to corrupt if unplugged unsafely. Security policies often govern how removable media can be used because of the risk of malware or data breaches. ITF+ expects you to understand both the usefulness and the risks.

7.10 Putting Internal Component Knowledge into Practice

THIS SECTION TIES THE internal component and storage concepts together into practical usage and troubleshooting. ITF+ questions will often hint at hardware or storage issues through symptoms. Your job is to recognize which component is likely involved.

- **Recognizing hardware-related symptoms**
- **Choosing appropriate storage for different needs**
- **Using simple internal checks in troubleshooting scenarios**

Hardware-related symptoms might include strange noises (like clicking from a failing HDD), random shutdowns (power or heat issues), or graphical artifacts (possible GPU problems). Performance issues under load may point toward CPU or RAM limitations. By matching symptoms to likely components, you can form better theories during troubleshooting. ITF+ scenarios frequently expect you to make these logical connections.

Choosing appropriate storage means understanding trade-offs between speed, capacity, and cost. For a gaming or productivity laptop, an SSD as the primary drive makes sense for speed. For a backup server or media archive, large HDDs might be more cost-effective. Hybrid and NVMe options fit when budgets allow and performance is a priority. Being able to recommend sensible combinations shows you understand infrastructure basics.

Simple internal checks might include visually inspecting components for loose cables, checking that drives are detected in firmware or the OS, and reviewing storage usage in system tools. While entry-level roles may not always open cases, you should still understand what someone *would* check if internal access is allowed. Combining physical awareness with software tools makes your troubleshooting more complete and grounded.

Practice Questions – Chapter 7 (25 Questions)

1. What is the primary role of the motherboard in a computer system?
A. To display images on the screen
B. To connect and allow communication among internal components
C. To permanently store user data
D. To provide internet service

2. Expansion slots on the motherboard are mainly used for:
A. Installing the operating system
B. Attaching add-on cards like graphics or network cards
C. Mounting hard drives
D. Cooling the CPU

3. The CPU is BEST described as:
A. Long-term storage for files
B. The main component that executes instructions and performs calculations
C. A device that only controls the monitor
D. A backup power source

4. Which factor is MOST associated with how many tasks a CPU can handle in parallel?

A. Screen size
B. Number of cores
C. Printer type
D. Fan color
5. Why is proper cooling important for the CPU?
A. It improves monitor brightness
B. It prevents overheating that can cause throttling or shutdowns
C. It makes the keyboard more responsive
D. It increases printer speed
6. Which statement correctly describes RAM?
A. It is non-volatile storage that persists when power is off
B. It is volatile memory used for active programs and data
C. It is a type of removable optical media
D. It is only used for backups
7. What happens to data stored in RAM when power is turned off?
A. It is saved permanently to the hard drive
B. It is retained until the RAM is removed
C. It is lost because RAM is volatile
D. It becomes read-only
8. Which of the following is a key difference between HDD and SSD technology?
A. HDDs use flash memory; SSDs use spinning platters
B. HDDs are always faster than SSDs
C. HDDs use spinning platters; SSDs have no moving parts
D. SSDs cannot store operating systems
9. A user complains about very slow boot times and long application launches on a system with an older HDD. Which upgrade is MOST likely to improve this?
A. Replace the monitor
B. Install an SSD as the primary drive
C. Add another printer
D. Downgrade the operating system
10. Which interface is commonly used by traditional hard drives and some SSDs, using flat data cables?
A. HDMI
B. SATA
C. RJ-45
D. PS/2
11. Which form factor is MOST common for laptop drives?
A. 3.5"
B. 2.5"
C. Full ATX
D. PCIe slot
12. What is an M.2 drive?
A. A large external hard drive
B. A small, card-like module that mounts on the motherboard, often used for SSDs
C. A type of CPU

D. A specific model of printer
13. A file system primarily:
A. Connects the CPU to the monitor
B. Manages how files and directories are stored and retrieved on a drive
C. Controls the temperature of the system
D. Protects the system from all malware
14. On a typical Windows system, user documents are MOST likely to be found under:
A. C:\Windows\System32
B. C:\Program Files
C. C:\Users<username>\Documents
D. D:\Drivers
15. Which of the following is a likely consequence of a system drive being almost completely full?
A. Increased internet speed
B. Faster boot times
C. Slower performance and possible errors during updates
D. Improved screen resolution
16. Why are backups important?
A. They speed up the CPU
B. They provide copies of data that can be restored after loss or corruption
C. They increase screen brightness
D. They eliminate the need for security software
17. A full backup is best described as:
A. Copying only the files changed today
B. Copying all selected data regardless of previous backups
C. A backup that never finishes
D. A backup that stores only system files
18. Which option describes a cloud backup?
A. Copying files to an external hard drive on your desk
B. Saving files on a USB stick
C. Sending encrypted copies of data to remote servers over the internet
D. Burning data to a DVD
19. CDs, DVDs, and Blu-ray discs are examples of:
A. Magnetic storage
B. Optical media
C. Flash-based storage
D. Virtual memory
20. Which device is MOST appropriate for quickly transferring a small set of files between two computers?
A. Internal HDD
B. USB flash drive
C. NAS used only for backups
D. CPU cooler
21. A user unplugs a USB flash drive while files are still being written. What is a possible result?
A. Faster performance
B. Improved audio quality

C. File corruption or incomplete files

D. Automatic upgrade of the operating system

22. A drive makes frequent clicking noises and sometimes disappears from the system. This MOST likely indicates a problem with:

A. The monitor

B. The HDD hardware

C. The keyboard

D. The CPU fan color

23. For an office workstation that regularly opens large applications and files, which is generally the BEST choice for the primary system drive?

A. A small SSD

B. A very large but slow tape drive

C. A floppy disk

D. A plotter

24. A user only needs cheap, high-capacity storage for long-term backups that aren't accessed often. Which storage type is MOST appropriate?

A. High-end NVMe SSD

B. Large-capacity HDD

C. Small USB thumb drive

D. Only cloud storage with very small limits

25. Which action is part of using internal component knowledge in troubleshooting?

A. Ignoring unusual noises inside the case

B. Checking whether the OS can see all installed drives and how much free space they have

C. Replacing components at random without diagnosis

D. Refusing to open system tools or look at storage information

Answer Key – Chapter 7 (with Explanations)

1. B – TO CONNECT AND allow communication among internal components

The motherboard is the central board that links the CPU, RAM, storage, and other components. It doesn't directly display images, store all user data by itself, or provide internet service.

2. B – Attaching add-on cards like graphics or network cards

Expansion slots (like PCIe) allow additional cards to be installed to extend system capabilities. Operating systems are installed on storage, not in expansion slots.

3. B – The main component that executes instructions and performs calculations

The CPU carries out program instructions and calculations, coordinating much of the system's work. It is not used for long-term storage or as a backup power source.

4. B – Number of cores

More cores allow a CPU to handle multiple tasks in parallel, improving multitasking and multi-threaded performance. Screen size, printer type, and fan color don't meaningfully affect CPU parallelism.

5. B – It prevents overheating that can cause throttling or shutdowns

Proper cooling keeps the CPU within safe temperature ranges. Overheating can force the CPU to slow down (throttle) or shut down the system to prevent damage.

6. B – It is volatile memory used for active programs and data

RAM holds data and programs currently in use and loses its contents when power is lost. Non-volatile storage like HDDs and SSDs persist after shutdown.

7. C – It is lost because RAM is volatile

By definition, volatile memory like RAM does not retain data without power. The system must load data back into RAM from storage at each startup.

8. C – HDDs use spinning platters; SSDs have no moving parts

HDDs are mechanical devices, while SSDs use solid-state flash memory. SSDs are typically faster and more shock-resistant, and they absolutely can store operating systems.

9. B – Install an SSD as the primary drive

Replacing an older HDD with an SSD (or adding an SSD and installing the OS on it) greatly improves boot and app launch times. Monitors and printers won't fix slow disk access.

10. B – SATA

SATA is a common interface for internal HDDs and many SSDs, using flat cables to connect drives to the motherboard. HDMI is for video, RJ-45 for network, and PS/2 for old keyboards/mice.

11. B – 2.5"

Laptops commonly use 2.5" drives due to their smaller form factor. 3.5" drives are typical in desktops, ATX refers to motherboard size, and PCIe slots are for cards, not standard drives.

12. B – A small, card-like module that mounts on the motherboard, often used for SSDs

M.2 drives are slim modules that plug into dedicated slots on the motherboard, frequently used by NVMe SSDs. They are not CPUs, printers, or large external drives.

13. B – Manages how files and directories are stored and retrieved on a drive

A file system organizes files, folders, and metadata on a storage device. It doesn't handle display output or block all malware by itself.

14. C – C:\Users<username>\Documents

On Windows, user documents are typically found within the user profile directory under C:\Users. System32 and Program Files contain OS and application files, not user documents.

15. C – Slower performance and possible errors during updates

A nearly full system drive can slow performance and prevent updates or temporary files from being written, causing various errors. It does not boost internet speed or resolution.

16. B – They provide copies of data that can be restored after loss or corruption

Backups are your safety net when data is lost due to hardware failure, deletion, or other issues. They don't directly speed hardware or replace security practices.

17. B – Copying all selected data regardless of previous backups

A full backup captures all chosen data in one operation. Incremental and differential methods copy changes relative to prior backups.

18. C – Sending encrypted copies of data to remote servers over the internet

Cloud backups involve sending copies of data to remote locations managed by providers. Local external drives and USB sticks are not cloud solutions.

19. B – Optical media

CDs, DVDs, and Blu-ray discs store data using optical methods. Magnetic storage includes HDDs and tapes; flash-based storage includes SSDs and USB drives.

20. B – USB flash drive

USB flash drives are ideal for quick, small file transfers between systems. Internal HDDs, NAS, and coolers don't offer the same portability and convenience for this purpose.

21. C – File corruption or incomplete files

Unplugging a drive while data is being written can interrupt the process, leading to corrupted or incomplete files. It does not improve performance or trigger OS upgrades.

22. B – The HDD hardware

Clicking noises and intermittent disappearance are classic symptoms of a failing hard drive. Monitors, keyboards, or fan colors don't typically cause these issues.

23. A – A small SSD

An SSD (even a smaller-capacity one) as the primary drive is usually best for applications and OS responsiveness in an office workstation. Tape, floppies, and plotters are not suitable primary system drives.

24. B – Large-capacity HDD

HDDs are cost-effective for high-capacity, infrequently accessed backups. High-end NVMe SSDs are faster but more expensive and unnecessary if speed is not a priority.

25. B – Checking whether the OS can see all installed drives and how much free space they have

Using system tools to verify drive detection and free space is a key part of hardware and storage troubleshooting. Ignoring symptoms or randomly swapping parts is inefficient and unprofessional.

Chapter 8

Networks, Internet Services, and Wireless Basics (Infrastructure – Part 3)

This chapter finishes the Infrastructure domain by focusing on how devices talk to each other over networks and the internet. You'll learn core networking concepts, common devices, addressing basics, and how wireless networking works. The goal is to give you a clear mental map of what happens between "I click a link" and "the page appears."

8.1 What a Network Is (and Why We Use Them)

AT ITS CORE, A NETWORK is simply a way for devices to share resources and information. ITF+ expects you to understand why networks exist and what basic benefits they provide. This section sets the foundation for everything that follows.

- **Definition of a network**
- **Benefits of networking devices**
- **Local vs. wide-area connections (high level)**

A **network** is a collection of interconnected devices—such as computers, printers, phones, and servers—that can communicate and share resources. These connections can be wired, wireless, or a mix of both. Networks can exist within a single room, across a building, or span cities and continents. When you save to a shared drive, print to a network printer, or access a website, you're using some form of network.

Networking devices brings clear benefits. Users can share files without carrying USB drives, access centralized printers, and collaborate through shared applications or cloud services. IT can manage software updates and security centrally instead of visiting every machine individually. Networks also make remote access possible, so employees can work from home or branch offices. Without networking, organizations would be far less efficient and flexible.

Local connections within the same building or home are often called **local area networks (LANs)**, while connections that span cities or regions—like the public internet—are part of **wide area networks (WANs)**. LANs usually offer higher speed and more control, while WANs connect those LANs together over longer distances. Understanding this distinction helps you interpret phrases like "on the local network" versus "over the internet."

8.2 Basic Networking Devices: Modem, Router, Switch

DIFFERENT DEVICES PLAY different roles in moving data around. ITF+ expects you to recognize the basic functions of modems, routers, and switches. Even in a small home network, you're likely to see some combination of these three.

- **Modem: connecting to the ISP**
- **Router: directing traffic and assigning addresses**
- **Switch: connecting local wired devices**

A **modem** connects your local network to your internet service provider (ISP). It converts signals from the ISP's medium—like cable, DSL, or fiber—into digital signals usable by your local network devices. Without a modem, your home or office wouldn't be able to reach the internet. Some devices combine modem and router functions into a single box, which can confuse users about what does what.

A **router** sits between your local network and other networks, such as the internet. It directs data packets to their correct destinations and often provides **NAT (Network Address Translation)** and basic firewall functions. Most home routers also assign IP addresses to devices via DHCP. When users say "my Wi-Fi router," they're usually referring to a device that acts as router, switch, and wireless access point in one.

A **switch** connects multiple wired devices within the same local network. It forwards data only to the specific port where the destination device resides, which is more efficient than older hubs that sent all traffic everywhere. Switches are common in offices and network closets, where many desktops and printers need wired connections. In small setups, a few switch ports may be built into the router itself.

8.3 IP Addresses and Basic Addressing Concepts

EVERY DEVICE ON A NETWORK needs an address so data knows where to go. ITF+ doesn't require deep networking skills, but you should understand basic IP addressing concepts. This helps you follow troubleshooting steps and recognize simple network issues.

- **IP addresses as numerical identifiers**
- **Private vs. public IP addresses (high level)**
- **Dynamic addressing with DHCP**

An **IP address** is a numeric label assigned to each device on a network, allowing data to be routed to and from it. In IPv4, addresses are usually written as four numbers separated by dots, like 192.168.1.10. When you visit a website, your device uses IP addresses behind the scenes to contact the correct server. Without these addresses, networked devices wouldn't know where to send responses.

Private IP addresses are used inside local networks and are not routable on the public internet. **Public IP addresses** are globally unique and used on the internet-facing side of routers and servers. Your home devices often use private addresses like 192.168.x.x, while your router has a public address assigned by your ISP. NAT on the router translates between many private internal addresses and the single public address.

Most devices get their IP addresses automatically using **DHCP (Dynamic Host Configuration Protocol)**. A DHCP server—often the router—leases an address to each device that connects, along with other settings like the default gateway and DNS servers. This automation makes network configuration easier for users and reduces errors. Understanding that addresses can be dynamic helps explain why a device's IP might change over time.

8.4 DNS, URLs, and How We Reach Websites

HUMANS DON'T LIKE TYPING IP addresses all day, so we use names instead. ITF+ wants you to know the relationship between URLs, domain names, and DNS. This section explains the "phone book of the internet" in simple terms.

- **Domain names and URLs**
- **DNS as a name-to-address translator**

- **What happens (high level) when you enter a web address**

A **domain name** is the human-friendly name of a site or service, such as example.com. A **URL (Uniform Resource Locator)** includes the domain plus additional details like the protocol (https://) and path (/page1). When you type a URL into your browser, you are telling it what resource you want and where to find it. Domain names are easier for people to remember than IP addresses.

DNS (Domain Name System) is like the internet's phone book. It translates domain names into IP addresses so computers can connect to the right servers. When your device needs to contact example.com, it asks a DNS server for the corresponding IP address. If DNS is misconfigured or not working, you may see "server not found" errors even if your internet connection is otherwise fine.

At a high level, when you enter a web address, your device first uses DNS to find the server's IP address. Then it contacts that IP using the appropriate protocol (usually HTTP or HTTPS). The server receives the request, processes it, and sends back the web page data. Your browser interprets this data and displays it as text, images, and interactive elements. Understanding this flow helps you reason about where things might be going wrong.

8.5 Wired Network Basics: Ethernet and Cabling

WIRED NETWORKS ARE still widely used because they're stable and fast. ITF+ expects you to recognize basic wired networking concepts and cabling. This section covers Ethernet and what typical wired connections look like.

- **Ethernet as the common wired LAN technology**
- **RJ-45 connectors and twisted-pair cables**
- **Benefits and trade-offs of wired connections**

Ethernet is the dominant technology for wired local area networks. It defines how data is formatted and transmitted over cables between devices like PCs, switches, and routers. Ethernet speeds range from older 10/100 Mbps to 1 Gbps and beyond. On the exam, you don't need to memorize all variants; just know that Ethernet is the typical wired standard.

Ethernet cables often use **twisted-pair** wiring with **RJ-45 connectors** at the ends. These connectors look wider than phone jacks and typically click into network ports on devices. The cables are sometimes called Cat5e, Cat6, or similar, indicating category and performance levels. Recognizing an RJ-45 cable and port is essential when you're plugging in or diagnosing wired connections.

Wired connections offer benefits like consistent speed, low latency, and resistance to wireless interference. They're often preferred for servers, desktops, and devices that require steady, high-throughput connections. The trade-off is reduced mobility: devices must be near outlets or have cables run to them. Understanding when wired is better than wireless helps you answer scenario-based questions about network choices.

8.6 Wireless Network Basics: Wi-Fi Concepts

WIRELESS NETWORKS PROVIDE flexibility and convenience, especially for mobile devices. ITF+ expects a basic understanding of Wi-Fi concepts and common issues. This section focuses on what you need to know at the fundamentals level.

- **Wi-Fi as wireless LAN technology**

- **SSID and basic security (passwords)**
- **Strengths and limitations of Wi-Fi**

Wi-Fi is a wireless LAN technology that uses radio signals to connect devices to a network via access points or routers. It operates on specific frequency bands, typically 2.4 GHz and 5 GHz, with newer standards offering higher speeds and capabilities. Wi-Fi allows laptops, phones, and tablets to connect without cables, enabling flexible workspaces and mobility. Even so, devices must be within range of the signal.

Each Wi-Fi network is identified by an **SSID (Service Set Identifier)**, which is the network name you see when you browse available Wi-Fi lists. Most networks are secured with a password using standards like WPA2 or WPA3. Users must enter the correct password to join the network, which helps prevent unauthorized access. Changing the SSID and password from default values is a basic security best practice.

Wi-Fi's strengths include convenience, mobility, and easy connection of many devices. Its limitations include potential interference from walls, other wireless devices, and distance. Speeds can vary depending on signal strength and network congestion. Understanding these trade-offs helps you troubleshoot complaints like "the Wi-Fi is weak in the back room" or decide when a wired connection might be more reliable.

8.7 Internet Connection Types (Home and Small Office)

THERE ARE MULTIPLE ways to connect to the internet, especially in home and small office settings. ITF+ expects you to recognize the main connection types and their general characteristics. This section summarizes the most common options.

- **Cable and DSL connections**
- **Fiber connections**
- **Cellular and hotspot options**

Cable internet uses the same coaxial infrastructure as cable TV providers, offering high speeds suitable for many homes and small businesses. **DSL (Digital Subscriber Line)** uses telephone lines but separates voice and data so they can function simultaneously. Both typically provide "always-on" connectivity, with speed depending on plan and distance from provider equipment. These technologies are widely available in many regions.

Fiber internet uses fiber-optic cables to transmit data as light, offering very high speeds and low latency. Fiber connections can support large uploads and downloads, making them ideal for heavy cloud usage, media production, and business needs. However, fiber availability may be limited in some areas compared to cable or DSL. Knowing that fiber usually represents the "top end" of consumer connections helps in scenario questions about performance needs.

Cellular connections use mobile networks (3G, 4G, 5G) to provide internet access, often through phones, mobile hotspots, or built-in cellular modems in laptops. These are useful for on-the-go connectivity or in locations without wired broadband. However, they may have data caps, variable speeds, and higher latency. Tethering a laptop to a phone's hotspot is a common way to connect temporarily when Wi-Fi isn't available.

8.8 Common Network and Internet Issues (User-Level)

EVEN BASIC USERS OFTEN encounter network problems. ITF+ wants you to recognize typical symptoms and reasonable first steps. This section frames network issues from a user-level troubleshooting perspective.

- **No connection vs. slow connection**
- **Local vs. internet-wide problems**
- **Simple checks: cables, Wi-Fi status, and power**

A **no connection** situation might show as a red X or no Wi-Fi icon, websites failing to load at all, or "no network" messages. A **slow connection** means some things still work but sluggishly—pages take long to load, video buffers, or large downloads crawl. Distinguishing between "nothing works" and "everything is just slow" helps you decide whether to suspect a complete outage, congestion, or a device-specific issue.

Understanding whether the issue is **local** or **internet-wide** is important. If only one device can't connect but others are fine, the problem is likely on that device. If all devices in the house are offline, the router, modem, or ISP may be at fault. Sometimes specific websites are down while others work, indicating a server or service-specific issue rather than your connection. Asking "does this happen on other sites or devices?" is a key question.

Simple checks often resolve common problems. For wired connections, confirm cables are plugged in securely and check link lights on network ports or switches. For Wi-Fi, ensure the device's Wi-Fi is turned on, the correct SSID is selected, and the password is correct. Power-cycling the modem/router (turning it off, waiting a bit, and turning it on) can fix temporary glitches—though this should be done carefully and not constantly. These basic steps often appear as options in exam scenarios.

8.9 Network Security Basics (User Perspective)

NETWORKING INTRODUCES security risks, which you'll explore more deeply in the Security domain. For now, ITF+ expects basic awareness of common security practices for networks. This section covers simple, user-facing protections.

- **Securing Wi-Fi networks with passwords**
- **Avoiding open and unknown networks**
- **Basic router security hygiene (high level)**

Securing Wi-Fi networks with strong passwords helps prevent unauthorized users from joining and consuming bandwidth or accessing internal resources. Encryption standards like WPA2 or WPA3 protect data in transit between devices and access points. Weak or default passwords make it easier for attackers or neighbors to gain access. Encouraging users to choose strong, unique Wi-Fi passwords is a simple but powerful security step.

Open networks (those without passwords) and unknown public Wi-Fi can be risky. On unsecured networks, others may potentially eavesdrop on traffic or attempt attacks on connected devices. When using public Wi-Fi, it's wise to avoid accessing sensitive accounts unless proper encryption (HTTPS, VPN) is in place. ITF+ wants you to recognize that "free Wi-Fi" may come with security trade-offs.

Basic router security hygiene includes changing default admin usernames and passwords, applying firmware updates, and disabling remote management features unless needed. Default credentials are widely known and can be exploited by attackers if left unchanged. While entry-level users may not handle all router configuration, appreciating these best practices helps you understand why security-conscious setups behave the way they do.

8.10 Putting Networking Basics Together

THIS FINAL SECTION ties together networking devices, addressing, wireless, and basic troubleshooting into a coherent picture. ITF+ questions often give you small network scenarios and ask what's happening or what you should do. Having a big-picture view helps you reason through those situations.

- **Seeing the "path" from device to internet and back**
- **Relating user complaints to specific layers (device, network, internet)**
- **Using basic checks before advanced steps**

When you browse a website, your device connects to a Wi-Fi access point or Ethernet switch, which forwards data to the router, then to the modem, then out to the ISP and the wider internet. Replies come back along the same path in reverse. Knowing this chain helps you mentally locate where a problem might be: is the device not on Wi-Fi, is the router down, or is the ISP offline? Each link in the chain can be tested or checked.

User complaints can often be mapped to specific parts of the system. "Only this laptop can't get online" suggests a device configuration or Wi-Fi issue. "Nothing in the building can reach any site" suggests a router, modem, or ISP outage. "One website won't load but others do" hints at a site-specific or DNS problem. Thinking in terms of scope (one device, many devices, one site, many sites) is a powerful troubleshooting shortcut.

Basic checks—like verifying Wi-Fi is enabled, ensuring cables are plugged in, confirming SSID and password, and power-cycling equipment when appropriate—should come before complex diagnostics. Many exam questions will include tempting advanced options alongside these simple steps. ITF+ rewards candidates who choose the safe, logical first actions aligned with an entry-level support role.

Practice Questions – Chapter 8 (25 Questions)

1. Which statement BEST describes a network?
A. A single standalone computer with no connections
B. A collection of interconnected devices that share resources and information
C. A device that prints documents
D. A type of storage drive

2. A home router is primarily responsible for:
A. Cooling the CPU
B. Displaying images on the monitor
C. Directing traffic between the local network and other networks
D. Storing all user files permanently

3. A modem's main role is to:
A. Connect a local network to an internet service provider
B. Provide Wi-Fi inside a building
C. Print over the network
D. Assign usernames to users

4. A switch is used to:
A. Connect multiple wired devices on the same local network
B. Provide fiber internet from the ISP
C. Translate domain names into IP addresses

D. Handle all wireless connections

5. An IPv4 address typically looks like:

A. www.example.com

B. C:\Users\Name

C. 192.168.1.25

D. 08:AF:23:99:11:CD

6. Which statement BEST describes a private IP address?

A. It is publicly visible on the internet and always globally unique

B. It is used only by servers and never by home devices

C. It is used inside local networks and not directly reachable from the public internet

D. It cannot be assigned by DHCP

7. DHCP is used primarily to:

A. Translate domain names to IP addresses

B. Automatically assign IP addresses and related settings to devices

C. Provide wireless encryption

D. Increase storage space on a server

8. DNS can be described as:

A. A file system for organizing folders

B. A hardware device that prints documents

C. A naming system that translates domain names to IP addresses

D. A type of wireless encryption

9. When you type https://www.example.com into a browser, the text www.example.com is:

A. An IP address

B. A MAC address

C. A domain name

D. A DNS server

10. Ethernet is BEST described as:

A. A cloud storage service

B. The common wired LAN networking technology

C. A type of wireless mobile network

D. A backup method

11. Which connector is MOST commonly associated with Ethernet cables?

A. USB Type-A

B. RJ-45

C. HDMI

D. 3.5mm audio jack

12. Which of the following is an advantage of using a wired Ethernet connection instead of Wi-Fi?

A. Greater mobility

B. Typically more stable speed and lower interference

C. No need for cables at all

D. Works only for laptops

13. A Wi-Fi network name is more formally called a(n):

A. URL

B. IP

C. SSID
D. DNS
14. Why should you secure a Wi-Fi network with a strong password?
A. To reduce monitor brightness
B. To keep unauthorized users from connecting and protect data in transit
C. To make the router quieter
D. To eliminate the need for backups
15. Which situation BEST indicates a problem on only one device, not the entire network?
A. All computers in the office cannot reach any website
B. Only one laptop cannot connect, while others are online
C. All users report a city-wide outage
D. The ISP reports a backbone failure
16. A user reports that some websites load fine, but one specific site always fails. What is the MOST likely type of issue?
A. Complete loss of internet service
B. A problem specific to that website or its DNS resolution
C. The user's monitor is broken
D. The router's power supply has failed
17. Which of the following is a common symptom of a **slow** connection rather than **no** connection?
A. Pages never load at all
B. "No network" icon with a red X
C. Websites eventually load but take a long time and videos buffer frequently
D. Devices cannot see any Wi-Fi networks
18. In a typical home network, which device is MOST likely to combine router, switch, and wireless access point functions in one box?
A. NAS device
B. Multi-function printer
C. All-in-one home gateway
D. Desktop PC
19. Which of the following is a common home/small-office broadband connection type that uses existing cable TV lines?
A. DSL
B. Fiber
C. Cable internet
D. Dial-up over acoustic couplers
20. Which internet connection type uses mobile phone networks (like 4G/5G) for data?
A. Cable
B. DSL
C. Cellular
D. Fiber
21. When troubleshooting "no Wi-Fi" on a laptop, which basic check is MOST appropriate to try first?
A. Replace the modem
B. Ensure the laptop's Wi-Fi is turned on and the correct SSID is selected
C. Rebuild the entire network from scratch

D. Upgrade the operating system

22. Why is connecting to unknown open public Wi-Fi potentially risky?

A. It always damages your hardware

B. Others on the network may attempt to intercept or tamper with your traffic

C. It prevents you from ever using Ethernet again

D. It automatically deletes all your files

23. Which security best practice applies to home routers?

A. Always leave default admin passwords unchanged

B. Disable all encryption to make the network faster

C. Change default admin passwords and apply firmware updates when appropriate

D. Share the admin password with all guests

24. A user reports that every device in the home suddenly loses access to all websites at the same time. Which is the BEST first step?

A. Check if the home router/modem has power and indicator lights

B. Replace the hard drive in one PC

C. Reinstall the OS on the user's laptop

D. Change the printer ink

25. Why is it helpful to distinguish between "one device" and "many devices" when diagnosing network issues?

A. It determines what type of printer to buy

B. It helps you narrow down whether the problem is local to a device or affects shared equipment/ISP

C. It only affects the color of network cables

D. It is required to calculate storage capacity

Answer Key – Chapter 8 (with Explanations)

1. B – A COLLECTION of interconnected devices that share resources and information

A network links multiple devices so they can communicate and share things like files, printers, and internet access. A single standalone computer is not a network by itself.

2. C – Directing traffic between the local network and other networks

A router connects your local network to external networks (like the internet) and decides where data packets go. It doesn't primarily cool CPUs or store all user files.

3. A – Connect a local network to an internet service provider

The modem interfaces with your ISP's infrastructure and converts signals to something your router/local network can use. Wi-Fi, printing, and user accounts are handled by other components.

4. A – Connect multiple wired devices on the same local network

Switches provide multiple network ports for wired devices and forward traffic only to relevant ports, improving efficiency. They do not provide ISP connectivity or DNS resolution.

5. C – 192.168.1.25

IPv4 addresses are typically dotted decimal numbers. URLs, file paths, and MAC addresses have different formats.

6. C – It is used inside local networks and not directly reachable from the public internet

Private IP ranges are used for internal addressing and are not routed across the public internet. Routers and NAT bridge private and public addressing.

7. B – Automatically assign IP addresses and related settings to devices

DHCP hands out IP addresses, subnet masks, gateways, and DNS info so devices don't need manual configuration. DNS handles name resolution, not DHCP.

8. C – A naming system that translates domain names to IP addresses

DNS resolves human-friendly domain names into numeric IP addresses so systems can connect. It is not a file system, printer, or encryption method.

9. C – A domain name

www.example.com is the domain part of the URL. The full https://www.example.com is a URL; the IP address and DNS server are separate concepts.

10. B – The common wired LAN networking technology

Ethernet defines how data is transmitted over wired LANs. It is not a cloud service, wireless standard, or backup technique.

11. B – RJ-45

RJ-45 connectors are characteristic of twisted-pair Ethernet cables. USB, HDMI, and 3.5mm jacks serve different purposes (peripherals, video, audio).

12. B – Typically more stable speed and lower interference

Wired Ethernet avoids many interference issues and is often more consistent than Wi-Fi. Wi-Fi offers more mobility but can be less stable.

13. C – SSID

The SSID is the broadcast name of a Wi-Fi network. URLs, IPs, and DNS are different parts of the networking stack.

14. B – To keep unauthorized users from connecting and protect data in transit

A strong Wi-Fi password and encryption prevent unauthorized access and help secure wireless traffic. It doesn't affect monitor brightness or backups directly.

15. B – Only one laptop cannot connect, while others are online

If only one device has issues while others work, the problem is likely with that device's configuration or hardware, not the entire network or ISP.

16. B – A problem specific to that website or its DNS resolution

If most sites work but one consistently fails, the issue is probably with that site or how its name is resolved. A total loss of internet would affect all sites.

17. C – Websites eventually load but take a long time and videos buffer frequently

This describes degraded performance, not a complete outage. No connection would mean pages never load and icons often show no network available.

18. C – All-in-one home gateway

Many home gateway devices combine modem, router, switch, and Wi-Fi access point features in one box. NAS, printers, and PCs usually serve narrower roles.

19. C – Cable internet

Cable internet uses coaxial lines from cable TV providers. DSL uses telephone lines, fiber uses fiber optics, and dial-up is an older, much slower option.

20. C – Cellular

Cellular data uses mobile networks to provide internet access, often via phones or hotspots. Cable, DSL, and fiber are wired broadband technologies.

21. B – Ensure the laptop's Wi-Fi is turned on and the correct SSID is selected

This is a simple, device-level check that often fixes "no Wi-Fi" issues. Replacing the modem or rebuilding the whole network is excessive as a first step.

22. B – Others on the network may attempt to intercept or tamper with your traffic

Open public Wi-Fi can expose you to eavesdropping or attacks, especially if encryption isn't used at higher layers. It doesn't inherently destroy hardware or files.

23. C – Change default admin passwords and apply firmware updates when appropriate

Changing defaults and updating firmware improve security. Leaving defaults or disabling encryption are dangerous practices, and sharing admin credentials widely is insecure.

24. A – Check if the home router/modem has power and indicator lights

If all devices lose internet at once, checking the shared equipment's power and status lights is a logical first step. Reinstalling OSs or swapping hard drives won't help with a network-wide issue.

25. B – It helps you narrow down whether the problem is local to a device or affects shared equipment/ISP

Scope (one vs. many devices) is a key diagnostic clue. It points you toward either device-specific fixes or shared infrastructure/ISP investigations.

Chapter 9

Operating Systems (Applications & Software – Part 1)

This chapter introduces operating systems (OSs), the software layer that makes hardware usable and runs your applications. You'll see how different OS types compare, what common desktop and mobile systems look like, and how user accounts and files are managed. The goal is to give you a clear, practical understanding of what an OS does so later software and security topics make more sense.

9.1 What an Operating System Is and Does

AN OPERATING SYSTEM is the core software that makes everything else on a computer possible. ITF+ expects you to understand the basic functions it performs. This section sets the foundation for all OS-related questions on the exam.

- **OS as the bridge between hardware and applications**
- **Resource management (CPU, memory, storage)**
- **User interfaces and services**

The operating system sits between the hardware and your applications, acting as a **bridge**. When you open a web browser, the OS loads it into memory, schedules CPU time for it, and handles its requests to read/write files or talk to the network. Without an OS, users would have to interact with hardware at a very low level, which isn't practical. Recognizing this bridging role helps you see why the OS must load before any normal applications can run.

The OS handles **resource management**, deciding which programs get CPU time, how memory is allocated, and how files are stored on disks. It coordinates device access so multiple applications can share hardware safely and efficiently. For example, it ensures two programs don't try to write to the same file in a conflicting way. When systems feel sluggish, it's often because resources are heavily used and the OS is juggling many competing demands.

Operating systems provide **user interfaces** and **system services**. Graphical user interfaces (GUIs) show windows, menus, and icons, while command-line interfaces (CLIs) accept text commands. Services include user account management, printing, networking, and security features like authentication. Understanding that the OS is responsible for these core capabilities helps you interpret error messages and know where to configure key settings.

9.2 Desktop and Laptop Operating Systems

DESKTOPS AND LAPTOPS commonly run a handful of major operating systems. ITF+ wants you to recognize these OS families and their general characteristics. This section helps you identify what environment you're dealing with when someone says "my computer."

- **Microsoft Windows**
- **Apple macOS**
- **Linux distributions (high level)**

Microsoft Windows is widely used on business and home PCs. It features a familiar GUI with a Start menu, taskbar, and File Explorer for file management. Different editions exist (such as Home and Pro), but they share a common look and feel. Many applications and games are developed primarily for Windows, which is why it remains so prevalent. IT support roles often involve working heavily with Windows systems.

Apple macOS runs on Apple's Mac computers. It has its own interface conventions, including the Dock, Finder, and menu bar at the top of the screen. macOS integrates tightly with other Apple services and devices, such as iCloud and iPhones. While it plays a smaller role in many corporate environments than Windows, macOS is common in creative fields and among certain professionals. Recognizing its look and basic structure is important for cross-platform support.

Linux distributions (often called "distros") are open-source operating systems that come in many flavors, such as Ubuntu, Fedora, or Debian. They may offer GUIs similar to other OSs, but they are also known for strong command-line capabilities. Linux is popular for servers, development environments, and some desktops, especially in technical and open-source communities. At the ITF+ level, you only need to know that "Linux" refers to a family of related systems, not one single product.

9.3 Mobile Operating Systems

MOBILE DEVICES LIKE smartphones and tablets use operating systems designed for touch, mobility, and app stores. ITF+ expects you to recognize the major mobile OSs and their general characteristics. This section draws the connection between desktop and mobile OS concepts.

- **Android**
- **iOS and iPadOS**
- **Similarities and differences with desktop OSs**

Android is a mobile OS used by many manufacturers on smartphones and tablets. It includes a home screen with app icons, notification areas, and settings menus optimized for touch. Users download apps from the Google Play Store and sometimes other sources. While built on Linux at a low level, Android presents a very different user experience focused on mobile use. Support often involves managing apps, permissions, and connectivity.

iOS and iPadOS are Apple's mobile operating systems for iPhones and iPads, respectively. They feature a clean, touch-centric interface, app grid, Control Center, and tight integration with Apple's ecosystem (such as iCloud and Apple ID). Apps are primarily installed through the Apple App Store. Security and privacy controls are built into the OS, often in ways that limit how much users and apps can modify system behavior. Recognizing this environment is important when helping users with Apple mobile devices.

Despite differences in appearance, mobile OSs share common ideas with desktop OSs. They manage resources, provide user interfaces, handle file storage, and control access to hardware like cameras and sensors. However, they often emphasize battery life, sandboxed apps, and simple update mechanisms. Knowing that mobile devices are also computers with OSs helps you apply similar concepts across device types.

9.4 32-bit vs. 64-bit and System Requirements (High Level)

YOU MAY SEE TERMS LIKE 32-bit and 64-bit in OS documentation or system specs. ITF+ expects a basic understanding of what these mean in practical terms. This section also touches on checking system requirements for software.

- **32-bit vs. 64-bit OS (conceptual)**
- **Impact on memory addressing**
- **Checking system requirements before installing software**

A **32-bit** operating system processes data in chunks of 32 bits, while a **64-bit** OS handles 64-bit chunks. Modern systems are typically 64-bit, which allows them to handle more data per operation and support more RAM. Many newer applications are designed for 64-bit environments. You don't need to know the math; just understand that 64-bit systems are now standard and generally more capable.

One major difference is **memory addressing**. 32-bit OSs have a relatively low RAM limit (commonly around 4 GB), while 64-bit OSs can use much more memory, which is essential for modern workloads. If you try to run memory-hungry applications on a 32-bit system, you'll quickly hit limitations. ITF+ may test whether you understand that a 64-bit OS is required to take full advantage of larger amounts of RAM.

Before installing software, it's important to **check system requirements**. These lists typically specify minimum OS versions, processor type, RAM, storage space, and sometimes graphics capabilities. Installing software on systems that don't meet these requirements can lead to crashes, poor performance, or failure to install. Understanding this helps you answer scenario questions where the best solution is to verify compatibility rather than immediately blame "bugs."

9.5 Files, Folders, and Extensions in the OS

OPERATING SYSTEMS ORGANIZE data using files and folders, and they often use extensions to identify file types. ITF+ expects you to navigate and understand this structure. This section reinforces how the OS manages everyday data.

- **Folders (directories) as containers**
- **File extensions and default applications**
- **Basic file operations (copy, move, delete, rename)**

Folders (or directories) are containers used to organize files and other folders. Users can create folders by project, date, or content type to keep their data structured. The OS displays folder hierarchies in file management tools like File Explorer, Finder, or similar. A well-organized folder structure makes it easier to locate and back up important files. IT support often involves helping users find where something is actually saved.

File extensions are suffixes on file names after a dot, such as .docx, .xlsx, .jpg, or .mp4. The OS uses extensions to determine which default application should open a file. For example, .pdf files might open in a PDF reader, while .jpg files open in an image viewer. Changing extensions improperly can make files unopenable, while understanding them helps you know what kind of content a file likely contains.

Basic file operations include **copying**, **moving**, **deleting**, and **renaming** files and folders. These actions are performed through GUI tools (drag-and-drop, right-click menus) or command-line utilities. Deleting often moves files to a temporary location first (like a Recycle Bin) before permanent removal. ITF+ may test whether you understand these operations conceptually and know their impact on where files live.

9.6 User Accounts, Permissions, and Profiles

OPERATING SYSTEMS SUPPORT multiple users, each with their own settings and access rights. ITF+ expects you to understand basic user account concepts and why permissions matter. This section ties OS use to security and personalization.

- **User accounts and login**
- **Standard vs. administrator accounts (high level)**
- **User profiles and personal settings**

User accounts represent individual users on a system. Each account typically has a username and password (or another authentication method) and determines what that user can access. When you log in, the OS loads settings and data associated with that account. Multiple people can share a computer while keeping their files and preferences separate using different accounts.

Accounts can have different **privilege levels**, such as standard (limited) and administrator (elevated). Standard accounts can use most applications and change personal settings but cannot make major system-wide changes. Administrator accounts can install software, change system settings, and manage other accounts. Using administrator privileges only when necessary reduces the risk of accidental or malicious changes. ITF+ wants you to recognize why running everything as admin is risky.

A **user profile** includes personal settings like desktop background, application preferences, browser bookmarks, and user-specific folders. When you log in, the OS loads your profile so the environment feels familiar. Problems with user profiles can cause missing icons, reset settings, or access issues. Understanding that profiles store per-user configuration helps explain why one user might see issues another on the same machine does not.

9.7 OS Settings, Control Panels, and System Tools

OPERATING SYSTEMS PROVIDE centralized places to view and change system settings. ITF+ expects you to recognize these tools and what they're generally used for. This section introduces where you'd go to configure things like devices, accounts, and updates.

- **Control Panel / Settings apps**
- **System information and device management tools**
- **Task Manager and similar utilities**

On desktop OSs, **Control Panel** (Windows) and **Settings** apps (on Windows, macOS, and mobile systems) provide organized access to configuration options. You can adjust display settings, network connections, user accounts, and more. While layouts differ across OSs, the idea of a central settings hub is universal. Recognizing that "this kind of change belongs in Settings" is part of basic IT literacy.

System information and **device management tools** show hardware details and driver status. In Windows, tools like "System Information" or "Device Manager" list installed hardware and driver health. On macOS and Linux, similar utilities exist under different names. These tools help you verify that devices are recognized by the OS and working correctly. ITF+ may reference them in troubleshooting or configuration scenarios.

Task Manager on Windows (and equivalents like Activity Monitor on macOS) shows running processes, CPU and memory usage, and sometimes network and disk activity. These tools help diagnose performance issues and identify unresponsive applications. Knowing they exist and what they show is important for understanding how to check what the system is actually doing.

9.8 OS Updates, Patches, and Stability

OPERATING SYSTEMS ARE not static; they receive updates that fix bugs, add features, and patch security vulnerabilities. ITF+ expects you to understand the basic importance of OS updates. This section explains why updates matter and how they can impact system behavior.

- **Security patches and bug fixes**
- **Feature updates vs. critical updates**
- **Basic update settings and scheduling**

Security patches close vulnerabilities that attackers could exploit, while **bug fixes** correct errors that cause crashes or incorrect behavior. Keeping an OS up to date is one of the most important security and stability practices. Ignoring updates for long periods increases risk, especially when a system is exposed to the internet. ITF+ will often treat "apply updates" as a reasonable step in security or stability scenarios.

Feature updates introduce new capabilities, interface changes, or major enhancements. **Critical updates** focus on urgent security or stability issues. While feature updates can sometimes be deferred in business environments to avoid disruption, critical patches are usually applied more quickly. Understanding this distinction helps explain why some updates feel bigger and take longer than others.

Most OSs provide **update settings** that let users choose how and when updates install—such as automatic installs, scheduled times, or manual approvals. Scheduling updates outside of peak work hours can reduce interruptions. However, delaying updates indefinitely is not advisable. ITF+ expects you to know that update configuration is part of managing system reliability and security.

9.9 Application Installation, Removal, and Compatibility

OPERATING SYSTEMS PROVIDE mechanisms for installing, managing, and removing applications. ITF+ expects basic awareness of how this works and what can go wrong. This section explains high-level application lifecycle concepts.

- **Installing applications from trusted sources**
- **Uninstalling and cleanup**
- **Compatibility and version issues**

Installing applications typically involves downloading an installer, running it, and following prompts, or using an app store or package manager. It's important to use trusted sources—official sites, stores, or organizational repositories—to reduce malware risk. The OS may prompt for administrator privileges when an installation affects system-wide components. Understanding this process helps you support users who aren't sure how to install software safely.

Uninstalling applications removes them from the system, usually through built-in tools like "Add or Remove Programs" in Windows or moving apps to the Trash on macOS. Proper uninstallation helps free storage and prevent leftover services or startup items from slowing the system. Some applications leave behind configuration files, but most user-facing components are removed. ITF+ may test that you know removing apps is done through OS tools, not simply deleting icons.

Compatibility issues arise when software requires a different OS version, bitness (32-bit vs. 64-bit), or dependencies than what's installed. Attempting to run incompatible applications can lead to errors or crashes. Sometimes older programs need compatibility modes or updated versions. Checking documentation and system requirements is a standard first step when apps won't install or run as expected.

9.10 OS Concepts in Troubleshooting Scenarios

THIS FINAL SECTION ties OS concepts into practical troubleshooting thinking. Many ITF+ questions will describe OS-related issues and ask what you should look at or do. Knowing what the OS is responsible for helps you choose reasonable answers.

- **Linking symptoms to OS components (accounts, updates, resources)**
- **Deciding when OS updates or reinstalls are appropriate**
- **Using OS tools as part of a structured troubleshooting approach**

OS-related symptoms might include slow performance, failed logins, missing user settings, or frequent crashes. For example, if only one user's desktop looks wrong, a profile issue is more likely than a hardware failure. If many apps crash after an update, you might suspect a bad patch or driver. Thinking about which OS component is involved—accounts, file system, drivers, or updates—helps you form targeted theories.

OS updates or reinstalls are **last-resort** or **escalation** steps, not first moves. Before reinstalling an entire OS, you should check simpler possibilities like storage space, corrupted user profiles, or problematic applications. In an entry-level role, major OS reinstalls may require approval or escalation. ITF+ expects you to choose the least disruptive reasonable action that could resolve the issue.

Using OS tools—such as Task Manager, file explorers, device managers, and settings panels—is part of structured troubleshooting. These tools help you gather evidence instead of guessing. For example, Task Manager can show whether a slowdown is due to CPU, RAM, or disk usage. Combining this information with the troubleshooting methodology from earlier chapters makes you more effective and aligns with how professionals actually work.

Practice Questions – Chapter 9 (25 Questions)

1. Which statement BEST describes an operating system?
A. A hardware device that cools the CPU
B. The core software that manages hardware and provides services to applications
C. A program used only to browse the internet
D. A storage medium for backups

2. Which of the following is NOT typically a responsibility of an operating system?
A. Managing CPU and memory usage
B. Providing a user interface
C. Directly manufacturing hardware components

D. Handling file storage and retrieval
3. Which desktop operating system is most commonly associated with the Start menu and File Explorer?
A. Linux
B. iOS
C. Microsoft Windows
D. Android
4. macOS is primarily designed to run on which type of devices?
A. Apple Mac computers
B. Android smartphones
C. Generic tablets from any vendor
D. Home routers
5. Which of the following is TRUE about Linux from an ITF+ perspective?
A. It is a single, identical operating system used only on phones
B. It is a family of open-source operating systems called distributions
C. It is a hardware-only technology
D. It cannot be used on servers
6. Which operating systems are most commonly used on smartphones?
A. Windows and macOS
B. Android and iOS
C. Linux and FreeBSD only
D. DOS and OS/2
7. A 32-bit operating system is MOST likely limited in which area compared to a 64-bit OS?
A. Screen resolution
B. Maximum usable RAM
C. Number of keyboard keys
D. Printer compatibility
8. Which is a good reason to check system requirements before installing software?
A. To see if it will make the CPU cooler
B. To ensure the system meets the OS, RAM, and storage needs of the software
C. To confirm the color of the user interface
D. To reduce the need for backups
9. Which statement BEST describes a file extension?
A. A security feature that encrypts files
B. A suffix that indicates the file type and helps the OS choose an application to open it
C. A part of the CPU
D. The top-level folder on a drive
10. The folder structure used to organize files is generally called:
A. A BIOS
B. A directory tree
C. A firewall
D. A kernel
11. A user wants to remove a program from Windows. What is the MOST appropriate method?
A. Delete the desktop icon only
B. Use "Add or Remove Programs" / "Apps & Features" to uninstall it

C. Turn off the computer
D. Delete random system files
12. User accounts in an operating system are primarily used to:
A. Control monitor brightness
B. Identify different users and control their access and settings
C. Replace the need for antivirus software
D. Provide additional storage space
13. A standard (non-admin) user account typically CANNOT:
A. Change their desktop wallpaper
B. Run most installed applications
C. Install system-wide software or change critical system settings
D. Save files in their documents folder
14. A user logs in and finds that their desktop icons and settings are missing, but other users on the same PC are fine. Which is the MOST likely explanation?
A. The CPU has failed
B. The monitor is broken
C. There may be a problem with that user's profile
D. All user accounts are corrupted equally
15. Which tool in Windows is commonly used to view running processes and resource usage like CPU and memory?
A. Device Manager
B. Task Manager
C. Control Panel
D. File Explorer
16. Why are operating system updates important from a security perspective?
A. They increase screen brightness
B. They apply patches that fix vulnerabilities attackers could exploit
C. They always improve gaming performance
D. They replace the need for passwords
17. Which best describes a **feature update** for an operating system?
A. A small patch that only changes one line of code
B. An update focusing solely on virus definitions
C. A larger update that may add new functionality or interface changes
D. A mandatory firmware replacement
18. Where are you MOST likely to adjust display resolution and network settings on a typical desktop OS?
A. Inside the CPU
B. In the system's Settings app or Control Panel
C. In the printer's ink cartridge
D. In the keyboard firmware
19. When installing software on a shared office computer, why might you need administrator rights?
A. To change the monitor color
B. Because system-wide installations affect all users and require elevated permissions
C. Because standard users cannot save any files
D. To reset the internet connection

20. Which of the following is a BEST practice when installing new software?
A. Always download from random websites to save time
B. Install multiple conflicting antivirus programs together
C. Use trusted sources like official vendor sites or app stores
D. Disable all OS updates first

21. A user reports that a newly installed program runs extremely slowly and occasionally crashes. Other programs are fine. Which is the BEST first step?
A. Reinstall the entire operating system
B. Check the program's system requirements and compare them to the PC's specs
C. Replace the monitor
D. Delete the user's profile

22. A user's PC is slow whenever many apps are open, and Task Manager shows RAM usage at 95%. What is the MOST likely explanation?
A. The keyboard is failing
B. The system is low on available memory
C. The mouse driver is missing
D. The monitor refresh rate is too high

23. Which of the following is usually a last-resort action after other OS troubleshooting steps fail?
A. Checking free disk space
B. Restarting a frozen application
C. Reinstalling the entire operating system
D. Closing unused browser tabs

24. Why is it better to remove software through OS tools rather than just deleting its files manually?
A. OS tools automatically make the screen brighter
B. OS uninstall tools clean up associated components and registry entries more safely
C. Manual deletion is always faster
D. Deleting files manually increases RAM

25. Which example shows using OS knowledge as part of structured troubleshooting?
A. Ignoring error messages and rebooting repeatedly
B. Using Task Manager to see which process is consuming high CPU and then investigating that application
C. Randomly deleting files until the system speeds up
D. Replacing hardware before checking software

Answer Key – Chapter 9 (with Explanations)

1. B – THE CORE SOFTWARE that manages hardware and provides services to applications

The OS coordinates hardware, runs applications, and provides user interfaces and core services. It is software, not hardware, and not just a browser.

2. C – Directly manufacturing hardware components

Operating systems manage resources, provide interfaces, and handle files, but they don't physically manufacture hardware. The other options are core OS responsibilities.

3. C – Microsoft Windows

Windows is known for its Start menu and File Explorer GUI components. Linux and Android can look different, and iOS is mobile-focused.

4. A – Apple Mac computers

macOS is designed for Apple's Mac hardware. iOS and iPadOS are used on phones and tablets, while routers typically run embedded or specialized OSs.

5. B – It is a family of open-source operating systems called distributions

Linux refers to many related distributions (distros), not a single product. It is common on servers and desktops, not just phones, and is software, not hardware.

6. B – Android and iOS

Android and iOS (plus iPadOS) dominate the smartphone OS market. Windows and macOS are desktop/laptop OSs.

7. B – Maximum usable RAM

32-bit OSs are limited in how much RAM they can address, commonly around 4 GB, while 64-bit OSs can use much more. Screen resolution and keyboard keys are unrelated to 32-bit vs. 64-bit.

8. B – To ensure the system meets the OS, RAM, and storage needs of the software

System requirements help you confirm that your device can run the software properly. Installing on underpowered systems often leads to poor performance or failures.

9. B – A suffix that indicates the file type and helps the OS choose an application to open it

Extensions like .docx or .jpg help the OS associate files with appropriate applications. They are not security features by themselves.

10. B – A directory tree

The directory (folder) tree describes how folders and files are organized hierarchically. BIOS, firewall, and kernel are different technical components.

11. B – Use "Add or Remove Programs" / "Apps & Features" to uninstall it

Using the OS's uninstall tools removes applications properly. Deleting only icons or random files can leave broken components behind.

12. B – Identify different users and control their access and settings

User accounts separate user data and permissions. They don't directly control brightness or replace antivirus software.

13. C – Install system-wide software or change critical system settings

Standard users are limited in what system-level changes they can make, which improves security. They can still personalize their environment and run most apps.

14. C – There may be a problem with that user's profile

If only one user sees missing settings while others are fine, the issue is likely with that specific profile. Hardware or system-wide failures would affect all users.

15. B – Task Manager

Task Manager shows running processes, CPU, memory, and more. Device Manager is for hardware/drivers; Control Panel and File Explorer handle settings and files.

16. B – They apply patches that fix vulnerabilities attackers could exploit

Security updates close known holes that attackers can use. While some updates may also impact performance, their primary security purpose is patching vulnerabilities.

17. C – A larger update that may add new functionality or interface changes

Feature updates introduce new capabilities or UI changes. Smaller patches and virus definitions are different kinds of updates.

18. B – In the system's Settings app or Control Panel

Display and network settings are typically configured through OS settings panels. CPU, printer ink, and keyboard firmware are not where these options live.

19. B – Because system-wide installations affect all users and require elevated permissions

Installing software for all users or modifying system components requires admin rights. Standard users typically can't make these changes.

20. C – Use trusted sources like official vendor sites or app stores

Trusted sources reduce malware risk and ensure you get legitimate, updated software. Random sites and conflicting antivirus setups are poor practices.

21. B – Check the program's system requirements and compare them to the PC's specs

If one new program misbehaves while others are fine, compatibility or resource requirements are suspect. Reinstalling the OS is excessive as a first step.

22. B – The system is low on available memory

High RAM usage when many apps are open indicates memory pressure. Keyboards, mice, and monitor refresh rates don't directly cause such symptoms.

23. C – Reinstalling the entire operating system

OS reinstall is a major step used only when other troubleshooting fails or is impractical. It is not a first-line action for routine issues.

24. B – OS uninstall tools clean up associated components and registry entries more safely

Using proper uninstall mechanisms removes applications more cleanly and avoids orphaned components. Manual deletion can leave behind broken entries and cause problems.

25. B – Using Task Manager to see which process is consuming high CPU and then investigating that application

This shows gathering data with OS tools and forming a targeted theory. Random deletion, ignoring errors, or replacing hardware without checking software are not structured approaches.

Chapter 10

Productivity, Collaboration, and Business Software

This chapter focuses on the software people use every day at work: office suites, collaboration tools, and basic business applications. You'll see how word processors, spreadsheets, and presentations differ, and how tools like email and videoconferencing fit into modern workflows. The goal is to help you recognize the main categories of business software and how they're used in real situations.

10.1 What Is Productivity Software?

"PRODUCTIVITY SOFTWARE" is a broad term for tools that help people get work done more efficiently. ITF+ expects you to recognize common examples and what they're generally used for. This section frames the rest of the chapter.

- **Definition and purpose of productivity software**
- **Common examples in office environments**
- **Installed vs. cloud-based tools**

Productivity software includes applications that help users create, edit, and manage information—things like documents, spreadsheets, presentations, and notes. These tools are used daily in offices, schools, and home businesses. They don't directly manage hardware; instead, they provide environments where people can write, calculate, and present ideas. Understanding this category helps you quickly identify what type of application might be needed in a scenario.

Common examples in office environments include word processors, spreadsheet programs, presentation software, email clients, calendar tools, and note-taking apps. Office suites bundle several of these into one package. Users may spend most of their day inside these applications, so performance and compatibility matter a lot. Recognizing names and roles of these programs helps you interpret user requests like "my spreadsheet won't open" or "I need to share this presentation."

Some productivity tools are installed locally on a computer, while others are **cloud-based**, running through a browser or streaming from remote servers. Cloud tools often allow real-time collaboration and easy access from multiple devices. Locally installed tools can work offline and sometimes offer more advanced features. ITF+ doesn't favor one over the other; it just expects you to understand that both models exist.

10.2 Word Processing Software

WORD PROCESSORS ARE used to create and edit text-based documents. ITF+ expects you to recognize their typical uses and basic features. This section covers what makes a word processor different from other applications.

- **Creating and formatting text documents**
- **Common features (spelling, styles, templates)**
- **Typical business use cases**

Word processing software focuses on **text documents** like letters, reports, memos, and essays. It allows users to type text, change fonts, adjust alignment, and insert headings or lists. Unlike plain text editors, word processors support rich formatting and page layout options. Understanding that these programs are built around text and layout helps you distinguish them from spreadsheets or presentation tools.

Common features include spell check, grammar suggestions, search and replace, and styles for headings and paragraphs. Styles make it easy to keep formatting consistent across a document and to generate tables of contents. Many word processors also offer templates for resumes, invoices, and business letters, which speed up document creation. Recognizing these features helps you answer questions about which tool to pick for a specific document task.

Business use cases include writing policies, drafting proposals, documenting procedures, and creating customer communications. Professionals rely on word processors to produce polished documents that can be printed, emailed, or shared as PDFs. When a scenario involves long text with paragraphs, headings, and pages, a word processor is usually the best fit.

10.3 Spreadsheet Software

SPREADSHEETS ARE USED to organize data into rows and columns and perform calculations. ITF+ expects a basic understanding of what spreadsheets are good for. This section focuses on their role in analysis and tracking.

- **Rows, columns, and cells**
- **Formulas and functions (high level)**
- **Common uses: budgets, logs, simple databases**

A **spreadsheet** organizes information into a grid of rows and columns, with each intersection being a **cell**. Cells can hold numbers, text, or formulas. This structure makes it easy to sort, filter, and visually scan data. Understanding this grid concept is essential for recognizing when a spreadsheet is the right tool.

Formulas and functions allow spreadsheets to perform calculations automatically. For example, a cell might contain a formula that sums a column (=SUM(A1:A10)) or averages values. When data changes, formulas update results without manual recalculation. Users can build models to track totals, forecast trends, or highlight values that meet certain conditions. You don't need to memorize functions for ITF+, but you should know that this is what makes spreadsheets powerful.

Common spreadsheet uses include budgeting, expense tracking, inventory lists, contact lists, and simple data analysis. Some people also use spreadsheets as basic databases or for simple reporting dashboards. When a scenario involves numbers, calculations, and structured lists, a spreadsheet application is typically the correct answer.

10.4 Presentation Software

PRESENTATION SOFTWARE is designed to create visual slide decks for meetings and talks. ITF+ wants you to know when a presentation tool is appropriate and what features it offers. This section highlights the visual communication role of these apps.

- **Slides as visual aids**
- **Text, images, charts, and multimedia**

- **Presenter tools and delivery options**

Presentation software lets users create **slides**—individual screens that show a combination of text, images, and other content. These slides act as visual aids to support spoken explanations. Unlike word processors, which focus on detailed text, presentations emphasize key points and visuals. Understanding this difference helps you choose the right tool for a talk or training session.

Slides can contain bullet lists, pictures, charts, diagrams, tables, and sometimes videos or audio clips. Templates and themes provide consistent colors and layouts, helping maintain a professional look. Presenters often use charts from spreadsheets or screenshots from other applications to illustrate their points. Recognizing these features helps you answer questions about how to communicate data in a meeting.

Presenter tools include slide show mode, speaker notes, and options to present on a second screen or projector. Some software supports remote presenting and sharing slides over the internet. Users can export presentations as PDFs or videos for distribution. When a scenario involves presenting information to a group, especially with visuals, presentation software is usually the correct choice.

10.5 Email, Calendars, and Contacts

COMMUNICATION AND SCHEDULING tools are core parts of business productivity. ITF+ expects you to understand how email, calendars, and contacts work together. This section explains their roles and how they're typically accessed.

- **Email clients and webmail**
- **Calendar scheduling and reminders**
- **Contact management and address books**

Email clients are applications that send, receive, and organize email messages. They can be installed programs or web-based interfaces accessed through a browser. Users can sort messages into folders, apply filters, and search their inbox. Understanding email tools is essential, since many workplace communications revolve around them.

Calendars help users schedule appointments, meetings, and reminders. Integrated calendar features let people invite others to events, see availability, and receive alerts before meetings start. In many office suites, calendars sync across devices and can show shared team or resource calendars. These features support efficient time management and coordination.

Contact management tools, often called **address books**, store information about people and organizations. Entries may include names, email addresses, phone numbers, job titles, and notes. Integration with email and calendars allows quick selection of recipients and meeting participants. ITF+ expects you to recognize these tools as part of standard business software environments.

10.6 Collaboration Tools and Real-Time Editing

MODERN WORKPLACES RELY heavily on collaboration software that lets multiple people work together. ITF+ expects you to recognize these tools and their main benefits. This section covers chat, shared documents, and real-time co-authoring.

- **Chat and messaging platforms**

- **Shared documents and cloud storage**
- **Real-time co-authoring and commenting**

Chat and messaging platforms provide quick, informal communication channels, often organized into channels or groups. They can include text, file sharing, emojis, and sometimes voice or video. Unlike email, which is slower and more formal, chat tools are often used for rapid questions and ongoing team discussions. Understanding their role helps you distinguish when a user might be referring to "messaging" versus "email."

Shared documents and cloud storage allow multiple users to access the same files from different locations. Files are stored on servers in the cloud, and permissions control who can view or edit them. Users no longer need to email documents back and forth; instead, they work from a single shared copy. This makes version control easier and reduces confusion. ITF+ may include scenarios where shared storage is the best solution for team collaboration.

Real-time co-authoring lets multiple people edit the same document at the same time, with changes appearing dynamically. Commenting features allow reviewers to leave notes or suggestions without altering the main text. These capabilities support group projects, document reviews, and collaborative brainstorming. Recognizing this real-time aspect helps you identify cloud-based collaboration tools in exam questions.

10.7 Videoconferencing and Remote Meetings

VIDEOCONFERENCING TOOLS have become essential for remote work and distributed teams. ITF+ expects you to understand what these tools do and common issues users encounter. This section outlines their functions and basic requirements.

- **Audio, video, and screen sharing**
- **Meeting links, participants, and controls**
- **Basic requirements: device, camera, mic, and network**

Videoconferencing applications combine **audio**, **video**, and sometimes **screen sharing** to simulate in-person meetings. Participants can see and hear each other and share presentations or applications on their screens. These tools support one-on-one calls, small group meetings, or large webinars. Recognizing them helps you interpret user complaints like "no one can hear me in the meeting."

Meetings are often joined via links sent in invitations or calendar events. Host controls allow muting participants, managing waiting rooms, recording sessions, or ending the meeting. Participants can usually turn their cameras and microphones on or off, and use chat features. Understanding these basic controls helps you answer scenario questions about managing remote meetings.

Basic requirements for successful videoconferencing include a device (computer, tablet, or phone), a camera and microphone (built-in or external), and a stable network connection. Poor audio or video quality often relates to bandwidth limitations or hardware issues. Helping users check their mic, speakers, and network connection is a common support task.

10.8 Databases and Line-of-Business Applications (High Level)

BEYOND GENERAL PRODUCTIVITY tools, many organizations use specialized applications to handle their core work. ITF+ expects a high-level understanding of what databases and line-of-business apps are. This section provides a simple introduction.

- **Databases as structured data storage**
- **Line-of-business (LOB) applications**
- **Examples: CRM, ERP, HR systems**

A **database** stores structured information in tables with fields and records, enabling efficient search, sorting, and reporting. While spreadsheets handle small datasets, databases are built for larger, more complex data relationships. They often power applications behind the scenes, so users interact with forms and reports rather than raw tables. ITF+ covers database fundamentals more deeply later, but here you just need to know they hold and organize data.

Line-of-business (LOB) applications are specialized programs built to support a specific organization or industry's main activities. They may handle inventory for a warehouse, patient records for a clinic, or ticketing for a support desk. These apps often sit on top of databases and enforce business rules. When a scenario mentions a "system" for doing a core job task, it's often a LOB application.

Examples of such systems include **CRM (Customer Relationship Management)** tools for tracking customer interactions, **ERP (Enterprise Resource Planning)** systems that integrate finance, supply chain, and operations, and HR systems for managing employees. ITF+ doesn't require detailed knowledge of each, just recognition that these are business-focused applications differing from general office tools.

10.9 Licensing, Subscriptions, and User Access

SOFTWARE ISN'T JUST about features; it's also governed by licensing and access models. ITF+ expects you to understand basic software licensing concepts. This section covers perpetual licenses, subscriptions, and user accounts.

- **Perpetual vs. subscription licensing**
- **Single-user vs. multi-user access**
- **Activation, sign-ins, and license enforcement**

Perpetual licenses are paid for once and let you use a specific version of software indefinitely, though updates may be limited. **Subscription licenses** charge recurring fees (monthly or yearly) and often include ongoing updates and cloud features. Many modern productivity and collaboration suites use subscription models. Recognizing these terms helps you interpret questions about how users access software over time.

Licenses can be **single-user**, tied to one person or device, or **multi-user**, allowing a certain number of users or seats. In business environments, licensing is often centralized so IT can assign and revoke access as staff join or leave. If someone can't use a program even though it's installed, a licensing limit or missing assignment may be the cause. ITF+ may present scenarios where the right action is to check license status.

Activation and sign-in requirements enforce licensing and personalize the experience. Users may need to log in with an account linked to a subscription, or enter a product key to activate software. If activation fails, the program may run in reduced functionality mode or stop working after a grace period. Understanding this helps you troubleshoot issues where features are disabled or warnings about "unlicensed product" appear.

10.10 Applying Software Knowledge in Scenarios

THIS FINAL SECTION ties productivity and business software concepts into exam-style thinking. Many ITF+ questions are really asking, "Which tool or step makes sense here?" Knowing the software landscape helps you answer confidently.

- **Choosing the right tool for the task**
- **Relating user complaints to application categories**
- **Using basic checks (updates, compatibility, network) before advanced fixes**

Choosing the right tool means matching the job to the software: word processors for documents, spreadsheets for numerical data and calculations, presentations for visual talks, email for formal messages, and chat tools for quick conversations. For collaboration, shared cloud documents and videoconferencing might be the best fit. ITF+ often frames questions by describing a need and asking which application category is appropriate.

User complaints can often be traced to specific application categories. "Numbers aren't adding correctly" points to a spreadsheet issue, while "my slides don't show on the projector" relates to presentation software and display settings. "I'm not receiving messages" could involve email or chat clients, depending on context. Translating these descriptions into software categories helps you pick relevant actions.

Basic checks include verifying the application is up to date, confirming the system meets requirements, checking network connectivity for cloud tools, and ensuring the user has the right access permissions. These steps usually come before drastic actions like reinstalling the OS. Applying the troubleshooting mindset from earlier chapters to software issues helps you answer exam questions in a calm, logical way.

Practice Questions – Chapter 10 (25 Questions)

1. Which of the following is the BEST description of productivity software?
A. Software used only by system administrators
B. Tools that help users create, edit, and manage information to get work done
C. Programs that control hardware drivers
D. Software used only for video games

2. A user needs to create a multi-page report with headings, paragraphs, and a table of contents. Which application type is MOST appropriate?
A. Presentation software
B. Spreadsheet software
C. Word processing software
D. Database management system

3. Which of the following is a common use for spreadsheet software?
A. Editing videos
B. Designing posters
C. Tracking a monthly budget with automatic totals
D. Recording audio tracks

4. Presentation software is primarily designed to:
A. Write detailed reports with page numbers
B. Create visual slide decks to support spoken presentations

C. Store structured data in tables
D. Send and receive email
5. Which statement BEST describes a cell in a spreadsheet?
A. A folder that stores documents
B. A single data entry box at the intersection of a row and column
C. A group of slides in a presentation
D. A command-line instruction
6. An email client is used to:
A. Compile source code
B. Send, receive, and organize email messages
C. Edit photographic images
D. Configure network switches
7. Calendars and scheduling tools in office suites are typically used to:
A. Track CPU usage
B. Schedule appointments, set reminders, and organize meetings
C. Manage device drivers
D. Monitor power supply voltages
8. A user wants to store names, phone numbers, and email addresses for coworkers. Which feature is MOST appropriate?
A. Contact list or address book
B. Disk defragmenter
C. Task Manager
D. Firewall settings
9. A chat/messaging platform in a business is BEST suited for:
A. Quick, informal communication and sharing files among team members
B. Long-term archival of legal documents
C. Managing hardware inventory alone
D. Compiling operating systems from source
10. Real-time co-authoring of documents typically requires:
A. Everyone to have physical access to the same USB drive
B. A shared document hosted on a cloud or network service
C. Offline-only desktop applications
D. A local printer connection
11. Which feature is commonly found in videoconferencing tools?
A. BIOS configuration
B. Disk partitioning
C. Screen sharing during meetings
D. Memory overclocking
12. A user complains that others can see and hear the meeting, but no one can hear them. Which is the FIRST thing to check?
A. Whether their microphone is muted in the videoconferencing app or system settings
B. Whether the router needs a firmware update
C. If their monitor supports 4K resolution
D. Whether the printer has paper

13. Which statement BEST describes a line-of-business (LOB) application?
A. A casual game installed on office PCs
B. A specialized program that supports a specific organization's core work
C. A generic text editor for personal notes
D. A default clock app on a phone
14. A CRM (Customer Relationship Management) system is primarily used to:
A. Track and manage interactions with customers and sales leads
B. Control CPU temperature
C. Manage disk partition tables
D. Configure routers
15. Which licensing model typically requires ongoing monthly or yearly payments and often includes updates?
A. Perpetual license
B. Subscription license
C. Trial version without expiry
D. Public domain
16. A single-user software license MOST likely:
A. Allows everyone in the company to use one copy simultaneously
B. Is only valid for servers
C. Is intended for use by one person or device
D. Requires no activation or sign-in ever
17. Why might an application display an "unlicensed product" or "activation required" message?
A. The CPU temperature is too low
B. The software's license has not been properly activated or assigned
C. The user has too much free disk space
D. The network cable is too short
18. A user needs to quickly share a live view of a presentation slide deck with remote coworkers. Which combination is MOST appropriate?
A. Word processor + local printer
B. Spreadsheet + USB flash drive
C. Presentation software + videoconferencing with screen sharing
D. Database + firewall rules
19. A manager wants several team members to edit the same document at the same time from different locations. Which solution is BEST?
A. Emailing copies back and forth and merging changes manually
B. Sharing a cloud-based document that supports real-time co-authoring
C. Printing the document and mailing it
D. Saving the file to a single user's desktop
20. Which issue is MOST likely related to a problem with an email or messaging client rather than with hardware?
A. Computer does not power on
B. User cannot send or receive messages but everything else on the PC works
C. Monitor displays no signal at all
D. Keyboard lights don't turn on

21. A user installs new business software, but it crashes frequently. Other programs work fine. What is the BEST first step?

A. Reinstall the operating system

B. Confirm the PC meets the software's system requirements and OS version

C. Replace the router

D. Reduce the monitor brightness

22. Which action BEST illustrates matching the correct tool to a task?

A. Using a spreadsheet to design a complex marketing flyer

B. Using word processing software to draft a company policy document

C. Using a presentation tool to store a backup of all files

D. Using a chat app to manage long-term financial records

23. A user says, "I can open the shared spreadsheet in my browser, but when I disconnect from the internet, I can't edit it anymore." What is the MOST likely reason?

A. The file is infected with malware

B. The browser cannot open any file

C. The spreadsheet is hosted as a cloud-based document that requires connectivity for editing

D. The keyboard layout changed

24. A subscription-based office suite expires and isn't renewed. What is a possible effect?

A. The computer's CPU speed increases

B. The applications may enter reduced functionality mode or stop working fully

C. The operating system automatically reinstalls

D. All local documents are deleted immediately

25. Which example shows using basic software troubleshooting steps before advanced actions?

A. Immediately reinstalling the OS when one app won't start

B. Checking for application updates and verifying login/license status when a cloud app fails to open

C. Replacing the hard drive before testing anything

D. Deleting random system files to "clean up" the PC

Answer Key – Chapter 10 (with Explanations)

1. B – TOOLS THAT HELP users create, edit, and manage information to get work done

Productivity software includes word processors, spreadsheets, presentations, email, and similar tools. It's not limited to admins or games and doesn't primarily control hardware drivers.

2. C – Word processing software

Word processors are ideal for long, formatted text documents with headings, pages, and tables of contents. Spreadsheets focus on grids and calculations; presentations focus on slides.

3. C – Tracking a monthly budget with automatic totals

Spreadsheets excel at numerical data, calculations, and totals. Video editing and poster design are better suited to specialized media or graphics tools.

4. B – Create visual slide decks to support spoken presentations

Presentation software's primary purpose is slide-based visual communication. Detailed reports belong in word processors; data storage belongs in databases.

5. B – A single data entry box at the intersection of a row and column

Cells are the basic units of a spreadsheet grid. Folders, slide groups, and commands are different concepts.

6. B – Send, receive, and organize email messages

Email clients manage email communication and often integrate with calendars and contacts. They don't compile code or configure network hardware directly.

7. B – Schedule appointments, set reminders, and organize meetings

Calendars help manage time and events. CPU usage and power voltages are handled by other tools and hardware monitoring systems.

8. A – Contact list or address book

Address books store details about people like names and contact info. Disk defragmenters and Task Manager serve very different purposes.

9. A – Quick, informal communication and sharing files among team members

Chat platforms support rapid team communication. Long-term archives and inventory management are usually handled by other tools.

10. B – A shared document hosted on a cloud or network service

Real-time co-authoring requires multiple users to access the same document from a shared location, usually in the cloud. USB drives and local printers don't support live collaboration.

11. C – Screen sharing during meetings

Screen sharing is a core feature in videoconferencing tools. BIOS setup, networking, and overclocking are unrelated to typical meeting software.

12. A – Whether their microphone is muted in the videoconferencing app or system settings

If others can see and hear the meeting but not the user, mic muting is a common cause. Checking this is a simple, logical first step.

13. B – A specialized program that supports a specific organization's core work

LOB applications are tailored for key business processes, such as inventory or patient management. Games and generic note apps are not considered LOB systems.

14. A – Track and manage interactions with customers and sales leads

CRM systems help manage customer relationships, track communication, and follow up on opportunities. They do not directly manage hardware.

15. B – Subscription license

Subscription licenses involve recurring payments and often include ongoing updates and cloud services. Perpetual licenses are one-time purchases.

16. C – Is intended for use by one person or device

Single-user licenses are designed for one user or one machine, depending on the terms. Company-wide usage would require different licensing.

17. B – The software's license has not been properly activated or assigned

"Unlicensed" or "activation required" messages indicate licensing or activation issues, not hardware or cable length problems.

18. C – Presentation software + videoconferencing with screen sharing

Creating slides and sharing them live via screen sharing matches the requirement exactly. Printing or using USB drives doesn't provide real-time remote viewing.

19. B – Sharing a cloud-based document that supports real-time co-authoring

Cloud documents with co-authoring are ideal for simultaneous editing from different locations. Emailing copies or printing creates version-control headaches.

20. B – User cannot send or receive messages but everything else on the PC works

If the rest of the system works but messaging doesn't, the issue likely lies with the email/chat app or its configuration, not basic hardware.

21. B – Confirm the PC meets the software's system requirements and OS version

If only one new app misbehaves, compatibility or insufficient resources may be the cause. Checking requirements is a sensible first step.

22. B – Using word processing software to draft a company policy document

Word processors are designed for text-heavy policy documents. Spreadsheets, presentations, and chat logs are poor primary tools for that job.

23. C – The spreadsheet is hosted as a cloud-based document that requires connectivity for editing

If the document is cloud-based, offline editing may be limited or unavailable. This explains why editing stops when the internet connection is lost.

24. B – The applications may enter reduced functionality mode or stop working fully

When subscriptions lapse, software may still open but not allow editing, or may stop functioning beyond basic viewing. It does not automatically delete documents or reinstall OSs.

25. B – Checking for application updates and verifying login/license status when a cloud app fails to open

This shows logical, low-impact troubleshooting steps aligned with how cloud apps work. Reinstalling OSs, replacing drives, or deleting random files is excessive and risky.

Chapter 11

Web Browsers, Cloud Apps, and Software Licensing

This chapter focuses on how users interact with the web and cloud-based software, and how licensing works behind the scenes. You'll learn browser basics, common web issues, what "the cloud" really means, and revisit software licensing in a bit more depth. The goal is to link everyday internet use with the technical concepts ITF+ expects you to know.

11.1 What a Web Browser Is and Does

WEB BROWSERS ARE THE primary tools people use to access websites and many cloud applications. ITF+ expects you to understand their basic purpose and behavior. This section sets the stage for everything web-related in this chapter.

- **Definition and purpose of a web browser**
- **Common examples and cross-platform availability**
- **How browsers display web content**

A **web browser** is an application that requests, receives, and displays web pages from servers on the internet or local networks. When you type a URL or click a link, the browser sends an HTTP/HTTPS request and then renders the response. Browsers interpret HTML, CSS, JavaScript, and other web technologies to show pages with text, images, forms, and interactive features. Without a browser, most users would have no practical way to navigate the web.

Common examples include Chrome, Edge, Safari, Firefox, and various mobile browsers. Many are available across multiple platforms, so a user might use the same browser on a phone, tablet, and desktop. Different browsers may have slightly different interfaces and performance characteristics, but they all serve the same core purpose. Recognizing these names and icons helps you interpret user questions like "my browser isn't working."

Browsers **render** web content by interpreting HTML structure, applying styles from CSS, and executing JavaScript for interactivity. They may load additional resources like images, fonts, and videos as needed. When pages don't display correctly, it can be due to browser compatibility, blocked scripts, extensions, or network issues. Understanding this rendering process helps you think about where problems might occur.

11.2 Basic Browser Features and Navigation

BROWSERS INCLUDE COMMON navigation and management features to help users move around the web. ITF+ expects you to recognize these standard elements. This section covers the basics of everyday browser use.

- **Address bar and search**
- **Tabs, back/forward, and refresh**
- **Bookmarks and history**

The **address bar** lets users type URLs directly, such as https://example.com, and often doubles as a search box. If the browser can't interpret what you typed as a URL, it sends it to a search engine instead. This unified bar simplifies navigation but can confuse some users who think they're on a search site when they're actually in the browser itself. Understanding this helps you explain what's happening when users "search" from the top bar.

Tabs allow multiple web pages to be open within one browser window. Users can switch between tabs, close them, or open links in new tabs to keep their place. Navigation buttons like **Back**, **Forward**, and **Refresh** control page history and reloading. When a page freezes or doesn't seem to update properly, refreshing or opening it in a new tab are simple troubleshooting steps.

Bookmarks let users save favorite sites for quick access later, organized into folders if needed. **History** records recently visited sites, which can be useful when someone wants to return to a page but doesn't remember the exact address. At the same time, history can be cleared for privacy. ITF+ expects you to know that these features exist and how they support everyday browsing.

11.3 Cookies, Cache, and Basic Privacy Concepts

BROWSERS STORE DATA locally to improve performance and remember preferences. ITF+ expects you to understand cookies and cache at a high level, along with basic privacy concerns. This section demystifies those terms.

- **Cookies as small pieces of website data**
- **Cache as stored copies of web content**
- **Privacy implications and clearing data**

Cookies are small pieces of data stored by websites on your device via the browser. They might remember login status, preferences, or items in a shopping cart. Some cookies are essential for site functionality; others track user behavior for analytics or advertising. If cookies are disabled or deleted, you may be logged out or lose saved preferences. Knowing this helps you understand why "clearing cookies" can both fix and disrupt things.

The **cache** stores copies of web resources (like images, scripts, and pages) to load them faster on subsequent visits. Instead of downloading the same content again, the browser can reuse cached versions when appropriate. However, outdated or corrupted cache data can cause display problems or prevent new versions of a page from showing. Clearing the cache forces the browser to fetch fresh content, which can fix some issues.

Privacy concerns arise because cookies and certain cached data can reveal browsing habits, especially when third-party tracking cookies are involved. Browsers offer privacy features like "private/incognito windows," cookie controls, and the ability to clear browsing data. ITF+ expects you to know that these tools exist and that clearing cookies/cache is a common troubleshooting and privacy step.

11.4 Browser Extensions, Pop-Ups, and Security Warnings

BROWSERS CAN BE EXTENDED with add-ons and may display security-related messages. ITF+ expects awareness of how extensions, pop-ups, and warnings affect browsing. This section connects convenience with risk.

- **Browser extensions and their uses**
- **Pop-ups and blockers**
- **Security warnings (certificates and unsafe sites)**

Browser extensions (or add-ons) are small programs that add features to the browser, such as ad-blocking, password management, or developer tools. While many extensions are useful, poorly designed or malicious ones can slow down browsing or create security risks. If a browser becomes unstable, disabling extensions is a common diagnostic step. ITF+ may include scenarios where an extension is the likely culprit.

Pop-ups are new windows or tabs opened by websites, sometimes for legitimate purposes like logins or notifications, but often for ads or spam. Modern browsers include pop-up blockers that can be toggled on or off or configured per site. Users may need to allow pop-ups temporarily for certain business tools. Understanding this helps you troubleshoot when a user says "nothing happens when I click this button" and a blocked pop-up is the reason.

Browsers display **security warnings** when certificates are invalid, sites are flagged as unsafe, or connections are not properly encrypted. For example, a warning may appear for sites without valid HTTPS certificates. Users should generally be cautious about proceeding past such alerts, especially on unknown sites. ITF+ expects you to recognize that these warnings exist to protect users from potential attacks or fraud.

11.5 Common Browser and Web Issues (User-Level)

MANY USER COMPLAINTS relate to the browser "not working right." ITF+ expects you to recognize common symptoms and simple fixes. This section emphasizes user-level troubleshooting steps.

- **Pages not loading or loading slowly**
- **Pages not displaying correctly**
- **Basic fixes: refresh, try another browser, clear cache/cookies**

If pages **don't load at all**, the problem could be network-related, DNS-related, or a site outage. If they **load slowly**, it might be due to a slow connection, overloaded server, or heavy content like large images and videos. Asking whether other sites are affected helps determine if the issue is widespread or specific to one site. ITF+ may present scenarios where this distinction leads to the correct answer.

When pages **don't display correctly**, you might see missing images, strange layouts, or buttons that don't work. This could be caused by outdated cache, blocked scripts, incompatible extensions, or older browser versions. Trying another browser or using an incognito window can help isolate whether the issue is browser-specific. If the page works elsewhere, something in the original browser environment is likely the problem.

Basic user-level fixes include refreshing the page, closing and reopening the browser, clearing cache and cookies, and disabling suspicious extensions. Trying a different browser or device can confirm whether the issue is local. These non-destructive steps are usually preferable to more extreme actions like reinstalling the OS.

11.6 What "The Cloud" Really Means

"THE CLOUD" IS A BUZZWORD that shows up everywhere, but its basic meaning is straightforward. ITF+ expects you to understand cloud computing at a conceptual level. This section explains what cloud services are and how users interact with them.

- **Cloud as remote computing resources**
- **Cloud storage vs. cloud applications**
- **Benefits: access, scalability, and reduced local requirements**

Cloud computing refers to using resources—such as servers, storage, and applications—that run in remote data centers and are accessed over the internet. Instead of running everything on local hardware you own, you rent capacity and services from providers. To users, this often looks like logging into a website or app that "just works" without them worrying about the servers behind it.

Cloud storage services let users store files remotely and access them from multiple devices. **Cloud applications** (SaaS—Software as a Service) run on provider infrastructure and are accessed via browsers or lightweight clients. Examples include online office suites, CRM systems, and collaboration platforms. Users may not even realize they're "using the cloud"—they just know their data is available wherever they log in.

Benefits of cloud services include easy access from anywhere with an internet connection, scalability (resources can grow or shrink based on demand), and reduced need for powerful local hardware. However, they depend on network connectivity and involve trusting providers with data. ITF+ wants you to understand these trade-offs, not to manage cloud infrastructure.

11.7 Cloud vs. Local Applications: Pros and Cons

USERS AND ORGANIZATIONS often choose between cloud-based and locally installed software. ITF+ expects you to compare these options at a basic level. This section highlights the main pros and cons of each model.

- **Cloud (SaaS) advantages and limitations**
- **Local (on-premises) software advantages and limitations**
- **Hybrid approaches (using both)**

Cloud applications (SaaS) offer **easy access**, automatic updates, and integrated collaboration features. Users can log in from different devices without installing full software everywhere. Licensing is often subscription-based, and data is stored centrally. However, cloud apps generally require a reliable internet connection and raise questions about data privacy and compliance.

Local software installed on the user's device can work offline and may provide deeper integration with hardware or advanced features. Organizations have more direct control over where data is stored and how the software is configured. However, local software requires manual installation, updates, and sometimes more powerful hardware. Managing many copies across a company can be complex.

Many environments use a **hybrid approach**, combining cloud and local tools. For example, a user might have a locally installed office suite that can also save documents to cloud storage. Or a company might host some applications on-premises while using cloud services for others. ITF+ expects you to recognize that real-world setups often blend both models.

11.8 Software Licensing Models (Deeper Dive)

YOU'VE ALREADY SEEN basic licensing concepts; here we go a little deeper. ITF+ expects awareness of how software can be licensed and how this affects usage. This section reviews and expands licensing ideas.

- **Per-device, per-user, and concurrent licensing**
- **Freeware, shareware, and open source (high level)**
- **License compliance and audits (conceptual)**

Per-device licensing ties the license to a specific machine, while **per-user licensing** ties it to an individual regardless of which device they use. **Concurrent licensing** allows a pool of licenses that can be used by a limited number of users at the same time. For example, a lab might have 20 concurrent licenses, with any 20 users able to use the software simultaneously. Understanding these models helps explain why some users may be blocked from accessing a program when limits are reached.

Freeware is software that is free to use but not necessarily open to modification. **Shareware** is typically a trial or limited version that encourages purchase of a full license. **Open-source software** makes its source code available for inspection, modification, and redistribution under specific licenses. ITF+ doesn't expect you to memorize license names, just to recognize these general categories.

License compliance means using software within the terms set by its license: not exceeding seat counts, not sharing keys improperly, and following usage restrictions. Organizations may face software audits, where vendors check for compliance. Non-compliance can lead to legal or financial penalties. At an entry level, you should understand that license management is important and that using unlicensed software is not acceptable.

11.9 Web App and Browser Security Basics (User Perspective)

WEB APPS AND BROWSERS introduce specific security considerations. While the Security domain covers more detail, ITF+ expects basic awareness here as well. This section touches on safe browsing behaviors and web app security basics.

- **Recognizing secure connections (HTTPS)**
- **Avoiding phishing and suspicious links**
- **Logging out on shared or public devices**

HTTPS indicates an encrypted connection between your browser and the website, shown as a padlock icon and https:// in the address bar. This protects data from eavesdropping in transit. Users should be cautious when entering passwords or payment information on non-HTTPS sites. While HTTPS doesn't guarantee a site is trustworthy, its absence on sensitive pages is a red flag.

Phishing attempts to trick users into revealing sensitive information by pretending to be legitimate sites or messages. Suspicious links in emails or messages may lead to fake login pages. Users should verify URLs, be wary of urgent or unexpected requests, and avoid clicking unknown attachments or links. ITF+ expects you to identify phishing-like behavior in scenarios.

Logging out of web apps on shared or public devices prevents others from using your session. Simply closing the browser may not always end the session, especially if cookies remain. Logging out and clearing browsing data where appropriate reduces the risk of unauthorized access. This is particularly important for email, banking, and other sensitive accounts.

11.10 Troubleshooting Cloud and Browser-Based Applications

FINALLY, WE TIE CLOUD and browser knowledge into practical troubleshooting. ITF+ questions often describe issues with web apps or cloud services and ask what to do. This section reinforces simple, logical steps.

- **Checking connectivity and service status**
- **Verifying login, licensing, and permissions**

- **Using browser troubleshooting steps (different browser, incognito, clear cache)**

For cloud and web apps, **network connectivity** is a primary dependency. If a cloud app fails, checking whether other websites load is a quick first step. Sometimes, the service itself may be down—status pages or internal announcements can confirm that. ITF+ scenarios may reward answers that recognize an external outage rather than blaming local hardware.

Login, licensing, and permissions issues are also common. If a user can't access a cloud app but others can, their account might lack the necessary license or permission. Verifying that the user is using the correct credentials and that their subscription or seat is active is often the right move. ITF+ may frame this as "user receives error that they are not authorized" and expect you to think about account-level problems.

Browser troubleshooting steps include trying another browser, using an incognito/private window, disabling extensions, and clearing cache/cookies. These steps help isolate whether the problem is tied to the browser environment or the service itself. As with other troubleshooting, these are low-risk actions that should come before drastic measures like reinstalling the OS.

Practice Questions – Chapter 11 (25 Questions)

1. What is the primary purpose of a web browser?
A. To compile and run programming code only
B. To manage device drivers
C. To request, receive, and display web pages from servers
D. To defragment hard drives

2. Which of the following is an example of a web browser?
A. File Explorer
B. Chrome
C. Task Manager
D. Notepad

3. The bar at the top of the browser where you type web addresses is called the:
A. Status bar
B. Address bar
C. Scroll bar
D. Menu bar

4. Browsers primarily use which protocols to retrieve web pages?
A. FTP/SMTP
B. HTTP/HTTPS
C. DHCP/DNS
D. POP/IMAP

5. A browser "tab" is best described as:
A. A storage device inside the computer
B. A single instance of a web page within a browser window
C. A type of RAM
D. A network port on a switch

6. Cookies in a web browser are:
A. Programs that update hardware drivers
B. Small pieces of data stored by websites to remember information

C. Viruses that always harm your computer
D. Audio settings for streaming music
7. The browser cache is used to:
A. Store copies of web content to speed up future loads
B. Replace RAM in the computer
C. Store the operating system
D. Control printer settings
8. Which action is commonly suggested when a web page layout appears broken or outdated?
A. Clear the browser cache and refresh the page
B. Replace the hard drive
C. Change the CPU
D. Reinstall the operating system
9. Browser extensions are:
A. Built-in CPU features
B. External devices used to extend monitor size
C. Add-on programs that enhance or modify browser functionality
D. Special types of network cables
10. A user clicks a link and nothing seems to happen, but a small icon appears in the browser's address bar indicating something was blocked. Which is the MOST likely cause?
A. The monitor lost power
B. A pop-up was blocked by the browser
C. The CPU overheated
D. The keyboard driver failed
11. "The cloud" is best described as:
A. A local folder on your hard drive
B. Remote computing resources and services accessed over the internet
C. A type of physical cable
D. A built-in feature of all CPUs
12. Which statement BEST describes a cloud storage service?
A. It stores files only on local USB drives
B. It provides remote file storage accessible from multiple devices over the internet
C. It is used only to store operating systems
D. It is a type of CPU
13. Which is a limitation of cloud-based applications compared to local software?
A. They can never be updated
B. They require no hardware at all
C. They usually depend on an internet connection to function
D. They cannot support multiple users
14. Per-user software licensing means:
A. The license is tied to a particular device regardless of who uses it
B. Any number of users can access it at the same time
C. Each licensed individual is allowed to use the software, possibly on multiple devices
D. Only administrators can use the software
15. Concurrent licensing allows:

A. Unlimited users at all times
B. Only one user to ever use the software
C. A specified number of users to use the software at the same time
D. No network connectivity
16. Freeware is:
A. Software that is free to use but not necessarily open-source
B. Always open-source and modifiable
C. A trial version that always expires after one day
D. Only for testing hardware
17. Open-source software is characterized by:
A. Source code being secret and proprietary
B. Source code being available to view and modify under certain licenses
C. Always costing more than proprietary software
D. Requiring special hardware to run
18. Which indicator in a browser suggests that the connection to a website is encrypted?
A. A floppy disk icon
B. A padlock icon and https:// in the address bar
C. A printer icon
D. A red X over the network icon
19. A user receives an email with a link to "verify their account now" from an unknown sender. Which risk is this MOST likely an example of?
A. Hardware failure
B. Phishing attempt
C. Disk fragmentation
D. Local software licensing error
20. Why is it important to log out of web applications on shared or public computers?
A. To make the browser run faster
B. To avoid wearing out the keyboard
C. To prevent others from accessing your accounts and data
D. To increase network speed
21. A user reports that a cloud-based app won't load, but other websites work fine. What is the BEST first step?
A. Reinstall the operating system
B. Check the cloud service's status page or organizational announcements
C. Replace the router immediately
D. Delete all files on the user's PC
22. A user cannot sign in to a cloud app and receives a message about not having a license or permission. What is the MOST likely issue?
A. The monitor is broken
B. The user's account is not assigned the required license or role
C. The CPU is overheating
D. The network cable is unplugged
23. A website works correctly in one browser but not in another on the same computer. What is the BEST explanation?
A. The hard drive is failing

B. A browser-specific issue such as extensions or settings is affecting one browser
C. The power supply is overloaded
D. The printer is misconfigured
24. Which action is a reasonable browser-level troubleshooting step before attempting advanced OS fixes?
A. Clearing cache/cookies and trying the site in an incognito window
B. Replacing all internal components
C. Formatting the hard drive
D. Installing a new operating system
25. Why is software license compliance important for organizations?
A. It increases CPU clock speeds automatically
B. It ensures they are using software legally and avoids potential fines or legal issues
C. It improves screen resolution
D. It eliminates all security threats

Answer Key – Chapter 11 (with Explanations)

1. C – TO REQUEST, receive, and display web pages from servers
Browsers handle web requests and render content for users. They don't primarily manage drivers or defragment disks.

2. B – Chrome
Chrome is a web browser. File Explorer, Task Manager, and Notepad serve other roles in the OS.

3. B – Address bar
The address bar is where you type URLs and often perform searches. Status bars and scroll bars serve different interface functions.

4. B – HTTP/HTTPS
HTTP and HTTPS are the primary protocols for web page delivery. FTP and SMTP handle file transfer and email; DHCP and DNS handle configuration and name resolution.

5. B – A single instance of a web page within a browser window
Each tab hosts a separate page or site in the same browser window. It's not hardware or a network port.

6. B – Small pieces of data stored by websites to remember information
Cookies persist small bits of site data like login status or preferences. They are not always malicious but can have privacy implications.

7. A – Store copies of web content to speed up future loads
Cache improves performance by avoiding repeated downloads. It doesn't replace RAM or store the OS itself.

8. A – Clear the browser cache and refresh the page
Broken or outdated layouts are often fixed by clearing cache and reloading. Hardware changes or OS reinstalls are unnecessary first steps.

9. C – Add-on programs that enhance or modify browser functionality
Extensions add capabilities like ad-blocking or password management. They're software, not cables or hardware features.

10. B – A pop-up was blocked by the browser
Blocked pop-ups often cause "nothing happens" behavior when sites rely on pop-up windows. A small icon or message usually indicates blocking.

11. B – Remote computing resources and services accessed over the internet

"The cloud" refers to remote infrastructure and services, not local folders or cables.

12. B – It provides remote file storage accessible from multiple devices over the internet

Cloud storage hosts files on remote servers for access from various devices. Local USB storage is different.

13. C – They usually depend on an internet connection to function

Cloud apps rely on network connectivity; offline local apps can run without it. Cloud tools can be updated and support many users.

14. C – Each licensed individual is allowed to use the software, possibly on multiple devices

Per-user licenses focus on the person, not the machine. Per-device licenses tie to specific hardware.

15. C – A specified number of users to use the software at the same time

Concurrent licenses allow a pool of simultaneous uses up to a limit. More users than licenses must wait or be denied access.

16. A – Software that is free to use but not necessarily open-source

Freeware is cost-free but may remain closed-source. Open source is a separate concept.

17. B – Source code being available to view and modify under certain licenses

Open-source projects share source code under licenses that define how it may be used, modified, and redistributed.

18. B – A padlock icon and https:// in the address bar

These indicate an encrypted HTTPS connection. Icons like floppy disks or printers are unrelated.

19. B – Phishing attempt

Unexpected messages urging urgent "verification" via links are classic phishing signs. They aim to steal credentials or sensitive data.

20. C – To prevent others from accessing your accounts and data

Logging out on shared systems prevents someone else from using your active session. It doesn't directly change hardware performance.

21. B – Check the cloud service's status page or organizational announcements

If other sites work, the problem may be with the specific service. Status pages or IT announcements can confirm outages.

22. B – The user's account is not assigned the required license or role

License or permission errors usually reflect account configuration, not hardware problems.

23. B – A browser-specific issue such as extensions or settings is affecting one browser

When something works in one browser but not another, differences in extensions, cache, or settings are often to blame.

24. A – Clearing cache/cookies and trying the site in an incognito window

These are safe, standard browser troubleshooting steps and should be tried before extreme OS-level actions.

25. B – It ensures they are using software legally and avoids potential fines or legal issues

License compliance is about legal and contractual obligations. It doesn't directly change performance or automatically solve security threats.

Chapter 12

Programming Languages and Logic Basics (Software Development – Part 1)

This chapter introduces core software development ideas at the ITF+ level. You won't be asked to code like a professional developer, but you should recognize what programming languages are, what source code looks like, and how basic logic works. The goal is to make programming concepts feel understandable, not intimidating.

12.1 What Programming Is (Big Picture)

PROGRAMMING IS SIMPLY telling a computer what to do, step by step, using a language it can understand. ITF+ wants you to grasp this high-level idea rather than memorize syntax. This section sets the foundation for all software development concepts in the exam.

- **Programs as sets of instructions**
- **Source code and compilers/interpreters (very high level)**
- **Why programming matters in IT**

A **program** is a set of instructions that tells a computer how to perform a task. These instructions might process data, respond to user input, or interact with hardware and networks. When you run an application, you are really executing a program that a developer wrote to solve a particular problem. Thinking of programs as recipes helps: each step builds toward a final result.

Source code is the human-readable text written by programmers in a programming language. This code must be translated into machine language that the CPU can execute, either by a **compiler** (which converts code ahead of time) or an **interpreter** (which reads and executes code line by line). ITF+ doesn't expect you to know the details—just that code needs some process to become running software.

Programming matters in IT because almost every tool, operating system, and application is built from code. Even when you're not programming yourself, understanding what code is and how it behaves helps you troubleshoot, automate tasks, and communicate with developers. It also opens up future career paths if you choose to go deeper into software development.

12.2 Types of Programming Languages (High Level)

THERE ARE MANY PROGRAMMING languages, each with strengths and typical uses. ITF+ expects you to recognize common categories and a few language names. This section gives you a simple map of the language landscape.

- **Compiled vs. interpreted languages (conceptual)**
- **High-level vs. low-level languages**
- **Common examples: Python, Java, JavaScript, C, C#**

Compiled languages are translated into machine code before they run, often producing an executable file. **Interpreted languages** are executed line by line by an interpreter at runtime. Some languages use a mix of both approaches with intermediate bytecode. You don't need to classify every language; just know that the translation step can happen before or during execution.

High-level languages are closer to human language and abstract away hardware details, making them easier to write and understand. **Low-level languages** are closer to machine code and give more control over hardware, but are harder to work with. Most modern application development uses high-level languages because they speed up development and reduce errors. Low-level languages show up more in systems programming and embedded devices.

Common examples include **Python** (popular for scripting, automation, and data work), **Java** (often used for enterprise apps and Android development), **JavaScript** (used heavily in web pages and web apps), **C** and **C++** (systems and performance-focused programming), and **C#** (used with Microsoft's .NET ecosystem). You don't need to code in these for ITF+, but you should recognize their names and broad use cases.

12.3 Source Code, Syntax, and Errors

PROGRAMMING LANGUAGES have rules, just like human languages. ITF+ expects you to understand that code must follow specific syntax and that mistakes cause errors. This section explains how source code structure affects whether programs run.

- **Source code as structured text**
- **Syntax rules and common syntax errors**
- **Runtime errors vs. syntax errors (conceptual)**

Source code consists of lines of text following a language's rules for keywords, symbols, and structure. It might include variables, operators, functions, and comments. The way code is laid out affects how the computer interprets it, even though the computer doesn't "see" it as human-readable. Organized, readable code is easier for humans to maintain and debug.

Syntax rules define what valid code looks like, similar to grammar in a spoken language. Missing punctuation, incorrect keywords, or unbalanced parentheses can cause **syntax errors**. These errors usually prevent the program from running until they are fixed. Compilers and interpreters often point to the line where they first noticed a problem, which helps developers find and correct mistakes.

Runtime errors occur while a program is running, even if the syntax is correct. For example, dividing by zero, trying to access a file that doesn't exist, or using invalid input can trigger runtime errors. The program starts successfully but encounters a problem during execution. Understanding the difference between syntax errors and runtime errors helps you interpret error messages and think about where problems come from.

12.4 Variables and Data Types (Conceptual)

PROGRAMS WORK WITH data, and they need a way to store and label that data. ITF+ expects you to understand variables and basic data types conceptually. This section introduces how programs keep track of information.

- **Variables as named storage locations**
- **Common data types: numbers, text, booleans**
- **Why data types matter**

A **variable** is a named storage location that holds a value the program can use or change. You can think of it as a labeled box: the box has a name, and inside is the current value. Programs read from and write to variables as they compute results. Without variables, code would have no convenient way to remember important values.

Common **data types** include numbers (integers and decimals), text strings (sequences of characters), and booleans (true/false values). A program might store an age as an integer, a name as a string, and a "isActive" flag as a boolean. Even if a language hides some details, the underlying idea is that different kinds of data are represented differently.

Data types matter because they determine what operations make sense. You can add two numbers, but adding a number and a name may not be meaningful. Trying to treat text as a number, or vice versa, can cause runtime errors or unexpected results. Understanding that data has types helps you reason about program logic and potential bugs.

12.5 Operators and Basic Expressions

OPERATORS ARE SYMBOLS or words that tell a program how to manipulate values. ITF+ expects you to understand basic arithmetic and comparison operators conceptually. This section covers the building blocks of expressions.

- **Arithmetic operators** (+, -, *, /)
- **Comparison operators** (==, !=, >, <)
- **Expressions that produce results**

Arithmetic operators perform basic math: addition (+), subtraction (-), multiplication (*), and division (/). Programs use these operators to calculate totals, averages, or other numeric results. For example, a shopping cart program might multiply quantity by price to compute a subtotal. Even if you're not writing code, you'll often see these symbols in examples or scripts.

Comparison operators compare values and produce boolean results (true or false). Common ones include equality (==), inequality (!=), greater than (>), and less than (<). For instance, a program might check whether age >= 18 to determine if someone is allowed to access certain content. These comparisons are the foundation of decision-making in code.

An **expression** combines variables, values, and operators to produce a result. For example, total = price * quantity is an expression that computes a new total. Programs evaluate expressions repeatedly as they run, using the current values of variables. Understanding expressions helps you follow code logic at a high level, even without writing it yourself.

12.6 Basic Logic: If/Then Decisions

DECISION-MAKING IS at the heart of programming. ITF+ expects you to understand simple conditional logic, often phrased as "if this, then that." This section introduces the concept of branching in code.

- **If statements and conditions**
- **Else and else-if branches**
- **Using conditions to guide program flow**

An **if statement** checks a condition and runs certain code only if that condition is true. For example, "If password is correct, then log the user in" is a basic conditional. If the condition is false, the program skips that block of code. This allows programs to respond differently depending on input or state.

Else and **else-if** branches provide alternative paths. An else branch runs when the if condition is false, while else-if allows multiple conditions to be checked in sequence. For example, a program might check if a score is above 90, else-if above 80, else-if above 70, and else label it as failing. This branching structure mirrors how humans make multi-step decisions.

Conditions often use comparison operators, such as if (balance > 0) or if (userIsAdmin == true). By combining variables and comparisons, programs can make complex decisions about what to do next. Understanding this basic logic helps you interpret pseudocode and flowcharts used on the exam.

12.7 Logical Operators and Compound Conditions

SOMETIMES A PROGRAM needs to check more than one condition at once. ITF+ expects a conceptual understanding of logical operators like AND, OR, and NOT. This section explains how compound conditions work.

- **AND (&&) – both conditions must be true**
- **OR (||) – at least one condition must be true**
- **NOT (!) – reverses a condition**

The **AND** operator (often written as &&) requires that all combined conditions be true for the whole expression to be true. For example, a login system might require that both the username is correct **and** the password is correct. If either part fails, access is denied. This is useful for enforcing multiple requirements at once.

The **OR** operator (often written as ||) evaluates to true if **at least one** of the conditions is true. For instance, a promotion might apply if the user is a student **or** a senior. OR is used when any of several possibilities are acceptable. It broadens the set of conditions that allow certain code to run.

The **NOT** operator (often written as !) reverses a boolean value: true becomes false, and false becomes true. For example, if (!isComplete) means "if it is not complete." NOT is often combined with AND and OR to express more nuanced logic. Understanding these logical operators helps you decode compound conditions in pseudocode and exam questions.

12.8 Loops and Repetition (Conceptual)

PROGRAMS OFTEN NEED to repeat actions multiple times, such as processing every item in a list. ITF+ expects a conceptual understanding of loops. This section explains repetition without deep syntax details.

- **Why loops are used**
- **Common loop types: for and while (conceptual)**
- **Loop control and avoiding infinite loops**

Loops allow code to run repeatedly without writing the same instructions many times. For example, if you need to print all names in a list, a loop can process each name one after another. This makes programs concise and easier to maintain. Without loops, many tasks would require long, repetitive code.

A **for loop** is often used when you know how many times you need to repeat an action, such as "for each item in this list" or "repeat 10 times." A **while loop** repeats as long as a condition remains true, which is useful when the number of repetitions isn't known in advance. ITF+ doesn't require exact syntax, just the idea that these structures exist.

Loop control involves ensuring that loops eventually stop. If a loop's condition never becomes false, it creates an **infinite loop**, where the program gets stuck repeating forever or until interrupted. This can cause performance issues or crashes. Programmers must update variables or conditions inside loops to move toward completion.

12.9 Pseudocode and Flowcharts (Describing Logic)

YOU DON'T NEED TO WRITE real code for ITF+, but you may see pseudocode and flowcharts. These tools describe program logic in a language-neutral way. This section shows how they help express algorithms.

- **Pseudocode as structured plain language**
- **Flowcharts as visual logic diagrams**
- **Using these tools to understand and plan logic**

Pseudocode is a way of writing program logic in plain, structured language without worrying about exact syntax. It uses simple statements like "IF condition THEN do something ELSE do something else" and "FOR each item in list." Pseudocode is designed to be easy for humans to read and translate into any programming language. ITF+ uses it to test your understanding of logic, not your syntax skills.

Flowcharts use shapes and arrows to represent steps and decisions in a process. Rectangles represent actions, diamonds represent decisions, and arrows show the flow from one step to the next. Flowcharts make it easy to see the overall structure of a program's logic at a glance. They are especially helpful for visual thinkers or when explaining an algorithm to non-programmers.

Using pseudocode and flowcharts helps developers plan before writing actual code. They also help IT professionals understand what a script or program is supposed to do without diving into detailed syntax. On the exam, you may be asked to interpret simple pseudocode or flowcharts and predict outcomes or identify mistakes.

12.10 Algorithms and Problem-Solving Mindset

AN ALGORITHM IS JUST a step-by-step method for solving a problem. ITF+ expects you to understand algorithms at this conceptual level. This final section ties programming ideas to general problem-solving skills.

- **Algorithms as step-by-step procedures**
- **Breaking problems into smaller steps**
- **Relating programming logic to real-world tasks**

An **algorithm** is a clear set of steps to accomplish a task or solve a problem. Recipes, directions, and troubleshooting checklists are all real-world examples of algorithms. In programming, algorithms take input, perform operations, and produce output in a predictable way. You don't need to know complex algorithms for ITF+, just the idea that they are structured procedures.

Breaking problems into smaller steps is fundamental to both programming and IT work. Instead of thinking "fix this entire system," you might think "check power, then check network, then check application configuration." Each step is easier to reason about than the whole problem at once. This decomposition is exactly what algorithms and pseudocode capture.

Programming logic mirrors real-world tasks: "If the light is off, turn it on; else, leave it alone" is a simple conditional. "Repeat checking email every 5 minutes" is like a loop. Recognizing these parallels can make programming feel less abstract. ITF+ wants you to see that software development is just formalized problem-solving using precise instructions.

Practice Questions – Chapter 12 (25 Questions)

1. Which statement BEST describes a computer program?
A. A physical device used for cooling
B. A set of instructions that tells a computer how to perform tasks
C. A hardware component that stores electricity
D. A type of network cable

2. Source code is:
A. The binary data directly executed by the CPU
B. Human-readable instructions written in a programming language
C. Only the comments inside a program
D. A special type of hardware

3. A compiler is BEST described as a tool that:
A. Edits photos automatically
B. Translates source code into machine-readable form before execution
C. Manages network printers
D. Controls screen brightness

4. Which of the following is a high-level programming language commonly used for scripting and automation?
A. Python
B. HDMI
C. RJ-45
D. SSD

5. Which of the following is TRUE about high-level languages?
A. They are harder for humans to understand than machine code
B. They are closer to human language and abstract away hardware details
C. They can only run on mobile phones
D. They are only used for device drivers

6. A syntax error occurs when:
A. The program runs but receives invalid input
B. The code breaks the language's structural rules and cannot be parsed
C. The hard drive fails
D. The network cable is unplugged

7. Which is an example of a runtime error?
A. Missing semicolon that prevents compilation
B. Misspelled keyword that causes the code to fail to parse

C. Dividing a number by zero during program execution
D. Using a modern browser to open a webpage

8. A variable in programming is best described as:
A. A permanent hardware setting
B. A named location in memory that holds a value
C. A type of network protocol
D. A physical storage device

9. Which data type is MOST appropriate to represent whether a user has agreed to terms (yes/no)?
A. Integer
B. String
C. Boolean
D. Floating-point number

10. The expression total = price * quantity is an example of:
A. A network configuration
B. A mathematical expression using variables and an operator
C. A file system command
D. A hardware diagnostic tool

11. Which operator is commonly used to test if two values are equal in many programming languages?
A. =
B. ==
C. !=
D. <>

12. An if statement is primarily used to:
A. Store large amounts of data
B. Repeat a block of code a fixed number of times
C. Make decisions based on whether a condition is true or false
D. Define a new data type

13. Which of the following best describes the AND logical operator?
A. The condition is true if at least one part is true
B. The condition is true only if both parts are true
C. The condition is always true
D. The condition is always false

14. A loop in programming is used to:
A. Randomly shut down the computer
B. Repeat a block of code multiple times
C. Change the screen resolution
D. Format a hard drive

15. Which type of loop is typically used when you know exactly how many times you want to repeat an action (conceptually)?
A. If loop
B. For loop
C. While loop that never ends
D. Hardware loop

16. An infinite loop occurs when:

A. The program executes only once
B. The loop condition never becomes false, so the loop never ends
C. The CPU is turned off
D. The hard drive is full
17. Pseudocode is:
A. Executable code that runs directly on hardware
B. Structured, human-readable descriptions of logic without strict syntax
C. A type of compiled binary
D. Only a type of error message
18. Flowcharts are used to:
A. Visualize program logic with shapes and arrows showing steps and decisions
B. Install device drivers
C. Manage user passwords
D. Format network packets
19. An algorithm is BEST described as:
A. A random sequence of commands
B. A step-by-step procedure for solving a problem
C. A hardware error in the CPU
D. A type of network router
20. Which of the following is a compound condition using logical operators?
A. x + y
B. if (age > 18 && hasID == true)
C. total = price * quantity
D. print("Hello")
21. Which situation is MOST like an if/else decision in everyday life?
A. Brushing your teeth in the morning
B. "If it's raining, take an umbrella; else, don't."
C. Breathing automatically
D. Counting to 10 repeatedly
22. Which everyday example is MOST similar to a loop?
A. Turning on a light switch once
B. "Check for new email every 5 minutes."
C. Writing your name one time on a form
D. Taking a single photo
23. Why is data typing important in programming?
A. It ensures the program is always fast
B. It helps determine which operations are valid on specific kinds of data
C. It increases hard drive capacity
D. It controls network bandwidth
24. A program needs to process every record in a list of 1,000 customers. Which concept is MOST relevant?
A. Single if statement only
B. A loop to iterate through each customer record
C. A network firewall rule
D. Screen resolution settings

25. Why does ITF+ focus on pseudocode and logic instead of specific language syntax?

A. Because syntax is never important in real life

B. Because logical thinking and problem-solving are language-agnostic skills

C. Because no one uses programming languages anymore

D. Because only hardware matters in IT

Answer Key – Chapter 12 (with Explanations)

1. B – A SET OF INSTRUCTIONS that tells a computer how to perform tasks

A program is essentially a list of instructions executed by the computer to accomplish specific goals. It is not hardware or a cable.

2. B – Human-readable instructions written in a programming language

Source code is what developers write and edit. It must be translated into machine code before the CPU can execute it.

3. B – Translates source code into machine-readable form before execution

Compilers convert source code into an executable or intermediate form. They don't edit photos or manage devices.

4. A – Python

Python is a high-level language often used for scripting and automation. HDMI, RJ-45, and SSD are hardware/connection-related terms.

5. B – They are closer to human language and abstract away hardware details

High-level languages are designed to be more readable and easier to work with than low-level machine code. They can run on many platforms via compilers/interpreters.

6. B – The code breaks the language's structural rules and cannot be parsed

Syntax errors violate language rules, preventing compilation or interpretation. Invalid input or hardware problems are different kinds of issues.

7. C – Dividing a number by zero during program execution

Runtime errors happen while the program is running, even if the syntax is valid. Division by zero commonly causes such an error.

8. B – A named location in memory that holds a value

Variables store values that can change as the program runs. They are not physical devices or protocols.

9. C – Boolean

A boolean represents true/false or yes/no states. Integers and strings can encode similar information, but booleans are the most appropriate type conceptually.

10. B – A mathematical expression using variables and an operator

This expression computes a result using variables price and quantity with the multiplication operator, then stores it in total.

11. B – ==

In many languages, == is used to test equality, while = assigns values. != is inequality; <> is used in some languages but not as broadly.

12. C – Make decisions based on whether a condition is true or false

If statements control branching by checking conditions and executing code selectively. Loops and storage have different roles.

13. B – The condition is true only if both parts are true

AND requires all combined conditions to be true; OR only needs one; "always true/false" would not describe a useful logical operator.

14. B – Repeat a block of code multiple times

Loops handle repetition. They don't directly control hardware or formatting tasks like drive formatting.

15. B – For loop

For loops are often used when the number of iterations is known ahead of time. While loops handle conditions that may depend on runtime events.

16. B – The loop condition never becomes false, so the loop never ends

Infinite loops are caused by conditions that never change to stop the loop. This can hang programs or consume resources indefinitely.

17. B – Structured, human-readable descriptions of logic without strict syntax

Pseudocode expresses logic in plain language that looks code-like but isn't tied to a specific language's rules.

18. A – Visualize program logic with shapes and arrows showing steps and decisions

Flowcharts map logic visually, showing how control flows through actions and decisions.

19. B – A step-by-step procedure for solving a problem

Algorithms are structured methods for solving problems or performing tasks, not hardware or random commands.

20. B – if (age > 18 && hasID == true)

This condition uses AND (&&) to combine two checks. The other options do not demonstrate compound logical conditions.

21. B – "If it's raining, take an umbrella; else, don't."

This mirrors an if/else structure. The other options are automatic or one-time actions.

22. B – "Check for new email every 5 minutes."

Repeating the same action on a schedule is like a loop. The other examples are one-time actions.

23. B – It helps determine which operations are valid on specific kinds of data

Data types ensure that operations make sense (e.g., adding numbers vs. concatenating strings). They don't directly control hardware or bandwidth.

24. B – A loop to iterate through each customer record

Processing each item in a list is a classic use case for loops. Single if statements or display settings won't handle repeated processing.

25. B – Because logical thinking and problem-solving are language-agnostic skills

ITF+ focuses on foundational logic that applies across languages. Specific syntax can vary, but the underlying problem-solving approach is universal.

Chapter 13

Algorithms, Pseudocode, and Scripting Concepts (Software Development – Part 2)

This chapter builds on basic programming logic and focuses more on algorithms, pseudocode, and scripting in real IT environments. You'll see how small scripts help automate tasks, how pseudocode describes solutions, and how input/output and errors are handled. The goal is to make "coding" feel like a natural extension of everyday problem-solving.

13.1 Algorithms in Everyday IT Work

ALGORITHMS AREN'T JUST for advanced programmers; they show up in regular IT tasks too. ITF+ wants you to connect the idea of algorithms to real-world procedures. This section grounds the concept in everyday work.

- **Algorithms as repeatable procedures**
- **Examples in troubleshooting and support**
- **Importance of clarity and order**

An **algorithm** is a repeatable procedure: a clear list of steps that, if followed, should lead to a consistent result. In IT, that might be a checklist for resetting a password, a sequence for configuring a router, or steps to deploy software. These procedures are algorithms, even if you never write them in code. Thinking of them this way helps you recognize structure and repeatability.

Troubleshooting guides are practical examples of algorithms. For instance, a help desk script might say: "1) Verify power; 2) Check network connection; 3) Restart the device; 4) Check logs; 5) Escalate." Each step is ordered and often depends on the outcome of previous steps. Following this algorithm helps first-level support handle many issues consistently.

Clarity and order are essential. If steps are ambiguous ("do something until it works") or in the wrong sequence (reinstalling the OS before checking the cable), results become unpredictable and wasteful. Good algorithms are specific, ordered, and testable—you can follow them and see whether they work. ITF+ wants you to see algorithms as practical tools, not just abstract math.

13.2 Pseudocode Structure and Conventions

PSEUDOCODE IS A WAY to write algorithms in a code-like style without worrying about actual syntax. ITF+ uses pseudocode to test logical thinking. This section shows typical pseudocode structures so you can read and reason about them.

- **Basic statements (assignment, input, output)**
- **IF/ELSE and loops in pseudocode**
- **Indentation and readability**

Basic pseudocode statements might look like SET total = 0, READ userInput, or DISPLAY "Hello". These lines describe actions like assigning values, getting input, and showing output. They aren't tied to any one programming language, but they resemble what real code does. Learning to read these statements helps you follow algorithm descriptions on the exam.

IF/ELSE and loops appear in pseudocode just like in real languages. For example:

IF score >= 60 THEN DISPLAY "Pass" ELSE DISPLAY "Fail".

Loops might be written as FOR EACH item IN list or WHILE count < 10. The exact wording can vary, but the logic is the same: conditions guide decisions, and loops repeat actions. ITF+ may ask you what output such pseudocode produces.

Indentation and spacing in pseudocode make it easier to see which lines belong to which blocks (such as inside an IF or loop). Indented lines show that they are part of a condition or repeated block. While computers don't run pseudocode, humans definitely benefit from readable structure. Being able to visually follow blocks of logic is a big part of understanding it.

13.3 Reading Pseudocode: Following the Flow

ITF+ WILL SOMETIMES present pseudocode and ask you what it does. You don't have to write perfect pseudocode yourself, but you should be able to follow it. This section focuses on tracing logic step by step.

- **Tracking variables and values through steps**
- **Understanding branches (different paths)**
- **Predicting final output or result**

To read pseudocode, track variables as they change. If you see SET x = 5 followed by SET x = x + 2, you should know that x now equals 7. As you move line by line, mentally update each variable's value. This is like keeping a little table of current values in your head (or on scratch paper during the exam).

Branches introduce different possible paths. For example, IF temperature > 100 THEN DISPLAY "Hot" ELSE DISPLAY "OK" will show different outputs depending on the temperature value at that moment. When tracing pseudocode, you must decide whether each condition is true or false and follow the appropriate branch. Only the chosen path's statements actually execute.

Predicting final output or results means following the entire pseudocode sequence from start to finish. You combine variable tracking with branch decisions and loop repetitions. ITF+ questions might ask, "What does this program display when input is 3?" Your job is not to worry about syntax, but to carefully simulate the logic.

13.4 Scripting vs. Full-Scale Programming

IN IT, YOU'LL HEAR about "scripts" and "applications." ITF+ expects you to understand the difference at a high level. This section explains where scripting fits into everyday IT work.

- **Scripts as small, task-focused programs**
- **Common scripting environments (shell, PowerShell, Python, etc.)**
- **When scripting is useful in IT roles**

A **script** is typically a smaller program designed to automate a specific task or sequence of tasks. Examples include cleaning up temporary files, adding users to a system, or renaming a batch of files. Scripts are often interpreted and run on demand, rather than packaged as large applications. They're practical tools for making repetitive work easier.

Common scripting environments include shell scripts (Bash on Linux/macOS, batch files on Windows), **PowerShell** on Windows, and languages like **Python** or JavaScript. These environments provide commands and functions tailored to working with files, processes, and system configuration. IT professionals frequently use scripts in these environments to automate routine tasks.

Scripting is useful whenever you repeat the same steps regularly or need to perform operations on many objects (like hundreds of user accounts or log files). Instead of clicking through menus or typing commands manually each time, a script does it for you consistently. ITF+ expects you to recognize scripting as part of an IT toolkit, even if you don't write complex scripts yet.

13.5 Common Scripting Uses in IT

SCRIPTS SHOW UP ALL over IT environments. ITF+ wants you to recognize typical scripting use cases so you can see where they fit. This section highlights examples you're likely to encounter.

- **Automation of repetitive tasks**
- **System administration and configuration**
- **Data extraction and reporting**

Automation of **repetitive tasks** is one of the biggest wins from scripting. For example, a script might back up certain folders daily, rotate logs weekly, or clean temp directories. Once written and scheduled, the script runs without manual intervention, saving time and reducing human error. This is especially helpful for tasks that must happen consistently.

System administration scripts manage users, services, and configuration settings. PowerShell scripts might create user accounts in bulk, assign permissions, or configure system policies. Shell scripts on servers can start or stop processes, update software, or monitor system health. Recognizing these uses helps you understand why IT professionals value scripting skills.

Data extraction and reporting scripts gather information from logs, databases, or APIs and convert it into human-readable reports. For example, a script might scan logs for errors and summarize them, or query a system for all active accounts. These reporting scripts support decision-making and troubleshooting by turning raw data into useful insights.

13.6 Input, Processing, and Output in Scripts

SCRIPTS, LIKE OTHER programs, often follow a simple pattern: get input, process it, and produce output. ITF+ expects you to understand this basic structure. This section shows how scripts interact with data and users.

- **Input sources (user, files, systems)**
- **Processing: applying logic and algorithms**
- **Output: screen, files, or other systems**

Input can come from user prompts (like "Enter your name"), configuration files, command-line arguments, or other systems (such as log files or network responses). A script might read a list of servers from a file or accept a filename as a parameter. Understanding input sources helps you see how flexible scripts can be.

Processing is where the script applies logic and algorithms to the input. It may filter data, perform calculations, check conditions, or transform values. For example, a script might read a list of numbers and compute their average, or parse log entries and extract error messages. This is where concepts like variables, loops, and conditionals come into play.

Output can be printed to the screen, written to files, sent over the network, or passed to other programs. A script that cleans up files might output a summary of what it deleted. A reporting script might generate a CSV file for import into a spreadsheet. Recognizing input–process–output patterns helps you mentally organize what a script is doing.

13.7 Error Handling and Basic Script Safety

EVEN SIMPLE SCRIPTS can fail or cause problems if they're not written carefully. ITF+ expects basic awareness of error handling and safety practices. This section explains how scripts can handle unexpected situations.

- **Common errors (bad input, missing files, permissions)**
- **Simple error messages and logging**
- **Safe practices: test, backup, and least privilege**

Common errors in scripts include invalid user input, missing or locked files, and insufficient permissions to perform actions. For example, a backup script might fail if the destination drive is full or unavailable. Good scripts anticipate these possibilities and check conditions before proceeding. Recognizing these failure points helps you think about how scripts should behave.

Simple error handling might involve displaying clear error messages or writing to log files. For instance, a script could print "Error: File not found" and exit gracefully instead of crashing with a cryptic system error. Logging allows admins to review what went wrong later. Even basic error handling is better than none, especially for scripts used by others.

Safe scripting practices include testing scripts in a non-production environment, keeping backups of important data, and running scripts with the least privileges necessary. For example, a file-cleanup script should be tested on sample folders before running on critical directories. Running scripts as a high-privilege admin unnecessarily increases the risk of serious damage if there's a mistake.

13.8 Script Execution Environments and Permissions

SCRIPTS DON'T RUN IN a vacuum; they depend on an environment and permissions. ITF+ expects you to recognize that scripts need the right context to work. This section covers where scripts run and what access they need.

- **Interpreters and shells**
- **Execution policies and permissions**
- **Platform differences (Windows vs. Linux/macOS)**

Scripts rely on **interpreters** or **shells** like Bash, PowerShell, or a Python interpreter. These environments understand the script's language and execute the instructions. If the necessary interpreter isn't installed or configured, the script won't run. Knowing which environment a script requires is basic but important.

Execution policies and permissions control whether scripts are allowed to run and what they can access. For example, Windows PowerShell has policies that can restrict unsigned scripts from running. File permissions determine whether a script can read, write, or execute. When a script fails immediately with a "permission denied" or "policy" message, these controls are often the cause.

Different platforms have different default scripting environments. Windows emphasizes PowerShell and batch files, while Linux and macOS favor Bash and other shells. Path formats and commands can also vary. ITF+ doesn't expect you to memorize all differences, but you should know that scripts often need adjustment when moved between platforms.

13.9 Basic DevOps and Automation Concepts (High Level)

MODERN IT INCREASINGLY blends development and operations work, a trend often called DevOps. ITF+ doesn't go deep into DevOps, but it does expect basic awareness of automation trends. This section connects scripts to bigger automation ideas.

- **Automation to reduce manual work and errors**
- **Infrastructure as code (conceptual)**
- **Continuous tasks (backups, deployments, monitoring)**

Automation reduces manual work by replacing repetitive tasks with scripts and tools. This makes processes faster, more consistent, and less error-prone. Instead of following a written checklist by hand, a well-designed automation pipeline can perform those steps in seconds. Understanding this helps you see why scripting and automation are valued skills.

Infrastructure as code is the idea of managing servers, networks, and configurations using code and scripts, rather than manual setup. Tools read configuration files and automatically create or update environments. While ITF+ doesn't test specific tools, you should understand that infrastructure itself can be scripted and version-controlled like software.

Continuous tasks—such as nightly backups, automated deployments, and system monitoring—are often orchestrated by scripts or automation tools. Logs, alerts, and dashboards show the results. Entry-level IT roles may involve maintaining or triggering these automations, even if you didn't build them. Recognizing this landscape helps you understand where scripting fits into modern IT.

13.10 Problem-Solving with Algorithms and Scripts

THIS FINAL SECTION brings everything together: algorithms, pseudocode, and scripting as tools for solving IT problems. ITF+ emphasizes thinking logically about tasks you might automate. This is where "knowing concepts" starts to feel practical.

- **Translating manual tasks into step-by-step procedures**
- **From pseudocode to script (high level)**

- **Choosing when scripting is appropriate**

Translating a manual task into steps is the first move. For example: "1) List files in folder; 2) Find those older than 30 days; 3) Move them to an archive folder; 4) Log the results." That's an algorithm in plain language. Once you have the steps, you can represent them in pseudocode or a flowchart that captures decisions and loops.

From pseudocode to script simply means turning those structured steps into real commands in a scripting language. You map "LIST files" to a directory listing command, and "IF older than 30 days" to a date comparison. While ITF+ doesn't require you to write full scripts, understanding this translation helps you collaborate with people who do.

Choosing when scripting is appropriate is also important. If a task is one-time and simple, manual action might be fine. If it's frequent, complex, or involves many items, scripting is often the better choice. ITF+ wants you to recognize those situations on the exam—where the right answer is to automate or at least consider a script.

Practice Questions – Chapter 13 (25 Questions)

1. Which statement BEST describes an algorithm in an IT context?
A. A physical server in a data center
B. A random series of commands typed into a shell
C. A clear, ordered set of steps used to solve a problem or perform a task
D. A specific brand of scripting language

2. Pseudocode is primarily used to:
A. Execute code faster than compiled languages
B. Describe program logic in a readable way without strict language syntax
C. Replace all real programming languages
D. Configure network switches directly

3. In pseudocode, which line is MOST likely an assignment statement?
A. IF x > 10 THEN
B. DISPLAY "Hello"
C. SET count = 0
D. WHILE count < 5

4. When reading pseudocode, what is the BEST way to determine the final value of a variable?
A. Ignore all assignments and guess
B. Track how the variable's value changes line by line
C. Only read the first line of the pseudocode
D. Assume the variable never changes

5. A script is BEST described as:
A. A gigantic enterprise application that runs on many servers
B. A small, task-focused program often used for automation
C. A type of physical cable
D. A hardware-only feature

6. Which of the following is a common scripting environment used in Windows for system administration?
A. Bash shell
B. PowerShell
C. BIOS
D. HDMI

7. Which is an example of a task that is well-suited for scripting?
A. Physically replacing a broken hard drive
B. Cleaning temporary files from multiple computers every night
C. Installing a CPU into a motherboard
D. Changing the color of a monitor's plastic case
8. In the input–process–output model, which of the following is an example of **input** for a script?
A. A summary report saved to a file
B. A user typing a file name at a prompt
C. A loop that counts from 1 to 10
D. A log message written after completion
9. Which of the following is an example of **output** from a script?
A. An IF statement deciding between two paths
B. A user entering their age
C. A file generated with a list of all active user accounts
D. A variable being updated in memory
10. A script that runs nightly to back up a folder is mainly doing what for the IT team?
A. Increasing CPU speed
B. Automating a repetitive task to save time and reduce manual errors
C. Replacing the need for network cables
D. Eliminating all security threats
11. Which of the following is a common cause of errors in scripts?
A. Using a modern operating system
B. Invalid user input, missing files, or lack of permissions
C. Too much free disk space
D. Having a fast network connection
12. Why is it important to test a script in a non-production (lab) environment first?
A. So users can access it immediately
B. To avoid reading any documentation
C. To reduce the risk of damaging real systems or data if the script has bugs
D. To make the script run slower
13. A script fails with a "permission denied" message when trying to delete a file. What is the MOST likely cause?
A. The CPU is overheating
B. The script does not have sufficient file system permissions
C. The monitor resolution is too low
D. The computer is offline
14. Which phrase best describes an interpreter in the context of scripting?
A. A device that cools the CPU
B. A program that reads and executes script code line by line
C. A physical backup tape drive
D. A type of network router
15. On Windows, which scripting-related security feature may block unsigned scripts from running?
A. File Explorer
B. Execution policy
C. Screen saver

D. Device Manager

16. Which example BEST illustrates "infrastructure as code" (conceptual)?

A. Manually configuring every server using only GUI tools

B. Writing scripts and configuration files that automatically set up servers and services

C. Backing up only user documents

D. Using only hardware firewalls for protection

17. Which of the following is MOST like a scripted monitoring task?

A. Checking server logs manually once per year

B. A tool that regularly checks server health and writes alerts to a log

C. Replacing keyboards in an office

D. Manually installing RAM in a PC

18. A flowchart diamond shape usually represents:

A. A start or end point

B. A process/action step

C. A decision point with branches

D. A storage device

19. In pseudocode, which structure would MOST likely represent a loop?

A. IF score >= 50 THEN

B. SET x = 10

C. FOR EACH user IN userList

D. DISPLAY "Error"

20. A help desk script instructs staff: "1) Verify user identity; 2) Reset password; 3) Have user log in; 4) Confirm access; 5) Close ticket." This is BEST described as:

A. An unrelated list of random tasks

B. An algorithm for handling password reset requests

C. A hardware installation manual

D. A network topology map

21. Which situation suggests that scripting might be a good solution?

A. You need to install a single application on one PC once

B. You must create 200 user accounts with similar settings

C. You want to change your personal desktop wallpaper

D. You need to plug in a new mouse

22. A script that never exits a while loop because the loop condition is never updated is an example of:

A. Good performance optimization

B. A syntax error

C. An infinite loop

D. A correct algorithm

23. Why is logging helpful in scripts used in production?

A. It slows down the system to save power

B. It provides a record of what the script did and any errors that occurred

C. It hides all script activity from admins

D. It replaces the need for any monitoring tools

24. A script runs correctly on Linux but fails on Windows with path-related errors. What is the BEST explanation?

A. The CPU architecture is different
B. Differences in file path formats and environment between platforms
C. Windows does not support scripting
D. Linux is always bug-free

25. Why does ITF+ emphasize understanding logic and algorithms over writing full production scripts?
A. Because production scripts are never used in IT
B. Because foundational logic skills apply across many tools and languages
C. Because automation is not important
D. Because only network hardware is on the exam

Answer Key – Chapter 13 (with Explanations)

1. C – A CLEAR, ORDERED set of steps used to solve a problem or perform a task

Algorithms are structured procedures, not physical objects or brand names. They can be written or implemented in many ways.

2. B – Describe program logic in a readable way without strict language syntax

Pseudocode focuses on logic rather than language-specific rules, making it easier to understand and translate into real code.

3. C – SET count = 0

Assignment statements set variables to values. The other lines are conditional, output, or loop constructs.

4. B – Track how the variable's value changes line by line

Simulating execution and updating variable values as you go is the best way to understand final results.

5. B – A small, task-focused program often used for automation

Scripts automate specific tasks, while large applications are more complex and often have user interfaces.

6. B – PowerShell

PowerShell is a powerful scripting environment for Windows administration. Bash is more common on Linux/macOS.

7. B – Cleaning temporary files from multiple computers every night

Automating repetitive maintenance tasks is a classic use case for scripting. Hardware replacement and cosmetic changes are physical tasks.

8. B – A user typing a file name at a prompt

User input is a source of data for the script to process. Reports and logs are examples of output.

9. C – A file generated with a list of all active user accounts

Writing a report file is a form of output. Updating variables or making decisions is part of processing.

10. B – Automating a repetitive task to save time and reduce manual errors

Nightly backups performed by scripts reduce human effort and ensure consistency.

11. B – Invalid user input, missing files, or lack of permissions

These are common causes of script failures. OS modernity and fast networks don't inherently cause errors.

12. C – To reduce the risk of damaging real systems or data if the script has bugs

Testing in a lab allows you to find and correct problems safely before affecting production systems.

13. B – The script does not have sufficient file system permissions

"Permission denied" indicates access rights issues, not hardware, display, or connectivity problems.

14. B – A program that reads and executes script code line by line

Interpreters process scripts dynamically rather than compiling them into standalone binaries ahead of time.

15. B – Execution policy

PowerShell's execution policies can prevent unsigned or untrusted scripts from running as a security measure.

16. B – Writing scripts and configuration files that automatically set up servers and services

Infrastructure as code is about defining infrastructure in code so it can be created and managed automatically.

17. B – A tool that regularly checks server health and writes alerts to a log

Automated, scheduled monitoring tasks are often implemented using scripts and tools.

18. C – A decision point with branches

Diamonds in flowcharts represent decisions where the flow can go in different directions based on conditions.

19. C – FOR EACH user IN userList

This line clearly represents a loop that iterates over a list. IF statements and single DISPLAY lines are not loops.

20. B – An algorithm for handling password reset requests

The help desk script is a clear, ordered procedure—a textbook algorithm for a specific task.

21. B – You must create 200 user accounts with similar settings

High-volume, repetitive actions are ideal for scripting. One-time, simple tasks may not justify script creation.

22. C – An infinite loop

If a loop's condition is never changed so that it becomes false, the loop runs indefinitely, causing problems.

23. B – It provides a record of what the script did and any errors that occurred

Logs are essential for understanding script behavior and troubleshooting issues after the fact.

24. B – Differences in file path formats and environment between platforms

Windows and Linux use different path conventions and environment assumptions, which can break scripts written for one platform.

25. B – Because foundational logic skills apply across many tools and languages

ITF+ focuses on transferable, core skills like logic and algorithms that you can use regardless of the specific scripting language later.

Chapter 14

Security Fundamentals and Threat Awareness (Security – Part 1)

This chapter introduces the basics of cybersecurity at the ITF+ level. You'll learn what we're trying to protect, what the common threats are, and how attackers typically try to get in. The goal is to give you a "big picture" of security so later details about protections and best practices make more sense.

14.1 What Security Is Trying to Protect

BEFORE YOU CAN TALK about security, you have to know what's at stake. ITF+ expects you to understand the basic "CIA" concepts of security and what assets are being protected. This section lays that conceptual foundation.

- **CIA triad: Confidentiality, Integrity, Availability**
- **Assets: data, devices, and services**
- **Balancing security with usability**

The **CIA triad** describes three core security goals. **Confidentiality** means keeping data secret from unauthorized people. **Integrity** means ensuring data and systems are accurate and not tampered with. **Availability** means systems and data are accessible when needed by authorized users. Most security measures support one or more of these goals.

Assets include data (like customer records or financial information), devices (like laptops, servers, and phones), and services (like web applications, email, and cloud tools). Attackers may target any of these for theft, disruption, or damage. Understanding that security protects more than just "files" helps you see why networks, accounts, and physical devices all matter.

Security must be balanced with **usability**. If protections make systems too hard to use, people may find workarounds that weaken security. For example, overly strict password policies might lead users to write passwords on sticky notes. Good security design considers human behavior and tries to provide strong protection without making normal work impossible.

14.2 Common Threat Actors and Motivations

NOT ALL ATTACKERS ARE the same. ITF+ expects you to recognize different types of threat actors and why they might target systems. This section introduces the "who" and "why" behind many attacks.

- **Cybercriminals and financial motivation**
- **Insiders (malicious or careless)**
- **Hacktivists, nation-states, and other actors (high level)**

Cybercriminals are attackers primarily motivated by money. They may steal payment data, deploy ransomware, or commit fraud. Their goals include selling stolen data, extorting victims, or abusing systems for profit. Many common attacks, like phishing and ransomware, are driven by these financial motives.

Insiders are people already inside the organization—employees, contractors, or partners. Some insiders are malicious and intentionally steal data or sabotage systems. Others are simply careless, clicking on phishing links, losing devices, or misconfiguring systems. Insider risk is significant because insiders often have legitimate access that attackers normally try to gain.

Hacktivists, **nation-states**, and other advanced actors may be motivated by politics, ideology, espionage, or strategic advantage. They might target government agencies, critical infrastructure, or large corporations for disruption or intelligence gathering. ITF+ doesn't expect deep geopolitical knowledge—just awareness that not all attacks are about quick cash, and some are highly sophisticated and persistent.

14.3 Malware Basics: Viruses, Worms, and More

MALWARE IS A BROAD term for malicious software. ITF+ expects you to recognize major malware categories and what they generally do. This section explains the big picture without deep technical detail.

- **Malware as malicious software**
- **Viruses, worms, and Trojans (high level)**
- **Ransomware and spyware**

Malware is any software designed to harm systems, steal data, or perform unwanted actions. It can arrive via email attachments, infected downloads, removable media, or compromised websites. Once installed, malware may try to spread, hide, or contact remote servers for further instructions. Anti-malware tools are designed to detect and remove these threats.

A **virus** attaches itself to legitimate programs or files and spreads when those programs are run or files are shared. A **worm** spreads over networks without needing user action, exploiting vulnerabilities to move from system to system. A **Trojan** disguises itself as something legitimate, tricking users into running it (for example, a fake "free" game that secretly installs malware). Recognizing these categories helps you interpret exam scenarios.

Ransomware encrypts data and demands payment to restore access, often combining financial motivation with powerful disruption. **Spyware** secretly monitors user activity, capturing keystrokes, browsing history, or other sensitive information. These types of malware can cause serious damage to individuals and organizations, ranging from data loss to financial loss and reputation damage.

14.4 Social Engineering and Phishing Attacks

ATTACKERS OFTEN GO after people instead of breaking through technical defenses. ITF+ expects you to recognize social engineering tactics and phishing. This section highlights how attackers manipulate users.

- **Social engineering as manipulation of people**
- **Phishing emails and messages**
- **Spear phishing and other targeted attacks**

Social engineering involves tricking people into doing something that helps the attacker, such as revealing passwords, clicking malicious links, or bypassing procedures. Attackers might pretend to be IT staff, delivery personnel, or trusted contacts. They exploit curiosity, fear, urgency, or desire to help. Understanding that people can be "hacked" is key to modern security awareness.

Phishing is a common social engineering technique using email or messages. Attackers send messages that look legitimate—such as fake bank alerts or package notifications—containing malicious links or attachments. When users click, they may be taken to fake login pages or run malware. Phishing often uses urgent language to push users into quick, unthinking action.

Spear phishing is a more targeted version of phishing, where the attacker customizes the message for a specific person or group. They may reference real projects, colleagues, or details gleaned from social media. Because the message feels more personal and relevant, targets are more likely to trust it. ITF+ wants you to recognize that spear phishing is more focused and potentially more convincing than generic phishing.

14.5 Passwords, Authentication, and Access Control Basics

AUTHENTICATION IS HOW systems confirm you are who you claim to be. ITF+ expects you to know basic authentication concepts and why strong passwords matter. This section explains core access control ideas.

- **Passwords and passphrases**
- **Multi-factor authentication (MFA)**
- **Principle of least privilege**

Passwords are secret strings used to prove identity, while **passphrases** are longer, more memorable sequences of words. Strong passwords use sufficient length and a mix of characters to resist guessing and brute-force attacks. Reusing the same password across multiple sites is risky because a single breach can compromise many accounts. Educating users about good password habits is a foundational security step.

Multi-factor authentication (MFA) adds one or more extra verification steps beyond a password. Common factors include something you know (password), something you have (a phone, token, or smart card), and something you are (biometrics like fingerprints). MFA makes it much harder for attackers to access accounts, even if they steal or guess a password. ITF+ expects you to recognize MFA as a powerful protection.

The **principle of least privilege** means users and processes should have only the minimum access they need to do their jobs, and no more. This limits the damage if an account is compromised or misused. For example, a regular user account shouldn't have admin rights for everyday tasks. Applying least privilege reduces the "blast radius" of security incidents.

14.6 Physical Security and Device Protection

SECURITY ISN'T JUST about software; physical access matters too. ITF+ expects you to understand basic physical security measures. This section covers how organizations protect devices and locations.

- **Locks, badges, and secure areas**
- **Device protection: cables, locking stations, privacy screens**
- **Environmental and theft risks**

Organizations use physical controls like **locks**, **access badges**, and secure areas to limit who can reach sensitive equipment and documents. Server rooms may require keycards or codes to enter, and visitors might need escorts.

Controlling physical access is a critical part of protecting systems from tampering or theft. If someone can walk up and plug in a malicious device, many other defenses can be bypassed.

Individual **devices** can be protected with cable locks, docking stations with locks, and secure storage cabinets. **Privacy screens** help prevent shoulder-surfing, where someone nearby reads information off a display. Laptops and mobile devices should not be left unattended in public places. Simple measures like locking screens when stepping away go a long way.

Environmental risks include fire, water damage, power surges, and temperature extremes. Equipment should be placed in appropriate locations and sometimes protected with surge protectors or uninterruptible power supplies (UPS). Theft risks are higher in public or poorly secured areas. Security awareness includes recognizing when devices are physically at risk and taking steps to protect them.

14.7 Network and Wireless Security (High Level)

NETWORKS AND WIRELESS connections introduce specific security concerns. ITF+ doesn't require deep networking skills, but you should understand basic protections. This section highlights key network security concepts at a high level.

- **Firewalls and basic network filtering**
- **Securing Wi-Fi with encryption and passwords**
- **Avoiding unsafe public networks**

A **firewall** is a device or software that monitors network traffic and enforces rules about what can come in or go out. It can block unwanted connections while allowing necessary ones, acting like a security gate. Firewalls are commonly built into routers and operating systems. While configuration details can be complex, ITF+ mainly wants you to recognize that firewalls help control access and reduce exposure.

Securing Wi-Fi involves using strong **encryption** (such as WPA2 or WPA3) and unique passwords. Default router settings and passwords should be changed to prevent easy compromise. Open (unsecured) Wi-Fi networks allow anyone nearby to connect and potentially eavesdrop on traffic. Encrypted wireless networks protect data as it travels between devices and access points.

Public Wi-Fi in cafes, airports, or hotels can be risky. Attackers may snoop on traffic, set up fake hotspots, or attempt man-in-the-middle attacks. Users should avoid accessing sensitive accounts on untrusted networks or use additional protections like VPNs. ITF+ expects you to know that open and unknown networks carry higher risk than secured, trusted ones.

14.8 Data Security, Backups, and Encryption Basics

PROTECTING DATA IS a core security goal. ITF+ expects you to understand backups and basic encryption concepts. This section explains how data can be protected both at rest and in transit.

- **Backups as protection against loss and ransomware**
- **Encryption of data at rest and in transit (high level)**
- **Secure disposal of data and devices**

Backups create copies of important data stored elsewhere so that it can be restored if the original is lost, corrupted, or encrypted by ransomware. Regular backups, stored securely and preferably in multiple locations, are essential for business continuity. When ransomware hits, having good backups can be the difference between recovery and disaster. ITF+ connects backups to both availability and integrity.

Encryption transforms data into unreadable form unless you have the correct key to decrypt it. Data **at rest** (on disks or devices) can be encrypted so that stolen hardware doesn't immediately expose its contents. Data **in transit** (moving across networks) can be protected by protocols like HTTPS or VPNs. You don't need to know the math, just that encryption keeps data confidential from eavesdroppers.

Secure disposal of data includes properly wiping or destroying storage media before discarding or repurposing devices. Simply deleting files or formatting drives may not be enough, as data can sometimes be recovered. Organizations often use specialized tools or physical destruction to ensure sensitive data cannot be retrieved. ITF+ wants you to recognize that disposal is part of the data lifecycle.

14.9 Security Policies, Training, and User Responsibilities

TECHNOLOGY ALONE CAN'T secure an organization; people and policies are critical too. ITF+ expects you to understand the role of security policies and user training. This section explains how rules and awareness support protection.

- **Security policies and acceptable use**
- **User training and awareness programs**
- **Reporting incidents and suspicious activity**

Security policies are formal documents that define how systems and data should be used and protected. They may cover password rules, acceptable use of devices, remote access, and data handling requirements. Policies provide a consistent standard for behavior and give IT a basis for enforcing security. Users are expected to know and follow these rules as part of their job.

User training and awareness programs teach people how to recognize and respond to threats like phishing, social engineering, and unsafe browsing. Training may include simulated phishing tests, videos, or workshops. Well-informed users are less likely to fall for attacks and more likely to follow secure practices. ITF+ emphasizes that security is everyone's responsibility, not just IT's.

Reporting incidents and suspicious activity is a key user responsibility. If someone sees a strange email, unusual device behavior, or possible data exposure, they should report it through established channels. Early reporting allows IT to respond quickly, potentially containing damage. Failing to report issues can let attackers operate longer and cause more harm.

14.10 Security Mindset and Everyday Best Practices

THIS FINAL SECTION ties security concepts into practical, everyday behavior. ITF+ wants you to think like someone who cares about risk and takes small, consistent steps to reduce it. You don't need to be a security expert; you just need a security mindset.

- **Being cautious with links, attachments, and downloads**
- **Keeping software updated and patched**

- **Using layered defenses (defense in depth)**

Being cautious means pausing before clicking links, opening attachments, or downloading software—especially from unknown or unexpected sources. If a message feels suspicious, verify it through another channel (like calling the sender) before acting. This simple habit blocks many common attacks that rely on tricking users into doing something risky.

Keeping software updated ensures that known vulnerabilities are patched. Operating systems, browsers, and applications should receive regular updates, especially security fixes. Out-of-date software is a favorite target for attackers, who rely on users not patching. Encouraging and following update best practices is a major part of everyday security.

Defense in depth means using multiple layers of protection instead of relying on a single control. For example, you might have strong passwords, MFA, antivirus software, firewalls, backups, encryption, and user training all working together. If one layer fails, others still provide protection. ITF+ wants you to appreciate that security is most effective when multiple overlapping measures are in place.

Practice Questions – Chapter 14 (25 Questions)

1. The CIA triad in security stands for:
A. Confidentiality, Integrity, Availability
B. Control, Isolation, Access
C. Confidentiality, Identification, Authorization
D. Control, Integrity, Authentication

2. Confidentiality in the CIA triad primarily refers to:
A. Ensuring data is always backed up
B. Ensuring only authorized people can read data
C. Ensuring systems are always online
D. Ensuring data cannot be changed

3. Which of the following is an example of an **asset** that security aims to protect?
A. A strong password policy
B. A firewall rule
C. A database containing customer records
D. A troubleshooting flowchart

4. Cybercriminals are MOST often motivated by:
A. Reducing electricity usage
B. Financial gain
C. Improving system performance
D. Writing documentation

5. An **insider threat** is BEST described as:
A. Only attackers from foreign countries
B. Any threat from employees, contractors, or partners with internal access
C. A type of network cable
D. A problem that can only occur on the internet

6. Malware is:
A. Any legitimate software used for business
B. Only viruses that spread through email

C. Any malicious software designed to harm systems or data
D. Only software that slows down computers accidentally
7. A Trojan is BEST described as:
A. A self-replicating program that spreads across networks automatically
B. A malicious program disguised as legitimate software
C. A hardware device that prevents malware
D. A type of password manager
8. Ransomware typically:
A. Encrypts data and demands payment to restore access
B. Physically damages computer components
C. Only slows down the network
D. Uninstalls all other applications
9. Which of the following is a social engineering attack that uses emails or messages to trick users?
A. Port scanning
B. Phishing
C. Disk defragmentation
D. Packet sniffing
10. Spear phishing refers to:
A. Generic phishing sent to millions of random people
B. Phishing that targets specific individuals or organizations with customized messages
C. A network-based worm
D. A hardware-based attack on routers
11. Which is the BEST example of a strong password practice?
A. Using the same simple password on all accounts
B. Sharing passwords with coworkers for convenience
C. Using long, unique passwords or passphrases for each account
D. Writing passwords on sticky notes and putting them under the keyboard
12. Multi-factor authentication (MFA) improves security by:
A. Replacing passwords entirely
B. Requiring two or more forms of verification, such as a password and a code on your phone
C. Making passwords shorter
D. Eliminating the need for encryption
13. The principle of least privilege means:
A. Giving users full admin access to avoid help desk calls
B. Giving users only the minimum access they need to do their jobs
C. Letting all guests use administrator accounts
D. Never allowing any access to systems
14. A cable lock attached to a laptop is an example of:
A. Software patching
B. Physical security control
C. Network security device
D. Data backup solution
15. Why is using open, public Wi-Fi networks risky?
A. They always make devices run faster

B. Anyone nearby may be able to intercept or tamper with traffic
C. They automatically encrypt all data
D. They never require passwords
16. Backups are important in security because they:
A. Prevent all phishing attacks
B. Ensure there is a recoverable copy of data after loss, damage, or ransomware
C. Stop malware from ever running
D. Replace the need for firewalls
17. Encryption is primarily used to:
A. Increase network speed
B. Make data unreadable without the correct key
C. Compress files to save space
D. Update software automatically
18. Which of the following is an example of data **in transit** that can be protected with encryption?
A. Files stored on a powered-off external hard drive
B. Data being sent from a user's browser to a website
C. Old printed reports in a filing cabinet
D. A laptop turned off in a backpack
19. Security awareness training is intended to:
A. Teach users how to configure routers
B. Help users recognize threats like phishing and follow secure practices
C. Replace technical security controls entirely
D. Teach programming languages
20. Which user action is MOST appropriate when receiving a suspicious email asking for login credentials?
A. Reply with the requested information
B. Click all links to see what happens
C. Delete it or report it according to company policy
D. Ignore it and do nothing, without informing anyone
21. A **security policy** is:
A. A physical lock on a server room
B. A firewall device
C. A formal document describing rules and expectations for system and data use
D. A type of malware detection software
22. Why is it important to keep operating systems and applications updated?
A. Updates always make systems slower
B. Updates can include security patches that fix known vulnerabilities
C. Updates remove all passwords
D. Updates erase user data
23. The concept of **defense in depth** means:
A. Relying on just one really strong security control
B. Using multiple layers of security controls so if one fails, others still protect
C. Never backing up data
D. Only using physical locks, not software security
24. Which of the following is a good everyday security best practice?

A. Using the same password everywhere because it's easier to remember

B. Leaving your computer unlocked when you leave your desk

C. Being cautious with links and attachments from unknown sources

D. Sharing your login with a coworker if they need access

25. A user notices that files on their computer suddenly have strange extensions and can't be opened, and a note demands payment to restore them. This is MOST likely:

A. A hardware failure

B. A phishing attack

C. Ransomware infection

D. Normal OS behavior after an update

Answer Key – Chapter 14 (with Explanations)

1. A – CONFIDENTIALITY, Integrity, Availability

The CIA triad is a core security model describing the main goals of protecting information and systems.

2. B – Ensuring only authorized people can read data

Confidentiality focuses on keeping data secret from unauthorized viewers. Availability and integrity cover different goals.

3. C – A database containing customer records

A database of customer records is a valuable asset. Policies, firewall rules, and flowcharts help protect assets but are not assets themselves.

4. B – Financial gain

Most cybercriminals are motivated by money, using attacks like ransomware, fraud, and data theft to profit.

5. B – Any threat from employees, contractors, or partners with internal access

Insider threats involve people already trusted with some level of access, whether they are malicious or careless.

6. C – Any malicious software designed to harm systems or data

Malware is a broad term for harmful software, not legitimate programs or accidental performance issues.

7. B – A malicious program disguised as legitimate software

Trojans trick users into running them by pretending to be something harmless, then perform malicious actions.

8. A – Encrypts data and demands payment to restore access

Ransomware locks users out of their data and demands a ransom, often in cryptocurrency, to decrypt it.

9. B – Phishing

Phishing uses deceptive emails or messages to trick users into revealing information or running malware.

10. B – Phishing that targets specific individuals or organizations with customized messages

Spear phishing is highly targeted, using personal details to make attacks more convincing.

11. C – Using long, unique passwords or passphrases for each account

Strong, unique passwords or passphrases reduce the damage from any single breach and are harder to guess.

12. B – Requiring two or more forms of verification, such as a password and a code on your phone

MFA adds extra layers beyond passwords, making it harder for attackers to gain access.

13. B – Giving users only the minimum access they need to do their jobs

Least privilege limits damage if accounts are compromised or misused by restricting unnecessary access.

14. B – Physical security control

Cable locks protect devices from theft by physically anchoring them to furniture or structures.

15. B – Anyone nearby may be able to intercept or tamper with traffic

Open or untrusted Wi-Fi can allow eavesdropping and attacks like man-in-the-middle, making it risky.

16. B – Ensure there is a recoverable copy of data after loss, damage, or ransomware

Backups protect against many forms of data loss, including hardware failure and malicious encryption.

17. B – Make data unreadable without the correct key

Encryption scrambles data so only someone with the right key can read it, protecting confidentiality.

18. B – Data being sent from a user's browser to a website

Data moving across a network is "in transit" and can be protected with protocols like HTTPS.

19. B – Help users recognize threats like phishing and follow secure practices

Awareness training focuses on user behavior and recognizing social engineering and unsafe actions.

20. C – Delete it or report it according to company policy

Suspicious emails should be treated cautiously and reported so IT can investigate and warn others if needed.

21. C – A formal document describing rules and expectations for system and data use

Security policies define how users should behave and how systems should be managed from a security standpoint.

22. B – Updates can include security patches that fix known vulnerabilities

Keeping software updated closes holes attackers might exploit. Slowness and data erasure are not goals of updates.

23. B – Using multiple layers of security controls so if one fails, others still protect

Defense in depth is about overlapping protections, not relying on a single control.

24. C – Being cautious with links and attachments from unknown sources

Careful handling of links and attachments helps avoid malware and phishing attacks. The other options are insecure behaviors.

25. C – Ransomware infection

Encrypted files with a ransom note are classic signs of ransomware. Hardware failures or normal updates don't demand payments.

Chapter 15

Secure Practices, Policies, and Device Hardening (Security – Part 2)

This chapter goes deeper into the practical side of security: how to harden devices, apply secure settings, and follow policies in everyday work. You'll see how patching, antivirus, account control, and mobile protections all fit together. The goal is to give you a checklist-style mindset for keeping systems safer.

15.1 What "Hardening" a System Means

"HARDENING" IS A SECURITY term you'll see a lot in IT. ITF+ expects you to understand that it means making a system more resistant to attack. This section introduces the core idea.

- **Reducing attack surface**
- **Removing unnecessary services and software**
- **Applying secure configurations**

Reducing attack surface means limiting the number of ways an attacker can interact with or exploit a system. Every open port, enabled feature, or installed application is a potential entry point. Hardening aims to minimize these opportunities so attackers have fewer paths to try. In practice, that means being intentional about what is installed and enabled.

Removing **unnecessary services and software** is a key hardening step. If a feature or application isn't needed for business purposes, disabling or uninstalling it removes a potential vulnerability. This might include turning off unused remote access services or removing trial software. Fewer components means fewer patches to track and fewer weak spots to manage.

Applying **secure configurations** means setting options and policies in ways that favor security over convenience when reasonable. Examples include enforcing strong passwords, limiting failed login attempts, and requiring screen locks. Hardening guides and benchmarks often provide recommended settings. Even at an entry level, understanding that configuration choices affect security is important.

15.2 Patch Management and Software Updates

KEEPING SYSTEMS UPDATED is one of the most important security practices. ITF+ expects you to understand why patching matters and how updates are typically handled. This section focuses on the basics of patch management.

- **Patches and security updates**
- **Update sources and scheduling**
- **Risks of running outdated software**

Patches and **security updates** fix known vulnerabilities and software bugs. When vendors discover security flaws, they release patches to correct them before attackers can exploit those weaknesses widely. Applying these updates reduces the risk that known exploits will succeed. Ignoring patches leaves systems exposed to attacks that are well understood and often automated.

Update sources include built-in OS update mechanisms, application updaters, and sometimes centralized management tools in larger organizations. Scheduling updates is important: many systems can be set to install updates outside of business hours or with user approval. IT teams may test updates first in non-production environments to avoid surprises.

Running **outdated software** increases risk significantly. Attackers often scan the internet for systems with known, unpatched vulnerabilities. Popular exploit kits and malware campaigns specifically target unpatched systems because they are easier to compromise. For ITF+, you should see timely patching as a foundational security practice.

15.3 Anti-Malware, Antivirus, and Endpoint Protection

PROTECTING ENDPOINTS like desktops, laptops, and mobile devices requires dedicated security software. ITF+ expects you to know what antivirus and endpoint protection tools do at a high level. This section explains their role.

- **Traditional antivirus and anti-malware scanning**
- **Real-time protection and signatures**
- **Endpoint protection suites (high level)**

Traditional **antivirus** and **anti-malware** tools scan files and programs for known malicious code and suspicious behavior. They may perform scheduled scans of the entire system or quick scans of critical areas. When they find something flagged as malicious, they can quarantine or remove it. These tools are a key line of defense against common malware threats.

Real-time protection means the software actively monitors activity as it happens, such as files being downloaded or executed. It uses **signatures** (patterns of known malware) and sometimes heuristic or behavior-based detection. This allows it to block many threats before they run. Keeping definitions and engines up to date is essential for effectiveness.

Modern **endpoint protection suites** combine multiple capabilities: antivirus, firewall, device control, web filtering, and sometimes encryption and intrusion detection. They may report centrally to management consoles so IT can see the security status of many devices. At the ITF+ level, you just need to recognize that endpoints are protected by more than just basic antivirus.

15.4 Secure Configuration of User Accounts

HOW USER ACCOUNTS ARE set up has a huge impact on security. ITF+ expects you to understand basic secure account practices. This section connects account management to least privilege and safe usage.

- **Using standard accounts for everyday work**
- **Managing administrator and privileged accounts**
- **Disabling or removing unused accounts**

Using **standard (non-admin)** accounts for everyday tasks reduces the risk of accidental or malicious changes to system settings. If malware runs under a standard account, it usually has fewer capabilities than if it runs as an administrator. This containment is a simple but powerful defense. Users can elevate privileges only when needed for specific tasks.

Managing **administrator and privileged accounts** carefully is crucial. These accounts should have strong, unique passwords and often MFA enabled. Access should be limited to people who genuinely need it, and actions taken with these accounts may be logged or monitored. Sharing admin accounts is a bad practice because it obscures accountability.

Unused accounts—such as those belonging to former employees or generic test accounts—should be disabled or removed. Leaving dormant accounts active provides extra targets for attackers. If an attacker compromises an unused account with high privileges, they may gain wide access without being noticed quickly. Good account hygiene is part of device hardening.

15.5 Secure Settings: Password Policies and Account Lockout

SYSTEMS CAN ENFORCE security rules to help users make safer choices. ITF+ expects you to understand basic password policy settings and lockout options. This section explains how these controls work.

- **Password complexity and length requirements**
- **Password expiration and reuse rules (conceptual)**
- **Account lockout after failed attempts**

Password policies can require minimum length, a mix of character types, or both. Longer passwords or passphrases often provide better protection than short, complex ones. The goal is to make passwords harder for attackers to guess or crack with automated tools, while still being usable for humans. Balancing strictness and memorability is part of policy design.

Some environments use **password expiration** and reuse rules, such as requiring users to change passwords periodically and not reuse recent ones. The effectiveness of frequent forced changes is debated, but ITF+ wants you to recognize that such policies exist as a security measure. Reuse rules aim to prevent cycling through the same few passwords.

Account lockout policies temporarily lock an account after a certain number of failed login attempts. This helps defend against brute-force attacks where an attacker tries many passwords. Lockouts may last for a set time or require manual reset by an admin. However, if settings are too strict, legitimate users may lock themselves out more easily, so tuning is important.

15.6 Secure Use of Email and Web Browsing

EMAIL AND WEB BROWSERS are common attack paths. ITF+ expects you to know how user behavior and technical controls combine to reduce risk. This section focuses on safe usage habits and basic protections.

- **Recognizing and avoiding suspicious emails and links**
- **Using spam filters and safe browsing features**
- **Limiting risky downloads and browser extensions**

Recognizing suspicious emails involves checking sender addresses, looking for unexpected attachments, and being wary of urgent requests for sensitive information. Users should hover over links to see the real destination before clicking and be cautious about messages that don't match known communication patterns. Deleting or reporting suspicious messages is safer than investigating them by clicking.

Spam filters and **safe browsing** features help automatically block known malicious emails and dangerous websites. Many email providers and browsers maintain lists of phishing and malware sites and warn users when they try to visit them. While these tools are helpful, they're not perfect, so users still need to be skeptical and attentive.

Limiting risky downloads and browser extensions reduces the chance of installing unwanted or malicious software. Users should only download from trusted sources and install extensions from reputable publishers. Too many extensions can slow down browsing and increase the attack surface. Unused or suspicious extensions should be removed.

15.7 Mobile Device and Remote Work Security

MOBILE DEVICES AND remote work introduce unique security challenges. ITF+ expects basic awareness of mobile protections and remote access considerations. This section covers the essentials.

- **Screen locks, PINs, and biometric authentication**
- **Mobile device management (MDM) concepts (high level)**
- **Secure remote access (VPNs, company policies)**

Screen locks, **PINs**, and **biometric authentication** (like fingerprint or face recognition) protect mobile devices from casual access if lost or stolen. Devices should be set to lock automatically after a short period of inactivity. Combined with device encryption, this helps protect sensitive work email or documents stored on the phone or tablet.

Mobile Device Management (MDM) tools allow organizations to enforce security policies on mobile devices, such as requiring encryption, restricting app installations, or remotely wiping lost devices. MDM is especially important for bring-your-own-device (BYOD) environments where personal devices access company data. ITF+ doesn't require tool names—just the concept that mobile devices can be centrally managed.

Secure remote access often uses **VPNs (Virtual Private Networks)** to encrypt traffic between remote devices and company networks. Company policies may require VPN use on untrusted networks and prohibit storing certain data locally. Remote workers should follow these policies, keep their devices updated, and avoid using personal accounts or insecure apps for work tasks.

15.8 Secure Handling of Data and Documents

HOW USERS HANDLE DATA day to day affects security just as much as technical controls do. ITF+ expects you to know basic data handling practices. This section explains how to treat documents and sensitive information safely.

- **Classifying data (public, internal, confidential)**
- **Sharing documents securely**
- **Avoiding data leaks (printing, screenshots, removable media)**

Data **classification** labels information by sensitivity, such as public, internal use only, confidential, or highly restricted. Different classes require different protections: public info can be widely shared, while confidential data might require encryption and strict access control. Knowing classification helps users decide how and where data may be stored and shared.

Sharing documents securely may involve using approved cloud storage with proper permissions, encrypted email, or secure portals. Avoid sending confidential data through personal email or unapproved apps. Access should be granted only to people who need it, and sharing links should be configured to limit resharing where possible.

Avoiding data leaks includes being careful with printing, screenshots, and removable media like USB drives. Printed documents can be lost if left on printers or desks, so they should be collected promptly and shredded when no longer needed. Screens should not display sensitive data in public places, and USB drives should be encrypted or restricted by policy. Small user actions can make big differences in preventing leaks.

15.9 Incident Response Basics (User-Level)

EVEN WITH GOOD SECURITY, incidents still happen. ITF+ expects basic awareness of what to do when something goes wrong. This section focuses on user-level incident response behavior.

- **Recognizing signs of a security incident**
- **Immediate actions users should and should NOT take**
- **Reporting to the appropriate team or contact**

Signs of a **security incident** can include strange pop-ups, unexpected system slowdowns, missing or encrypted files, unknown programs appearing, or accounts behaving oddly. Unusual login alerts or emails about password changes you didn't make are also warning signs. Users don't have to diagnose the exact cause; they just need to recognize that something isn't normal.

Immediate user actions should be cautious and aligned with policy. Users should not try to "fix" malware by randomly deleting files or running unapproved tools. They also should avoid continuing to use a system that appears compromised for sensitive activity. Disconnecting from the network if instructed and preserving evidence can help IT investigate.

Reporting incidents quickly to the appropriate help desk, security team, or manager is critical. Many organizations have specific procedures or contacts for security issues. The sooner IT knows about an incident, the earlier containment and remediation can begin. Failing to report or delaying can allow attackers more time to cause damage.

15.10 Pulling It Together: Everyday Security Habits

THIS FINAL SECTION turns all these concepts into simple habits. ITF+ wants you to think like a security-conscious user or junior technician who makes good choices consistently. You don't need advanced tools; you need reliable routines.

- **Keep systems updated and protected**
- **Use strong authentication and secure settings**
- **Be alert, skeptical, and policy-aware**

Keeping systems updated and protected means turning on automatic updates where appropriate, verifying that antivirus or endpoint protection is running, and responding to update prompts in a timely way. It also includes avoiding unsupported or pirated software, which often lacks patches and may include malware. This habit addresses many common vulnerabilities with minimal extra effort.

Using strong authentication and secure settings includes choosing long, unique passwords or passphrases, enabling MFA whenever possible, and logging out or locking devices when not in use. It also means using standard accounts for routine work and reserving admin rights for specific tasks. These choices directly reduce the risk of account compromise and unauthorized changes.

Being alert and skeptical means questioning unusual requests, verifying emails or messages that ask for sensitive information, and following security policies and training. When in doubt, ask a supervisor or IT rather than guessing. Over time, these habits form a security mindset that supports all the technical defenses around you.

Practice Questions – Chapter 15 (25 Questions)

1. In security, "hardening" a system primarily means:
A. Making the case physically heavier
B. Adding as many new features as possible
C. Reducing vulnerabilities by securing configurations and removing unnecessary components
D. Disabling all security settings
2. Which action is an example of reducing a system's attack surface?
A. Installing every available browser extension
B. Uninstalling unused software and disabling unnecessary services
C. Sharing admin passwords with coworkers
D. Turning off automatic updates
3. Why are security patches and updates important?
A. They only add new visual themes
B. They fix known vulnerabilities that attackers might exploit
C. They always make computers much slower
D. They remove old documents
4. Running outdated software is risky because:
A. It is always faster than new software
B. Attackers often target known, unpatched vulnerabilities
C. It disables firewalls by default
D. It always causes physical damage to hardware
5. Traditional antivirus software primarily:
A. Designs secure networks
B. Scans for and removes known malicious software
C. Replaces the need for passwords
D. Configures physical locks
6. Real-time protection in antivirus/endpoint tools means:
A. The software runs only when you restart the computer
B. The software checks files and activity as they are accessed or executed
C. The software updates once a year
D. The software only scans at midnight

7. Which is the BEST practice regarding user account privileges?
A. Use an administrator account for all daily activities
B. Give all users the highest level of access possible
C. Use standard accounts for routine work and admin accounts only when needed
D. Share a single admin account with the entire team
8. Disabling or removing unused user accounts is important because:
A. It slows down login times
B. It creates more confusion for attackers
C. Unused accounts can be targets for attackers if left active
D. It prevents backups from running
9. A password policy that requires a minimum length and a mix of character types is intended to:
A. Make passwords easy to guess
B. Ensure all users have identical passwords
C. Make passwords harder to guess or crack
D. Eliminate the need for account lockout
10. An account lockout policy typically:
A. Locks accounts forever after one failed attempt
B. Locks accounts temporarily after several failed login attempts to slow brute-force attacks
C. Has no impact on security
D. Forces users to change their username
11. Which of the following is a safe email practice?
A. Opening all attachments to see what they are
B. Ignoring unexpected messages and never reporting them
C. Being cautious of unexpected attachments or links and reporting suspicious emails
D. Forwarding suspicious emails to friends so they can see them
12. Spam filters and safe browsing tools are designed to:
A. Increase hardware performance
B. Block or warn about known malicious emails and websites
C. Replace the need for antivirus software
D. Disable all encryption
13. Which is a recommended security setting for mobile devices?
A. Turn off all screen locks so the device is easy to use
B. Use a screen lock (PIN, password, or biometrics) and auto-lock after inactivity
C. Share your unlock code with coworkers
D. Disable updates to save battery
14. Mobile Device Management (MDM) tools allow organizations to:
A. Control only desktop computers
B. Physically lock all devices in a safe
C. Enforce security settings, push configurations, and remotely wipe managed mobile devices
D. Automatically replace broken screens
15. A VPN (Virtual Private Network) is primarily used to:
A. Increase the brightness of the screen
B. Encrypt network traffic between a device and a remote network
C. Speed up the CPU

D. Defragment the hard drive

16. Classifying data as public, internal, or confidential helps organizations:

A. Decide where to store backup power supplies

B. Determine what level of protection and sharing is appropriate for different types of information

C. Decide which users should be fired

D. Configure printer ink levels

17. Which action could lead to a data leak?

A. Using encrypted cloud storage with proper sharing settings

B. Printing a confidential report and leaving it on a shared printer

C. Locking your computer when leaving your desk

D. Using a privacy screen in a public place

18. A user notices unusual pop-ups and very slow performance, and antivirus shows multiple detections. What is the MOST appropriate action?

A. Ignore it and keep working

B. Attempt to delete random system files

C. Follow company policy to report the incident to IT or the help desk

D. Email the malware to coworkers as an example

19. Users should generally NOT:

A. Report suspicious activity

B. Run unapproved "cleanup" tools from unknown websites

C. Lock their screens when away

D. Follow security policy instructions

20. Why is quick reporting of security incidents important?

A. It reduces the need for training

B. It allows IT to respond quickly and potentially limit damage

C. It guarantees no data will ever be lost

D. It automatically fixes all vulnerabilities

21. Which is a good everyday security habit?

A. Turning off antivirus because it uses resources

B. Reusing the same password on all sites

C. Enabling automatic updates and keeping security tools up to date

D. Disabling all screen locks

22. Using a standard user account for everyday tasks and an admin account only for special tasks is an example of:

A. Social engineering

B. Malware analysis

C. Applying the principle of least privilege

D. Data classification

23. Which of the following is part of a secure browsing practice?

A. Installing every toolbar offered by websites

B. Only downloading software from trusted, reputable sources

C. Ignoring browser warnings about unsafe sites

D. Turning off all security prompts

24. A remote worker accesses company resources over public Wi-Fi at a café. Which measure BEST improves security in this scenario?

A. Connecting without any authentication

B. Using a VPN as required by company policy

C. Sharing the Wi-Fi password with everyone

D. Turning off the firewall

25. Defense in depth on an endpoint device could include:

A. Only a strong password

B. Only a firewall

C. Antivirus, a firewall, strong authentication, updates, and user training together

D. Disabling all logging and alerts

Answer Key – Chapter 15 (with Explanations)

1. C – REDUCING VULNERABILITIES by securing configurations and removing unnecessary components

Hardening is about making systems more resistant to attack, not physically changing the case or disabling protection.

2. B – Uninstalling unused software and disabling unnecessary services

Removing unneeded components reduces potential entry points and simplifies patching.

3. B – They fix known vulnerabilities that attackers might exploit

Security patches close holes discovered in software. Ignoring them leaves systems exposed.

4. B – Attackers often target known, unpatched vulnerabilities

Outdated software is easier to compromise because exploits are widely known and sometimes automated.

5. B – Scans for and removes known malicious software

Antivirus/anti-malware tools detect and remove or quarantine malicious code, forming a key part of endpoint protection.

6. B – The software checks files and activity as they are accessed or executed

Real-time protection monitors ongoing activity instead of only scanning on a schedule.

7. C – Use standard accounts for routine work and admin accounts only when needed

This limits potential damage if malware runs or mistakes are made, aligning with least privilege.

8. C – Unused accounts can be targets for attackers if left active

Dormant accounts, especially privileged ones, can be exploited if not disabled or removed.

9. C – Make passwords harder to guess or crack

Complexity and length make automated guessing attacks more difficult.

10. B – Locks accounts temporarily after several failed login attempts to slow brute-force attacks

Lockouts protect against repeated password guessing, though settings must be tuned to avoid hurting legitimate users.

11. C – Being cautious of unexpected attachments or links and reporting suspicious emails

Careful handling of unexpected emails helps prevent phishing and malware infections.

12. B – Block or warn about known malicious emails and websites

Spam filters and safe browsing lists help stop many threats before users even interact with them.

13. B – Use a screen lock (PIN, password, or biometrics) and auto-lock after inactivity

Screen locks and auto-lock reduce the risk of unauthorized access if a device is lost or left unattended.

14. C – Enforce security settings, push configurations, and remotely wipe managed mobile devices

MDM lets organizations manage and secure mobile devices that access corporate data.

15. B – Encrypt network traffic between a device and a remote network

VPNs protect data in transit on untrusted networks, such as public Wi-Fi.

16. B – Determine what level of protection and sharing is appropriate for different types of information

Classification guides decisions about storage, access, and sharing controls.

17. B – Printing a confidential report and leaving it on a shared printer

Unattended printed documents can be read or taken by unauthorized people, causing data leakage.

18. C – Follow company policy to report the incident to IT or the help desk

Quick reporting allows IT to investigate, contain, and remediate the issue safely.

19. B – Run unapproved "cleanup" tools from unknown websites

Unapproved tools may be malicious or harmful. Users should follow policy and use approved software.

20. B – It allows IT to respond quickly and potentially limit damage

Early detection and response can reduce the impact of incidents significantly.

21. C – Enabling automatic updates and keeping security tools up to date

Regular updates and active security tools address many common vulnerabilities.

22. C – Applying the principle of least privilege

This practice gives users only the rights needed to perform tasks, reducing risk.

23. B – Only downloading software from trusted, reputable sources

Trusted sources reduce the chance of downloading malware or unwanted software.

24. B – Using a VPN as required by company policy

A VPN encrypts traffic on public Wi-Fi, helping to protect sensitive company data.

25. C – Antivirus, a firewall, strong authentication, updates, and user training together

Defense in depth relies on multiple layers of security controls, not just a single measure.

Chapter 16

IT Support Roles, Troubleshooting, and Professionalism

This chapter focuses on the "people side" of IT: how support roles work, how to troubleshoot systematically, and how to behave professionally with users and teammates. You'll see how technical skills and soft skills combine to make an effective IT support person. The goal is to prepare you for entry-level help desk and support responsibilities that show up on the ITF+ exam.

16.1 IT Support Roles and Responsibilities

IT SUPPORT ROLES ARE often the first point of contact when something goes wrong with technology. ITF+ expects you to understand what these roles generally do. This section outlines the basics of help desk and support responsibilities.

- **Front-line (tier 1) support tasks**
- **Escalation to higher tiers (tier 2, tier 3)**
- **Documenting and tracking issues**

Front-line (tier 1) support handles initial user contact—answering calls, tickets, or chats when someone needs help. These technicians gather basic information, perform simple troubleshooting, and resolve common issues like password resets or basic configuration problems. They follow documented procedures and know when a problem is outside their scope. This role emphasizes communication as much as technical skill.

More complex problems are passed to **tier 2 or tier 3** support. Tier 2 may handle advanced configuration and deeper troubleshooting, while tier 3 often consists of specialists, engineers, or vendors. Escalation ensures that difficult issues get attention from people with the right expertise. Knowing when and how to escalate is part of being an effective tier 1 technician.

Documenting and tracking issues is done through ticketing systems or help desk tools. Each request gets a record describing the problem, troubleshooting steps taken, and final resolution. This documentation helps with follow-up, trend analysis, and knowledge sharing. ITF+ expects you to recognize that good documentation is a core support responsibility.

16.2 The Troubleshooting Methodology

TROUBLESHOOTING ISN'T random guessing; it follows a repeatable process. ITF+ expects you to know a basic troubleshooting methodology. This section outlines the classic step-by-step approach.

- **Identify the problem and gather information**
- **Establish a theory and test it**
- **Implement, verify, and document the solution**

The first step is to **identify the problem** and gather information from the user and the system. This includes asking clarifying questions, noting error messages, and observing symptoms. You want to understand what's happening, when it started, and what changed recently. Good information gathering often reveals obvious causes without needing complex analysis.

Next, you **establish a theory** of what might be causing the issue. This theory should be based on symptoms, knowledge of the system, and previous experience. You then **test** the theory by performing targeted actions or checks. If the theory is wrong, you revise it and test again, working from the most likely or simplest causes to more complex ones.

Once you find the cause, you **implement a solution**, verify that it works, and ensure the issue is truly fixed. Verification may include asking the user to test, monitoring the system, or checking logs. Finally, you **document** what happened and what resolved it, so the knowledge is available for future incidents. This structured approach is often what exam questions will reference.

16.3 Asking Effective Questions and Active Listening

TECHNICAL SKILL ALONE isn't enough; you need to communicate effectively with users. ITF+ expects you to recognize good questioning and listening techniques. This section focuses on how to gather information politely and efficiently.

- **Open-ended vs. closed-ended questions**
- **Clarifying and summarizing user statements**
- **Active listening and empathy**

Open-ended questions invite users to describe the problem in their own words (e.g., "Can you describe what happens when you try to print?"). **Closed-ended questions** get specific details (e.g., "Do you see any error message on the screen?"). Using a mix of both helps you get a broad picture and then drill down into specifics. Poor questions can confuse users or miss key information.

Clarifying and summarizing user statements shows you understand and gives them a chance to correct you. For example, "So to confirm, this started this morning after you installed the new app, correct?" This avoids assumptions and ensures you're working with accurate facts. It also builds user confidence that you're listening carefully.

Active listening means paying attention to the user's words and tone, not interrupting unnecessarily, and acknowledging their frustration. Simple phrases like "I understand this is frustrating; let's see what we can do" show empathy. Users are more cooperative when they feel heard and respected, which makes troubleshooting smoother.

16.4 Documenting Issues and Resolutions

GOOD DOCUMENTATION is a key part of professional IT support. ITF+ expects you to understand why accurate notes matter. This section covers what to record and how it helps the team.

- **Recording symptoms and environment details**
- **Documenting steps taken and outcomes**
- **Building a knowledge base over time**

Recording **symptoms** includes capturing error messages, user descriptions, and observed behavior. Environment details such as device type, OS version, network connection, and recent changes are also important. These details help you and others reproduce or analyze the issue later. Incomplete information makes follow-up harder.

Documenting **steps taken** and the outcome provides a clear history of what's been tried. If you need to escalate, the next technician can see what's already been done and avoid repeating unsuccessful steps. After resolution, notes can explain what fixed the problem and any side effects. This makes the support process more efficient and transparent.

Over time, documented issues and resolutions form a **knowledge base**—a repository of solutions and troubleshooting guides. Technicians can search it when similar problems arise, allowing faster resolutions and consistent handling. ITF+ recognizes knowledge sharing as a professional practice, not just a nice-to-have.

16.5 Prioritization and Impact (Severity vs. Urgency)

NOT ALL ISSUES ARE equal; some affect more people or critical services. ITF+ expects you to understand basic prioritization concepts. This section explains how severity and urgency influence support responses.

- **Severity: how big the impact is**
- **Urgency: how quickly it must be resolved**
- **Handling multiple tickets and expectations**

Severity refers to the impact of an issue on users or business operations. A complete outage of a production system is high severity, while a minor cosmetic bug affecting one user is low severity. High-severity issues often receive immediate attention and may trigger incident response processes. Understanding severity helps you triage tickets logically.

Urgency refers to how quickly an issue needs to be resolved. Some problems have deadlines (e.g., payroll system down on payday) or affect time-sensitive tasks. High urgency doesn't always mean high severity (and vice versa), but both factors are considered when prioritizing work. ITF+ expects you to recognize that a single user's minor issue usually ranks lower than a company-wide outage.

Handling multiple tickets means balancing priorities and setting **realistic expectations** with users. You may need to tell someone that their low-impact issue will be addressed after higher-priority problems. Communicating clearly and politely about timelines helps maintain trust, even when users have to wait.

16.6 Change Management and "What Changed?"

MANY PROBLEMS START after something changes. ITF+ expects you to recognize the importance of change management and the classic "what changed?" question. This section connects modifications to troubleshooting.

- **Recognizing changes as common causes of issues**
- **Change management processes (high level)**
- **Rolling back or undoing problematic changes**

A large percentage of IT issues occur after a **change**—installing new software, applying updates, modifying configurations, or changing hardware. Asking "What changed recently?" is a powerful troubleshooting question. If a system worked yesterday and fails today, recent changes are prime suspects. This simple insight can save a lot of time.

Change management processes formalize how changes are proposed, approved, tested, and deployed. They often include documenting the reason for change, potential impact, and rollback plans. Larger organizations use change management to reduce risk and avoid unplanned outages. At the ITF+ level, you should know that changes shouldn't be made randomly on production systems.

When a change causes problems, **rolling back** (undoing) the change is often the fastest way to restore service. This might involve uninstalling an update, reverting a configuration, or restoring from backup. Rolled-back changes can then be studied in a test environment to understand what went wrong before trying again.

16.7 Basic Troubleshooting of Hardware, OS, and Network Issues

SUPPORT TECHNICIANS deal with many kinds of problems. ITF+ expects broad awareness of common hardware, OS, and network symptoms. This section gives a high-level view of how these issues are approached.

- **Hardware issues: power, cables, and peripherals**
- **Operating system issues: performance, updates, and errors**
- **Network issues: connectivity and scope**

Hardware issues often involve **power**, **cables**, and **peripherals**. A monitor that won't turn on might have a loose power cable or be connected to the wrong port. A printer that doesn't respond might be turned off or unplugged. Basic checks—ensuring devices are powered, connected, and properly seated—solve many hardware problems without advanced tools.

Operating system issues can include slow performance, application crashes, or update failures. High CPU or memory usage, low disk space, or conflicting software can cause sluggishness. Updates may fix bugs but can also introduce new issues if they fail or conflict with existing software. Checking resource usage, recent updates, and error messages are common OS troubleshooting steps.

Network issues often show as no connection, intermittent connection, or some services working while others don't. Determining **scope** is crucial: does the issue affect one device, many devices, or only certain websites or apps? This helps you decide whether to focus on local configuration, network hardware, or external services like ISPs or cloud providers.

16.8 Customer Service, Professionalism, and Ethics

IT SUPPORT IS A CUSTOMER-facing role, even when the "customers" are coworkers. ITF+ expects you to recognize professional behavior and basic ethics. This section focuses on how you interact with people and handle sensitive information.

- **Polite, respectful communication even under stress**
- **Managing expectations and avoiding blame**
- **Confidentiality and ethical handling of data**

Professional support staff remain polite and respectful, even when users are frustrated or upset. They avoid sarcasm, judgmental language, or dismissive comments. Simple courtesies ("please," "thank you," "I appreciate your patience") can defuse tension. Remember that users are often stressed when technology fails, and you represent the IT team.

Managing expectations means being honest about what you can do and how long it might take, without making promises you can't keep. Avoid blaming users, even if they made a mistake; instead, focus on solving the problem and helping them avoid it in the future. Phrases like "Let's see what's going on" are more constructive than "You did it wrong."

Confidentiality and ethics require you to handle sensitive data carefully. You may see private emails, documents, or personal information while troubleshooting. You must not share or misuse this information and should only access what is necessary to do your job. Ethical behavior builds trust and is often enforced by company policies and laws.

16.9 Safety Considerations in IT Support

WORKING WITH HARDWARE and cables involves safety risks. ITF+ expects high-level awareness of physical and electrical safety. This section covers basic precautions support staff should follow.

- **Electrical and equipment safety**
- **Handling components and ESD (high level)**
- **Workspace organization and trip hazards**

Electrical safety includes unplugging devices before opening them, avoiding working on equipment in wet environments, and not overloading power strips. You should not attempt repairs beyond your training, especially on high-voltage equipment. When in doubt, follow manufacturer guidelines and safety policies. Safety comes before speed.

Handling internal components requires care to avoid **electrostatic discharge (ESD)**, which can damage sensitive electronics. At a basic level, this means grounding yourself (such as with an ESD strap or by touching grounded metal) and avoiding unnecessary contact with circuitry. Components should be stored and handled using anti-static bags or surfaces where possible.

Workspace organization matters too. Loose cables and clutter can create **trip hazards** and make equipment more likely to be damaged. Keeping the area tidy, labeling cables, and routing wires safely contribute to both safety and professionalism. Users are more confident in technicians who work in a clean, organized way.

16.10 Putting It Together: Being an Effective Entry-Level IT Professional

THIS FINAL SECTION ties together troubleshooting, communication, and professionalism into a picture of a successful entry-level IT worker. ITF+ wants you to see how all these skills work together on the job.

- **Combining technical and soft skills**
- **Using process and documentation consistently**
- **Continuous learning and improvement**

Effective IT professionals blend technical knowledge with **soft skills** like communication, patience, and empathy. You might know how to fix a problem, but you also need to explain what you're doing in plain language and keep the user informed. Good bedside manner turns stressful incidents into positive experiences and builds trust.

Using process and documentation consistently means following the troubleshooting methodology, recording what you do, and adhering to policies like change management. This creates predictable, repeatable outcomes and helps your team work together smoothly. Skipping steps or failing to document makes it harder to resolve recurring or complex issues.

Continuous learning is essential because technology and threats are always evolving. Reading documentation, learning from colleagues, taking courses, and reviewing past incidents all help you grow. ITF+ is a starting point: it gives you a foundation, but your effectiveness will come from applying these concepts and improving over time.

Practice Questions – Chapter 16 (25 Questions)

1. Which of the following BEST describes the role of a tier 1 help desk technician?
A. Designing enterprise network architecture
B. Handling initial user contact, resolving common issues, and escalating complex problems
C. Writing operating system kernels
D. Managing company finances

2. Why is documenting troubleshooting steps in a ticket important?
A. It makes the screen look busy
B. It helps other technicians see what has been tried and understand the resolution
C. It replaces the need to talk to users
D. It automatically fixes future issues

3. The FIRST step in a typical troubleshooting methodology is to:
A. Replace hardware
B. Escalate the issue
C. Identify the problem and gather information
D. Install new software

4. After forming a theory about the cause of a problem, what should you do NEXT?
A. Immediately reinstall the operating system
B. Test the theory with targeted actions
C. Close the ticket
D. Blame the user

5. Which question is an example of an open-ended question?
A. "Does your monitor turn on? Yes or no?"
B. "Do you see an error code 404?"
C. "Can you describe what happens when you try to print?"
D. "Is your computer plugged in?"

6. Which behavior BEST demonstrates active listening with a user?
A. Interrupting frequently to save time
B. Repeating back key points to confirm understanding
C. Ignoring user frustration and focusing only on the computer
D. Speaking in jargon the user won't understand

7. Why is it useful to ask "What changed recently?" during troubleshooting?

A. Changes are rarely related to problems
B. Most issues are random and unrelated to changes
C. Many problems start after a change such as an update or configuration change
D. It fills time while you think of something else
8. In a support environment, which issue would typically be assigned the HIGHEST priority?
A. One user's desktop wallpaper isn't displaying correctly
B. A company-wide email outage during business hours
C. A printer in a rarely used room is low on ink
D. A user wants a new screen saver
9. Severity in incident prioritization primarily measures:
A. How angry the user sounds
B. How much the issue impacts users or business operations
C. How long the technician has worked at the company
D. How colorful the error message is
10. Which of the following BEST describes escalation?
A. Ignoring the issue until it goes away
B. Passing the issue to a more experienced or specialized technician when appropriate
C. Restarting the computer repeatedly
D. Asking the user to fix it themselves
11. Which statement is MOST professional when dealing with a user who made a mistake?
A. "You broke it again."
B. "Why didn't you read the instructions?"
C. "Let's take a look at what happened and see how we can fix it."
D. "This is your fault, not mine."
12. Why should technicians avoid sharing admin passwords?
A. It makes logging in too easy
B. It prevents users from remembering passwords
C. It reduces accountability and increases security risks
D. It slows down the internet
13. Which action is part of ethical behavior in IT support?
A. Reading users' personal emails out of curiosity
B. Sharing confidential documents with friends
C. Accessing only the data you need to do your job and keeping it confidential
D. Posting screenshots of user desktops on social media
14. Why is electrical safety important when working inside a computer?
A. To improve network speed
B. To avoid damaging components and prevent personal injury
C. To make the screen brighter
D. To speed up troubleshooting
15. What is the MAIN purpose of using ESD precautions when handling internal components?
A. To protect components from dust only
B. To prevent static discharge that could damage sensitive electronics
C. To make components easier to see
D. To keep components warm

16. Which of the following is a good example of workspace safety?
A. Leaving cables running loosely across walkways
B. Keeping tools and components organized and cables routed to avoid tripping
C. Stacking heavy equipment precariously
D. Keeping drinks on top of computer cases
17. Why is building a knowledge base helpful to an IT support team?
A. It replaces the need for training
B. It provides a central place to store solutions and troubleshooting steps for future reference
C. It hides information from new staff
D. It eliminates the need for documentation
18. A user reports a problem and is clearly frustrated. Which response BEST demonstrates professionalism?
A. "Calm down; it's not that serious."
B. "That's not my problem."
C. "I understand this is frustrating. Let's see what we can do to get this working for you."
D. "You should have fixed this yourself."
19. Why is it important to verify the solution after you think you've fixed a problem?
A. To show off your skills
B. To ensure the issue is truly resolved and hasn't caused new problems
C. To make the user wait longer
D. To fill out more forms
20. Which is an example of a user-level sign that might indicate a security incident?
A. The office lights are off
B. Multiple strange pop-ups and unknown programs appearing suddenly
C. The keyboard is dusty
D. The mouse pad is worn out
21. What should a user generally do if they suspect their computer is infected with malware?
A. Keep using it for sensitive tasks
B. Download random "cleanup" tools from the internet
C. Report it according to company policy and wait for guidance
D. Turn off all security software
22. Which of the following is a good example of continuous learning for an IT professional?
A. Ignoring new technologies and procedures
B. Reviewing documentation, attending training, and learning from past incidents
C. Only fixing the same problem repeatedly
D. Refusing to read error messages
23. Why is it important to differentiate whether an issue affects one user or many users?
A. It determines the user's salary
B. It helps decide whether the problem is likely local or related to shared systems or services
C. It controls how bright the monitor should be
D. It determines what brand of computer to buy
24. Which behavior is appropriate when working remotely with a user over the phone or chat?
A. Using technical jargon without explanation
B. Speaking clearly, explaining steps in simple terms, and confirming understanding
C. Typing in all caps to show urgency

D. Refusing to repeat instructions

25. Which of the following BEST summarizes the role of an entry-level IT support professional?

A. Working alone and avoiding contact with users

B. Combining basic technical skills with communication, documentation, and professional behavior to support users

C. Only installing hardware and never troubleshooting

D. Managing company strategy and executive decisions

Answer Key – Chapter 16 (with Explanations)

1. B – HANDLING INITIAL user contact, resolving common issues, and escalating complex problems

Tier 1 support focuses on first-line assistance and escalation when needed, not high-level design or finance.

2. B – It helps other technicians see what has been tried and understand the resolution

Documentation supports teamwork, escalation, and future troubleshooting by preserving what happened.

3. C – Identify the problem and gather information

You must understand the problem and context before forming theories or taking major actions.

4. B – Test the theory with targeted actions

Testing confirms whether your theory is correct before implementing bigger changes.

5. C – "Can you describe what happens when you try to print?"

This invites a detailed description. The others are yes/no questions (closed-ended).

6. B – Repeating back key points to confirm understanding

This confirms you heard correctly and shows the user you are paying attention.

7. C – Many problems start after a change such as an update or configuration change

" What changed?" is a powerful question because changes are common root causes.

8. B – A company-wide email outage during business hours

This affects many users and critical communication, making it a high-priority incident.

9. B – How much the issue impacts users or business operations

Severity measures impact; urgency addresses how quickly it must be resolved.

10. B – Passing the issue to a more experienced or specialized technician when appropriate

Escalation ensures the right expertise is applied when tier 1 can't resolve an issue.

11. C – "Let's take a look at what happened and see how we can fix it."

This is professional, non-blaming, and focused on resolution.

12. C – It reduces accountability and increases security risks

Shared admin credentials make it hard to track actions and increase the chance of misuse.

13. C – Accessing only the data you need to do your job and keeping it confidential

Ethical behavior respects privacy and follows policies for handling sensitive data.

14. B – To avoid damaging components and prevent personal injury

Electrical safety protects both the technician and the equipment.

15. B – To prevent static discharge that could damage sensitive electronics

ESD can silently damage components, so precautions help keep them safe.

16. B – Keeping tools and components organized and cables routed to avoid tripping

An organized workspace reduces accidents and shows professionalism.

17. B – It provides a central place to store solutions and troubleshooting steps for future reference

Knowledge bases improve consistency and speed by reusing known solutions.

18. C – "I understand this is frustrating. Let's see what we can do to get this working for you."
This response shows empathy and a willingness to help, which is professional and calming.
19. B – To ensure the issue is truly resolved and hasn't caused new problems
Verification confirms success and prevents recurring or hidden issues.
20. B – Multiple strange pop-ups and unknown programs appearing suddenly
These are classic signs of possible malware infection or other security problems.
21. C – Report it according to company policy and wait for guidance
Following policy ensures the issue is handled properly by trained staff.
22. B – Reviewing documentation, attending training, and learning from past incidents
Continuous learning keeps skills current and improves future responses.
23. B – It helps decide whether the problem is likely local or related to shared systems or services
Scope (one vs. many users) guides where you focus your troubleshooting.
24. B – Speaking clearly, explaining steps in simple terms, and confirming understanding
Clear communication is essential, especially when you can't see the user's screen.
25. B – Combining basic technical skills with communication, documentation, and professional behavior to support users
Entry-level IT roles blend tech skills with strong people skills and good process habits.

Chapter 17

ITF+ Exam Strategy, Review, and Practice

This chapter is all about getting you across the finish line on the CompTIA ITF+ exam. You'll review core ideas, learn how questions are structured, and practice exam-day strategies. The goal is to make the content you've learned easier to recall under test conditions and to boost your confidence when you sit down for the real thing.

17.1 Understanding the ITF+ Exam Structure

KNOWING THE EXAM'S structure helps you feel less surprised on test day. ITF+ focuses on foundational IT concepts across several domains. This section gives a high-level reminder of what you're walking into.

- **Exam domains and coverage (conceptual)**
- **Question types (mostly multiple choice)**
- **Time management awareness**

The ITF+ exam is divided into domains such as IT concepts and terminology, infrastructure, applications and software, software development, database basics, and security. Each domain contributes a percentage to your total score, so you can't ignore any area completely. The material in this book maps to those domains so you've touched all the bases.

Most questions are **multiple choice**, with a single best answer among several options. Some questions may be scenario-based, describing a small situation and asking what you should do or which concept applies. Careful reading is essential; many wrong answers will be "partial truths" that sound plausible.

You'll have a fixed amount of time to answer all questions, so **time management** matters. You can't spend 10 minutes on a single item and still finish comfortably. Learning to move on from questions you're stuck on (and flag them for review) helps you avoid time crunch panic at the end.

17.2 Review: Core IT Concepts and Terminology

THIS BOOK STARTED BY building your foundation. ITF+ expects you to speak "IT language" at a basic level. This section reviews the big conceptual pillars from earlier chapters.

- **Hardware vs. software vs. services**
- **Data representations and storage basics**
- **Client, server, and networked environments**

You should be comfortable distinguishing **hardware** (physical devices), **software** (programs and OSs), and **services** (things like web hosting, email, and cloud platforms). Questions may ask you to categorize an item or identify which layer is responsible for a problem. Knowing where something "lives" helps you reason about what might be wrong.

Data basics include understanding that files, documents, images, and media are all stored as bits on storage devices. You don't need to do binary math, but you should know terms like **bit, byte, kilobyte, gigabyte**, and the idea of persistent storage vs. memory. This helps you interpret questions about capacity, file sizes, and performance.

Client–server environments involve devices (clients) accessing resources from other systems (servers) over networks. Basic understanding of this model helps you reason about where issues are originating—local device, server, or network. Many exam scenarios implicitly assume you recognize this structure even if they don't say "client-server" out loud.

17.3 Review: Infrastructure, Devices, and Networking

INFRASTRUCTURE QUESTIONS check that you understand how computers, peripherals, and networks fit together. This section reminds you of the big infrastructure ideas.

- **Common device types (PCs, laptops, mobiles, peripherals)**
- **Basic network concepts (LAN, internet, IP, Wi-Fi)**
- **Troubleshooting scope: one device vs. many**

Know the roles of **desktops, laptops, mobile devices**, and common peripherals like printers, scanners, and displays. Recognize ports and connection types conceptually (USB, HDMI, etc.) and what they're used for. You don't need pin-level details, just the "what goes where and why" level of understanding.

Networking basics include the idea of a **LAN** (local network), routers connecting to the internet, wired vs. wireless connections, and IP addresses as "logical addresses" on the network. Wi-Fi introduces security concerns like encryption and passwords. Recognizing when an issue sounds network-related (e.g., "no internet on multiple devices") helps you choose the right answer.

In troubleshooting, always consider **scope**: if only one device has a problem, check local settings or hardware first. If many users or systems are affected, the issue is more likely with shared resources (network, server, service provider). ITF+ will often test this reasoning indirectly through scenarios.

17.4 Review: Applications, Cloud, and Software Concepts

A BIG PORTION OF ITF+ is making sure you can identify what kind of software/tool is appropriate for a task. This section reviews how to think about applications and the cloud.

- **Matching tools to tasks (word processor vs. spreadsheet vs. presentation)**
- **Cloud storage and cloud applications (SaaS)**
- **Licensing basics (per-user, subscription, activation)**

Matching tools to tasks is exam gold. Long text documents → **word processors**; numerical analysis and calculations → **spreadsheets**; visual support for talks and meetings → **presentation software**. Email, calendars, contact lists, and collaboration tools each have their own typical use cases. Many scenario questions are really asking, "Which tool should they use?"

Cloud concepts include understanding that **cloud storage** keeps files on remote servers accessible from multiple devices, and **cloud applications** (SaaS) run in a provider's environment, usually via web browsers. Remember that cloud tools usually depend on internet connectivity and often use subscription licensing and sign-in for access.

Licensing basics: **per-device vs. per-user vs. concurrent**, perpetual vs. **subscription**, and the concept of **activation** or account-based access. When a question mentions "unlicensed product" or "no license assigned" errors, think about licensing and account configuration, not hardware failure.

17.5 Review: Software Development and Logic Essentials

YOU DON'T NEED TO WRITE code on the exam, but you do need to understand logic. This section reviews the key development concepts that ITF+ cares about.

- **Programs, source code, and scripting**
- **Variables, conditions, and loops (conceptual)**
- **Pseudocode and flowcharts**

Remember that a **program** is a sequence of instructions, and **source code** is the human-readable form. **Scripts** are smaller, task-focused programs often used for automation, especially in IT environments. Recognizing their role helps in scenario questions about automating repetitive tasks.

Core logic: **variables** hold data, **conditions** (if statements) decide what to do based on comparisons, and **loops** repeat actions. Logical operators (AND, OR, NOT) combine conditions. You may see simple pseudocode like IF age >= 18 THEN Display "Adult" and be asked what happens with different input values.

Pseudocode and **flowcharts** express logic in language-neutral ways. Diamonds usually mean decisions in flowcharts; arrows show control flow. On the exam, take pseudocode slowly: track variable values, follow branches, and count loop iterations for specific scenarios.

17.6 Review: Security Fundamentals and Best Practices

SECURITY IS A BIG PART of ITF+. This section reinforces the key security concepts and behaviors that appear again and again.

- **CIA triad and common threats**
- **Malware, phishing, and social engineering**
- **Passwords, MFA, and least privilege**

The **CIA triad**—Confidentiality, Integrity, Availability—is your mental anchor. Many questions can be framed as "Which of these protects confidentiality?" or "Which risk threatens availability?" Common threats include malware (viruses, worms, Trojans, ransomware) and misconfigurations or weak practices.

Phishing and **social engineering** target people, not just systems. Suspicious emails, unexpected links, fake login pages, or callers asking for passwords all fit this pattern. Know the difference between phishing and more targeted **spear phishing** (aimed at specific people or groups).

For defenses, strong **passwords/passphrases**, **multi-factor authentication (MFA)**, and the **principle of least privilege** are key. MFA is a favorite "best answer" in questions about improving account security. Least privilege explains why users shouldn't run as administrators for everyday work.

17.7 Review: Device Hardening and Safe Use

DEVICE HARDENING AND safe use combine technical settings with smart user behavior. This section recaps the key ideas from the security hardening chapters.

- **Patching and endpoint protection**
- **Secure configurations and account management**
- **Safe browsing and email habits**

Patching (applying OS and software updates) closes known vulnerabilities. Endpoint protection (antivirus/anti-malware suites) monitors for malicious code and behavior. Running outdated, unpatched systems is almost always a "bad idea" answer on the exam.

Secure configurations include disabling unused services, enforcing password policies, and controlling admin privileges. Disabling or removing unused accounts reduces potential footholds for attackers. If a question mentions old shared admin accounts or ex-employee accounts still active, that should ring alarm bells.

Safe browsing and email behavior includes avoiding unknown attachments, being cautious with links, recognizing warnings, and downloading only from trusted sources. When in doubt, the exam's "best practice" is almost always the cautious, policy-following option.

17.8 Exam Skills: Reading Questions and Eliminating Answers

SOMETIMES THE DIFFERENCE between passing and failing is how you read questions, not what you know. This section helps you answer smarter.

- **Identifying keywords and what's really being asked**
- **Eliminating obviously wrong answers**
- **Choosing the "best" answer among several that seem right**

Questions often include extra story details that don't matter. Focus on **keywords** about symptoms, scope (one user vs many), timing (after an update), and domain hints (security vs. networking vs. software). Then ask yourself, "What domain is this really testing?"

Eliminate obviously wrong answers first. If a solution is extreme ("reinstall the OS" for a minor issue), unsafe ("disable all security"), or clearly unrelated ("change the monitor's color" for a network issue), you can usually remove it. Narrowing choices from four to two increases your odds even when you're unsure.

Sometimes more than one answer looks reasonable; ITF+ wants the **best** one. Usually that means: lowest risk, least invasive, aligns with policies, and fits the problem's scope. For example, "check cable connections" is better than "replace all hardware" as a first step.

17.9 Exam-Day Strategy and Mindset

GOOD STRATEGY AND MINDSET help you use what you know effectively under pressure. This section covers practical test-day tips.

- **Pacing and flagging questions**
- **Handling tricky or unfamiliar questions**
- **Staying calm and avoiding overthinking**

Pace yourself: if you get stuck on a question, **flag it** and move on. Many exams let you revisit flagged items later. You want to reach every question at least once; don't burn too much time on one stubborn item early on.

For tricky or unfamiliar questions, use what you do know: identify the domain, rule out obviously wrong answers, and pick the choice that best fits general best practices (secure, safe, logical, non-destructive). Sometimes your job is to avoid wrong answers rather than know the perfect one.

Staying calm matters. If you hit a rough patch, take a breath, refocus on the current question, and apply your process. Don't let one confusing question rattle you. Often, later questions will jog your memory or clarify earlier concepts.

17.10 Putting It All Together: Final Review Plan

THIS LAST SECTION GIVES you a simple study and review plan using this book. ITF+ rewards broad familiarity more than extreme depth, so a balanced review works best.

- **Lightly review each domain, not just your favorites**
- **Focus on weak spots and repeat practice questions**
- **Simulate exam conditions at least once**

Plan to **review each domain**, even the ones you feel strong in. Skimming chapter summaries, headings, and key definitions helps refresh your memory. Don't let an entire area like security or software development become a blind spot.

Focus extra time on **weak spots**: the topics that confuse you or where you miss more questions. Re-do practice questions for those chapters, but also spend time understanding *why* the correct answers are right. Looking at explanations is more valuable than just memorizing letters.

Before the real exam, **simulate test conditions** at least once: timed, no notes, answering a full set of practice questions. This helps you get comfortable with pacing and builds confidence. When you can calmly work through a full practice set, you're much more likely to handle the real thing smoothly.

Practice Questions – Chapter 17 (25 Questions)

1. The ITF+ exam primarily focuses on:
A. Deep, specialized knowledge of a single technology
B. Foundational IT concepts across multiple domains
C. Advanced programming and algorithm design
D. Expert-level network engineering

2. Most ITF+ questions are:
A. True/false only
B. Essay questions requiring long written answers
C. Multiple choice with a single best answer
D. Hands-on lab simulations only
3. When a question describes a document with paragraphs, headings, and a table of contents, which application type is MOST appropriate?
A. Spreadsheet software
B. Word processing software
C. Presentation software
D. Database management system
4. A question describes a scenario where an employee needs to analyze sales data, calculate totals, and create basic charts. Which tool is BEST?
A. Email client
B. Word processor
C. Spreadsheet
D. Graphics editor
5. A scenario describes a user clicking a link in an email and being taken to a fake login page that steals credentials. This is an example of:
A. Port scanning
B. Phishing
C. Disk fragmentation
D. Printer sharing
6. The principle of least privilege suggests that:
A. Users should have full admin rights on all systems
B. Users should have only the minimum access needed to do their jobs
C. Guests should use administrator accounts
D. Everyone should share one account
7. A question mentions encrypted traffic between a user and a website. Which protocol is MOST likely being used?
A. HTTP
B. FTP
C. HTTPS
D. Telnet
8. On the exam, when a question asks for the "BEST first step" in troubleshooting, you should generally choose:
A. The most destructive option that guarantees a fix
B. A simple, low-risk action that gathers information or checks common causes
C. Reinstalling the operating system immediately
D. Replacing all hardware in the system
9. A scenario describes data being stored in tables with rows and columns, optimized for search and reporting. This MOST closely describes:
A. A web browser
B. A database
C. A firewall

D. A spreadsheet printer

10. A user can't access a cloud app, but other users can. The user's login is correct. What is the MOST likely problem?

A. The user's device is overheating

B. The user's account lacks the required license or permission

C. All network cables in the building are unplugged

D. The monitor is broken

11. Which exam strategy is MOST effective if you encounter a very difficult question?

A. Spend as much time as needed until you solve it, even if it takes 15 minutes

B. Guess randomly and submit the exam early

C. Eliminate wrong answers, choose the best remaining one, flag it, and move on

D. Skip it and never return to it

12. A question describes an issue affecting only one user's PC, while others are fine. Which is the MOST logical focus for initial troubleshooting?

A. The entire corporate network

B. The user's local device and settings

C. The ISP's data center in another country

D. Global internet routing tables

13. In a scenario, a user reports very slow performance, and Task Manager shows 98% CPU usage caused by a single application. What is the MOST likely explanation?

A. The monitor is using the wrong resolution

B. That specific application is consuming excessive CPU resources

C. The user's keyboard is malfunctioning

D. The hard drive is unplugged

14. A user complains that they cannot remember complex passwords. Which solution is MOST aligned with best practices?

A. Using very short, simple passwords

B. Using a long passphrase and/or a reputable password manager

C. Reusing the same password for all accounts

D. Writing passwords on sticky notes on the monitor

15. A scenario asks how to improve the security of accounts beyond just passwords. Which option is MOST appropriate?

A. Disabling all screen locks

B. Adding multi-factor authentication (MFA)

C. Turning off antivirus

D. Using unlicensed software

16. A question shows pseudocode:

```
SET x = 3
SET x = x + 2
DISPLAY x
```

What will be displayed?

A. 2

B. 3

C. 5

D. 6

17. A flowchart diamond usually represents:

A. Data storage

B. A decision point

C. A print command

D. A program start

18. A scenario describes an email that appears to be from IT asking users to "verify their password immediately by replying to this message." What is the BEST user response?

A. Reply with the password

B. Ignore it and delete it or report it according to policy

C. Forward it to friends for fun

D. Change the desktop wallpaper

19. When reading a multi-sentence exam question, you should FIRST:

A. Read the answer options and guess quickly

B. Focus on the last sentence only

C. Identify the key problem or question being asked

D. Count how many words are in the question

20. A scenario describes a backup process that runs every night and stores copies of important files in another location. This primarily protects against:

A. Slow CPU performance

B. Data loss from hardware failure or ransomware

C. Monitor glare

D. Weak Wi-Fi signals

21. A user says, "My internet doesn't work," but you find other apps are fine; only their web browser won't open pages. What is the MOST likely area to investigate first?

A. Global internet outage

B. The user's browser settings, cache, or extensions

C. All power outlets in the building

D. The BIOS configuration

22. A question describes a user accessing a shared document hosted online that multiple team members can edit at the same time. This is an example of:

A. Local file storage only

B. Cloud-based collaboration

C. A BIOS update

D. Offline backup

23. Which action is MOST aligned with good exam-day time management?

A. Spending equal time on every question, no matter how easy or hard

B. Spending 5–10 minutes on each tricky question

C. Answering easier questions first, flagging hard ones for later review

D. Leaving questions blank if they're confusing

24. A question describes an older system that cannot run newer software because it doesn't support 64-bit applications or more than 4 GB of RAM. This limitation is MOST likely due to:

A. The system being 32-bit

B. Using too many USB ports

C. Having a wireless mouse

D. A misconfigured browser

25. Why does this exam prep book spend so much time on explanations for practice questions (not just the correct letters)?

A. To make the book longer for no reason

B. Because understanding *why* an answer is correct strengthens your concepts and helps on new questions

C. Because you will see the exact same questions on the real exam

D. Because explanations are required by law

Answer Key – Chapter 17 (with Explanations)

1. B – FOUNDATIONAL IT concepts across multiple domains

ITF+ is an entry-level exam covering a wide range of basic IT topics, not deep specialization.

2. C – Multiple choice with a single best answer

Most questions are multiple choice; you must choose the best option based on concepts and context.

3. B – Word processing software

Word processors are designed for rich text documents with headings, paragraphs, and tables of contents.

4. C – Spreadsheet

Spreadsheets excel at numeric analysis, calculations, and generating charts from data.

5. B – Phishing

This is a classic phishing scenario: an email link takes the user to a fake login page to steal credentials.

6. B – Users should have only the minimum access needed to do their jobs

That's the essence of least privilege: limit access to reduce potential damage from compromise or mistakes.

7. C – HTTPS

HTTPS encrypts traffic between browser and website, protecting data in transit.

8. B – A simple, low-risk action that gathers information or checks common causes

Good troubleshooting starts with safe, easy checks, not drastic measures like reinstalling the OS.

9. B – A database

Databases store structured information in tables with rows and columns, optimized for search and reporting.

10. B – The user's account lacks the required license or permission

If others can access the app and the service is up, licensing or permissions for that account are likely at fault.

11. C – Eliminate wrong answers, choose the best remaining one, flag it, and move on

This balances good reasoning with time management, giving you a chance to revisit if needed.

12. B – The user's local device and settings

If only one PC is affected, focus on local causes before blaming the entire network or internet.

13. B – That specific application is consuming excessive CPU resources

Very high CPU usage by one app usually points to that app being the culprit, not the monitor or keyboard.

14. B – Using a long passphrase and/or a reputable password manager

Passphrases are easier to remember and more secure; password managers safely store complex passwords.

15. B – Adding multi-factor authentication (MFA)

MFA significantly strengthens account security beyond passwords alone.

16. C – 5

x starts at 3, then becomes 3 + 2 = 5, which is then displayed.

17. B – A decision point

Diamond shapes in flowcharts represent decisions that branch the flow based on conditions.

18. B – Ignore it and delete it or report it according to policy

This is a suspicious request; users should not send passwords via email and should follow policy.

19. C – Identify the key problem or question being asked

You need to understand what's being asked before analyzing the options effectively.

20. B – Data loss from hardware failure or ransomware

Backups protect against many types of data loss, including drive failure and malicious encryption.

21. B – The user's browser settings, cache, or extensions

If "internet" issues only affect the browser, check the browser environment before assuming global outages.

22. B – Cloud-based collaboration

Shared online documents with simultaneous editing are a hallmark of cloud collaboration tools.

23. C – Answering easier questions first, flagging hard ones for later review

This approach helps you secure points quickly and ensures you reach all questions within the time limit.

24. A – The system being 32-bit

32-bit systems are typically limited to around 4 GB of RAM and older 32-bit software.

25. B – Because understanding *why* an answer is correct strengthens your concepts and helps on new questions

Explanations deepen understanding so you can handle unfamiliar variations of the same concepts on the real exam.

ITF+ Full-Length Mock Exam

Instructions

This mock exam contains 75 multiple-choice questions, each with one best answer. To get the most benefit, try to simulate real exam conditions. Find a quiet place, set a timer for about 60–90 minutes (aim for roughly one minute per question), and complete the exam without using notes, the internet, or any reference materials. Scratch paper and a pen or pencil are fine if you want to jot down thoughts.

Work through the questions in order and answer **every** one. If you get stuck on a question, don't spend too long on it. Mark it, make your best guess, and move on—you can come back to it at the end if you have time. On the real exam, leaving questions blank or spending too much time on one item can hurt your overall score, so practice moving forward even when you're unsure.

As you answer questions, read each one carefully and pay attention to key words like "FIRST," "BEST," "MOST likely," "single user," "multiple users," or "after an update." These phrases often tell you exactly what the exam is really asking. Use elimination to your advantage: cross out obviously wrong options first, especially answers that are extreme, unsafe, or unrelated. In general, prefer solutions that are safe, non-destructive, logical first steps and that align with security and company policies.

When you finish the exam, use the answer key to check your work. For each question you missed, read the explanation and note the chapter and section reference (for example, "Ch 14.3 – Malware Basics"). Then go back to those sections in your book for a quick refresher. This will help you strengthen weak areas instead of just memorizing letters.

Finally, count how many questions you got correct and convert that to a percentage (correct ÷ 75 × 100). As a rough goal, try to work your way up to at least 80% on this mock exam before you sit the real ITF+ test. Pay special attention to patterns—if you consistently miss questions in one domain (like Security, Networking, or Software Development), focus your review there in your next study session.

Here's a **full-length 75-question ITF+ mock exam**.

All questions are multiple choice.

After the questions, you'll find a full **answer key** with:

- Correct answer
- Brief reasoning
- The **chapter & section** it's pulled from in this book (e.g., *"Ch 9.5 – Files, Folders, and Extensions in the OS"*).

ITF+ Mock Exam – 75 Questions

1–15: IT Concepts, Hardware, and Infrastructure

1. Which of the following is an example of **hardware**?

A. Web browser

B. Antivirus software

C. Printer

D. Cloud storage service

2. Which component is MOST responsible for performing calculations and processing instructions in a computer?

A. RAM

B. CPU

C. Hard drive

D. Power supply

3. RAM is BEST described as:

A. Long-term storage for files and documents

B. Temporary working memory used while the computer is running

C. A permanent backup location for data

D. A type of input device

4. Which device is primarily used to convert digital signals from a computer into a visual image on a screen?

A. Keyboard

B. Mouse

C. Monitor

D. Printer

5. A user wants to connect a modern external hard drive to their laptop. Which port type is MOST commonly used?

A. PS/2

B. VGA

C. USB

D. Parallel

6. Which storage technology typically offers the **fastest** access times for general use?

A. Traditional hard disk drive (HDD)

B. Solid-state drive (SSD)

C. Optical disc (DVD)

D. Magnetic tape

7. Which unit of measurement is the LARGEST?

A. Kilobyte (KB)

B. Megabyte (MB)

C. Gigabyte (GB)

D. Terabyte (TB)

8. A user complains their desktop PC will not power on at all—no lights or fans. Which is the MOST logical first check?

A. Update the OS

B. Verify the power cable and power strip are connected and switched on
C. Reinstall all drivers
D. Replace the monitor
9. A **client** in a client–server network is typically:
A. A database system that stores data
B. A device or application that requests services from a server
C. A firewall that filters traffic
D. A backup system
10. Which network type is used to describe a small network within a single building or office?
A. WAN
B. LAN
C. VPN
D. PAN
11. Which device typically provides **routing** between a local network and the internet?
A. Switch
B. Router
C. Hub
D. Access point
12. Wi-Fi is an example of:
A. A wired networking technology
B. A wireless networking technology
C. A storage protocol
D. A backup method
13. A user is connected to Wi-Fi but cannot access any websites, while others on the same Wi-Fi can. Which is the MOST likely first area to check?
A. The global internet
B. The user's device network settings or browser
C. The entire office LAN
D. The ISP's main router in another city
14. Which address uniquely identifies a device at the network (internet) layer?
A. MAC address
B. IP address
C. Serial number
D. Hostname only
15. Which connection type is typically used to attach a printer directly to a home network so multiple devices can print to it?
A. HDMI
B. Ethernet or Wi-Fi
C. PS/2
D. VGA

16–30: Operating Systems, Applications, and Cloud

16. The primary purpose of an **operating system** is to:

A. Design websites
B. Manage hardware resources and provide services to applications
C. Print documents
D. Replace network cables
17. Which of the following is a **desktop operating system**?
A. Android
B. Windows 11
C. iOS
D. Chrome (web browser)
18. Which of the following is a **mobile operating system**?
A. macOS
B. Linux (server edition)
C. Android
D. BIOS
19. A file named Report.xlsx is MOST likely associated with:
A. A word processor
B. A spreadsheet application
C. A presentation tool
D. A database server
20. Which of the following is typically used to create visual slides for a meeting?
A. Spreadsheet application
B. Word processor
C. Presentation software
D. Email client
21. Which is the BEST tool to track expenses, add them up automatically, and create simple charts?
A. Word processor
B. Spreadsheet
C. Presentation software
D. Text editor
22. A web browser's **cache** is primarily used to:
A. Store backups of all user files
B. Save copies of web content to speed up future visits
C. Encrypt emails automatically
D. Replace RAM
23. Cookies in a web browser are:
A. Files that always contain viruses
B. Small data pieces that websites store to remember information like logins or preferences
C. Backup copies of all documents
D. A type of encryption algorithm
24. Which statement BEST describes "the cloud" in IT?
A. A local folder on your laptop
B. Remote computing resources and services accessed over the internet
C. A specific brand of desktop PC
D. A type of firewall

25. A user is working in a **cloud-based document editor** and multiple team members can edit the document at the same time. This is an example of:

A. Local-only storage
B. Real-time collaboration using a SaaS app
C. BIOS configuration
D. Offline backup

26. Which situation BEST describes a **subscription license** for software?

A. One-time purchase that never needs to be renewed
B. Monthly or yearly payment that includes ongoing access and updates
C. Free software that is always open source
D. Software installed only from a DVD

27. A user sees "unlicensed product" on their office suite, and some features are disabled. The MOST likely cause is:

A. The monitor driver failed
B. The software has not been activated or assigned a valid license
C. The keyboard is unplugged
D. The ISP is down

28. Which is a typical advantage of **cloud applications** compared to locally installed software?

A. They never require internet access
B. They always run faster than local software
C. They can be accessed from multiple devices via a browser and are often updated automatically
D. They can never be used on mobile devices

29. A user wants to send and receive messages, organize folders, and search their inbox. Which application type is MOST appropriate?

A. Email client
B. Spreadsheet
C. Presentation tool
D. BIOS

30. A website address like https://www.example.com is called a:

A. IP address
B. URL
C. MAC address
D. File extension

31–45: Software Development, Databases, and Logic

31. Source code is BEST described as:

A. The binary instructions executed directly by the CPU
B. Human-readable instructions written in a programming language
C. The physical motherboard design
D. Network configuration settings

32. A **variable** in programming is:

A. A type of network cable
B. A named storage location in memory that holds a value

C. A special kind of CPU
D. A security certificate
33. Which data type is MOST appropriate to represent whether a user has agreed to terms (yes/no)?
A. Integer
B. String
C. Boolean
D. Floating point
34. The expression total = price * quantity is an example of using:
A. Variables and an arithmetic operator
B. File system commands
C. A network protocol
D. A system BIOS setting
35. An **if statement** in programming is mainly used to:
A. Store large amounts of data
B. Make decisions based on a condition being true or false
C. Change screen resolution
D. Format hard drives
36. Which logical operator means "both conditions must be true"?
A. OR
B. AND
C. NOT
D. XOR
37. A **loop** in programming is used to:
A. Execute code only once
B. Repeat a block of code multiple times
C. Turn off the computer
D. Change disk partitions
38. Pseudocode is:
A. Executable machine code
B. Structured, human-readable descriptions of program logic without strict syntax
C. A hardware blueprint
D. A type of network router
39. A flowchart diamond typically represents:
A. A data storage step
B. A decision point
C. A program start
D. User output
40. A **database** is BEST described as:
A. A collection of random files stored on a desktop
B. Structured data stored in tables with fields and records for efficient search and reporting
C. A type of graphics editor
D. A local text document
41. A table in a database contains:
A. Only one record for all data

B. Fields (columns) and records (rows)
C. Only files and folders
D. Only graphics
42. When a program runs correctly but crashes when trying to open a missing file, this is an example of a:
A. Syntax error
B. Runtime error
C. Power failure
D. Hardware upgrade
43. A script used to rename hundreds of files in a folder automatically is an example of:
A. A manual process
B. A small, task-focused program used for automation
C. A hardware component
D. A BIOS setting
44. Which list shows steps in the **input–process–output** model?
A. Display → Save → Print
B. Save → Delete → Exit
C. Get data → Apply logic → Produce results
D. Turn on → Turn off → Restart
45. A help desk has a written procedure: "1) Verify identity; 2) Reset password; 3) Have user log in; 4) Confirm access; 5) Close ticket." This sequence is BEST described as:
A. A random list
B. An algorithm for password resets
C. A hardware manual
D. A network diagram

46–60: Security Fundamentals and Device Hardening

46. In the **CIA triad**, the "C" stands for:
A. Control
B. Confidentiality
C. Compatibility
D. Compliance
47. Confidentiality in security focuses on:
A. Ensuring systems are always online
B. Ensuring only authorized people can read information
C. Ensuring data is easy to edit
D. Ensuring data is never backed up
48. Malware is:
A. Legitimate business software
B. Any malicious software designed to harm systems or data
C. Only viruses that spread via email
D. Just spam email
49. Ransomware typically:
A. Displays banner ads only

B. Encrypts data and demands payment to restore access
C. Installs printer drivers
D. Cleans temporary files
50. A fake email pretending to be from a bank that asks a user to click a link and "verify their password" is an example of:
A. Phishing
B. Port scanning
C. Backup
D. Load balancing
51. Multi-factor authentication (MFA) improves security by:
A. Removing passwords
B. Requiring two or more forms of verification
C. Shortening passwords to 4 characters
D. Turning off all security settings
52. The principle of **least privilege** means:
A. Give all users administrator rights
B. Give users only the minimum access needed to do their jobs
C. Allow guests to use admin accounts
D. Never let anyone log in
53. Which is a common reason why using open, public Wi-Fi is risky?
A. It always uses too much bandwidth
B. Attackers on the same network may be able to intercept traffic
C. It requires expensive hardware
D. It cannot be used with laptops
54. Backups are primarily used to:
A. Speed up gaming performance
B. Ensure there is a recoverable copy of data after loss or damage
C. Replace antivirus software
D. Increase screen brightness
55. Encryption makes data:
A. Larger in size only
B. Unreadable without the correct key
C. Automatically backed up
D. Always public
56. Which of the following is an example of **physical security**?
A. Firewall rules
B. Complex passwords
C. Cable lock on a laptop
D. Antivirus software
57. Hardening a system generally involves:
A. Installing every possible feature
B. Removing unnecessary services and applying secure settings
C. Disabling all security tools
D. Sharing all admin accounts

58. A password policy requiring a minimum length and mixed character types is intended to:
A. Make passwords easy to guess
B. Make passwords harder to guess or crack
C. Eliminate the need for usernames
D. Shorten all passwords to 4 characters

59. An account lockout policy that locks an account after several failed login attempts primarily protects against:
A. Phishing
B. Brute-force password guessing
C. Hardware failure
D. Slow networks

60. A user sees a message on their screen saying their files are encrypted and they must pay to recover them. What should they do FIRST according to best practice?
A. Immediately pay the ransom
B. Delete random files to free space
C. Report the incident to IT/security and follow company policy
D. Ignore it and keep working

61–75: Troubleshooting, Support, and Professionalism

61. The FIRST step in a typical troubleshooting process is to:
A. Replace hardware
B. Identify the problem and gather information
C. Reinstall the OS
D. Escalate to tier 3

62. A tier 1 help desk technician typically:
A. Designs enterprise networks
B. Handles initial user contact and resolves common issues
C. Writes operating system kernels
D. Manages company finances

63. Why is documenting troubleshooting steps in a ticket important?
A. It's optional and rarely helpful
B. It helps others see what has been tried and what resolved the issue
C. It replaces talking to users
D. It makes the ticketing system slower

64. Which question is an example of a **closed-ended** question?
A. "Can you describe everything you see on your screen?"
B. "What were you doing right before the error appeared?"
C. "Do you see an error message? Yes or no?"
D. "How often does this issue happen?"

65. A user is clearly frustrated. Which response BEST demonstrates professionalism and empathy?
A. "You must have done something wrong."
B. "Calm down, it's not a big deal."
C. "I understand this is frustrating. Let's see what we can do to fix it."
D. "This isn't my fault."

66. A user reports that only **their** PC cannot access the internet, while everyone else is fine. Which is the MOST logical initial focus?

A. Company-wide network outage
B. The user's local device network settings or cables
C. Global internet routing
D. The ISP's undersea cables

67. A common safety precaution when opening a desktop computer case is to:

A. Leave it plugged in and powered on
B. Work in a wet area for better cooling
C. Unplug power and avoid static discharge
D. Place drinks on top for convenience

68. Electrostatic discharge (ESD) precautions are used to:

A. Protect components from static electricity damage
B. Make components easier to see
C. Increase CPU speed
D. Clean dust from components

69. Why is it important to differentiate whether a problem affects many users or just one user?

A. To decide who should be fired
B. To determine if the issue is likely local or tied to shared systems
C. To change monitor brightness
D. To choose what printer to buy

70. A user thinks they might have malware on their system. Which action is MOST appropriate?

A. Download random "cleanup" tools from unknown websites
B. Turn off all security software
C. Report it according to company policy and wait for guidance
D. Email the suspicious files to coworkers

71. A support technician finishes a fix and immediately closes the ticket without verifying. This is a problem because:

A. Verification is unnecessary
B. The user might still have the issue or new issues caused by the fix
C. Tickets should never be closed
D. It makes the system too fast

72. A knowledge base in IT support is primarily used to:

A. Store hardware drivers only
B. Store documented solutions and troubleshooting steps for future reference
C. Hide information from new staff
D. Monitor network performance

73. A user working remotely on public Wi-Fi is required by company policy to use a VPN. The MAIN security benefit is that:

A. The VPN increases monitor brightness
B. The VPN encrypts traffic between the user and company network
C. The VPN speeds up all internet connections
D. The VPN replaces antivirus software

74. Which behavior is MOST aligned with good workplace ethics for IT staff?

A. Reading users' personal files out of curiosity
B. Sharing confidential information with friends
C. Only accessing data needed for work and keeping it confidential
D. Posting screenshots from user systems on social media
75. Which BEST describes the role of an entry-level IT support professional?
A. Working alone with no user contact
B. Combining basic technical skills with communication, documentation, and professionalism to support users
C. Writing advanced operating systems from scratch
D. Managing company strategy and legal compliance

Answer Key – With Reasoning & Section References

1. C – Printer
Hardware is physical components; a printer is a tangible device.
Ch 2.1 – What Is a Computer? (Hardware vs. Software)
2. B – CPU
The CPU performs calculations and executes instructions; it's the "brain" of the computer.
Ch 2.3 – Core Components: CPU, RAM, Storage
3. B – Temporary working memory used while the computer is running
RAM stores data currently in use; it's volatile and cleared when power is lost.
Ch 2.3 – Core Components: CPU, RAM, Storage
4. C – Monitor
The monitor outputs visual information from the computer to the user.
Ch 3.1 – Input vs. Output Devices
5. C – USB
Modern external drives typically use USB connections for data and power.
Ch 3.2 – Common Ports and Connectors
6. B – SSD
SSDs have no moving parts and provide faster access than HDDs or optical media.
Ch 4.1 – Storage Types and Performance
7. D – Terabyte (TB)
Order: KB < MB < GB < TB, so TB is largest.
Ch 4.2 – Capacity and Units (KB, MB, GB, TB)
8. B – Verify the power cable and power strip are connected and switched on
Always start with simple, low-risk checks like power and connections.
Ch 16.2 – Troubleshooting Methodology
9. B – A device or application that requests services from a server
Clients consume services; servers provide them.
Ch 5.1 – Clients, Servers, and Services
10. B – LAN
A local area network covers a limited area like one office or building.
Ch 5.2 – Network Types (LAN, WAN, etc.)
11. B – Router
Routers connect different networks, such as a LAN to the internet.
Ch 5.3 – Common Network Devices
12. B – A wireless networking technology
Wi-Fi is radio-based wireless networking.
Ch 5.2 – Network Types (LAN, WAN, etc.)
13. B – The user's device network settings or browser
If others on same Wi-Fi are fine, problem is likely local to that device or browser.
Ch 7.3 – Determining Scope of Network Problems
14. B – IP address
IP addresses identify devices on an IP network for routing.

Ch 5.4 – IP Addressing Basics

15. B – Ethernet or Wi-Fi

Network printers are typically connected via Ethernet or Wi-Fi so many devices can print.

Ch 3.4 – Printers and Print Options

16. B – Manage hardware resources and provide services to applications

The OS mediates between hardware and applications.

Ch 9.1 – What an Operating System Is and Does

17. B – Windows 11

Windows 11 is a desktop/laptop OS; Android/iOS are mobile.

Ch 9.2 – Desktop and Laptop Operating Systems

18. C – Android

Android is a mobile OS used on phones and tablets.

Ch 9.3 – Mobile Operating Systems

19. B – A spreadsheet application

.xlsx is a typical spreadsheet file extension.

Ch 9.5 – Files, Folders, and Extensions in the OS

20. C – Presentation software

Presentation tools are designed for slides and visual aids.

Ch 10.4 – Presentation Software

21. B – Spreadsheet

Spreadsheets are ideal for numeric tracking and calculations with charts.

Ch 10.3 – Spreadsheet Software

22. B – Save copies of web content to speed up future visits

Cache stores resources to avoid re-downloading, improving load times.

Ch 11.3 – Cookies, Cache, and Basic Privacy Concepts

23. B – Small data pieces that websites store to remember information like logins or preferences

Cookies store small pieces of site-specific information.

Ch 11.3 – Cookies, Cache, and Basic Privacy Concepts

24. B – Remote computing resources and services accessed over the internet

"The cloud" refers to remote services accessible via networks.

Ch 11.6 – What "The Cloud" Really Means

25. B – Real-time collaboration using a SaaS app

Cloud-based editors that support multiple simultaneous editors are SaaS collaboration tools.

Ch 10.6 – Collaboration Tools and Real-Time Editing

26. B – Monthly or yearly payment that includes ongoing access and updates

Subscriptions trade recurring fees for continued access and updates.

Ch 11.8 – Software Licensing Models (Deeper Dive)

27. B – The software has not been activated or assigned a valid license

"Unlicensed product" errors indicate licensing/activation problems, not hardware.

Ch 10.9 – Licensing, Subscriptions, and User Access

28. C – They can be accessed from multiple devices via a browser and are often updated automatically

Cloud apps are device-agnostic and provider-managed for updates.

Ch 11.7 – Cloud vs. Local Applications: Pros and Cons

29. A – Email client

Email clients handle sending, receiving, and organizing email.
Ch 10.5 – Email, Calendars, and Contacts
30. B – URL
The written web address is a URL (Uniform Resource Locator).
Ch 11.1 – What a Web Browser Is and Does
31. B – Human-readable instructions written in a programming language
Source code is what developers write before it's compiled/interpreted.
Ch 12.1 – What Programming Is (Big Picture)
32. B – A named storage location in memory that holds a value
Variables store data that can be read/updated during program execution.
Ch 12.4 – Variables and Data Types (Conceptual)
33. C – Boolean
Booleans represent true/false or yes/no states.
Ch 12.4 – Variables and Data Types (Conceptual)
34. A – Variables and an arithmetic operator
price and quantity are variables, * is an arithmetic operator.
Ch 12.5 – Operators and Basic Expressions
35. B – Make decisions based on a condition being true or false
If statements branch logic depending on conditions.
Ch 12.6 – Basic Logic: If/Then Decisions
36. B – AND
AND requires all combined conditions to be true.
Ch 12.7 – Logical Operators and Compound Conditions
37. B – Repeat a block of code multiple times
Loops are used for repetition.
Ch 12.8 – Loops and Repetition (Conceptual)
38. B – Structured, human-readable descriptions of program logic without strict syntax
Pseudocode describes logic in a language-neutral way.
Ch 12.9 – Pseudocode and Flowcharts
39. B – A decision point
Diamonds in flowcharts represent decisions/branches.
Ch 12.9 – Pseudocode and Flowcharts
40. B – Structured data stored in tables with fields and records for efficient search and reporting
That's the core idea of a database.
Ch 6.1 – What Is a Database?
41. B – Fields (columns) and records (rows)
Tables are organized with columns (fields) and rows (records).
Ch 6.2 – Tables, Fields, and Records
42. B – Runtime error
The program starts, but crashes when encountering missing resources at run time.
Ch 12.3 – Source Code, Syntax, and Errors
43. B – A small, task-focused program used for automation
Scripts automate repetitive tasks with short programs.
Ch 13.4 – Scripting vs. Full-Scale Programming

44. C – Get data → Apply logic → Produce results
That's the classic input → process → output pattern.
Ch 13.6 – Input, Processing, and Output in Scripts
45. B – An algorithm for password resets
It's a step-by-step procedure to handle a specific task—an algorithm.
Ch 13.1 – Algorithms in Everyday IT Work
46. B – Confidentiality
CIA = Confidentiality, Integrity, Availability.
Ch 14.1 – What Security Is Trying to Protect
47. B – Ensuring only authorized people can read information
Confidentiality protects against unauthorized disclosure.
Ch 14.1 – What Security Is Trying to Protect
48. B – Any malicious software designed to harm systems or data
Malware is a broad category for malicious software.
Ch 14.3 – Malware Basics: Viruses, Worms, and More
49. B – Encrypts data and demands payment to restore access
That's the hallmark behavior of ransomware.
Ch 14.3 – Malware Basics: Viruses, Worms, and More
50. A – Phishing
Fake messages pretending to be legitimate entities trying to steal data are phishing.
Ch 14.4 – Social Engineering and Phishing Attacks
51. B – Requiring two or more forms of verification
MFA adds extra verification factors beyond passwords.
Ch 14.5 – Passwords, Authentication, and Access Control Basics
52. B – Give users only the minimum access needed to do their jobs
Least privilege limits damage from misuse or compromise.
Ch 14.5 – Passwords, Authentication, and Access Control Basics
53. B – Attackers on the same network may be able to intercept traffic
Open Wi-Fi allows eavesdropping and man-in-the-middle attacks.
Ch 14.7 – Network and Wireless Security (High Level)
54. B – Ensure there is a recoverable copy of data after loss or damage
Backups support availability and recovery.
Ch 14.8 – Data Security, Backups, and Encryption Basics
55. B – Unreadable without the correct key
Encryption scrambles data so only key holders can read it.
Ch 14.8 – Data Security, Backups, and Encryption Basics
56. C – Cable lock on a laptop
Physical security controls access to devices themselves.
Ch 14.6 – Physical Security and Device Protection
57. B – Removing unnecessary services and applying secure settings
Hardening reduces attack surface and secures configuration.
Ch 15.1 – What "Hardening" a System Means
58. B – Make passwords harder to guess or crack
Length/complexity policies resist guessing and brute-force attacks.

Ch 15.5 – Secure Settings: Password Policies and Account Lockout

59. B – Brute-force password guessing

Lockouts slow/stop repeated login attempts.

Ch 15.5 – Secure Settings: Password Policies and Account Lockout

60. C – Report the incident to IT/security and follow company policy

Best practice is to involve security/IT, not pay or ignore ransomware.

Ch 15.9 – Incident Response Basics (User-Level)

61. B – Identify the problem and gather information

You must understand the issue before applying fixes.

Ch 16.2 – The Troubleshooting Methodology

62. B – Handles initial user contact and resolves common issues

Tier 1 deals with front-line issues and escalation.

Ch 16.1 – IT Support Roles and Responsibilities

63. B – It helps others see what has been tried and what resolved the issue

Documentation supports escalation, future reference, and knowledge-building.

Ch 16.4 – Documenting Issues and Resolutions

64. C – "Do you see an error message? Yes or no?"

Closed-ended questions elicit specific yes/no or limited responses.

Ch 16.3 – Asking Effective Questions and Active Listening

65. C – "I understand this is frustrating. Let's see what we can do to fix it."

Shows empathy and focuses on resolving the issue professionally.

Ch 16.8 – Customer Service, Professionalism, and Ethics

66. B – The user's local device network settings or cables

Scope suggests a local issue when only one user is affected.

Ch 16.7 – Basic Troubleshooting of Hardware, OS, and Network Issues

67. C – Unplug power and avoid static discharge

Unplugging and using ESD precautions protects both people and components.

Ch 16.9 – Safety Considerations in IT Support

68. A – Protect components from static electricity damage

ESD can damage sensitive electronics; precautions help prevent that.

Ch 16.9 – Safety Considerations in IT Support

69. B – To determine if the issue is likely local or tied to shared systems

Scope (one vs. many) guides where to troubleshoot first.

Ch 16.7 – Basic Troubleshooting of Hardware, OS, and Network Issues

70. C – Report it according to company policy and wait for guidance

Security incidents should follow formal reporting procedures.

Ch 15.9 – Incident Response Basics (User-Level)

71. B – The user might still have the issue or new issues caused by the fix

Verification confirms the solution actually worked and didn't create side effects.

Ch 16.2 – The Troubleshooting Methodology

72. B – Store documented solutions and troubleshooting steps for future reference

Knowledge bases support faster, more consistent resolutions.

Ch 16.4 – Documenting Issues and Resolutions

73. B – The VPN encrypts traffic between the user and company network

VPNs protect data in transit over untrusted networks.

Ch 15.7 – Mobile Device and Remote Work Security

74. C – Only accessing data needed for work and keeping it confidential

That's proper ethical handling of user data.

Ch 16.8 – Customer Service, Professionalism, and Ethics

75. B – Combining basic technical skills with communication, documentation, and professionalism to support users

Entry-level IT roles blend tech skills and soft skills to support users effectively.

Ch 16.10 – Being an Effective Entry-Level IT Professional

About the Author

CertiPrep Publishing specializes in high-quality certification exam prep books. We empower learners with expert resources to succeed in their professional certifications.

www.ingramcontent.com/pod-product-compliance
Lightning Source LLC
LaVergne TN
LVHW082333200926
848481LV00012B/3333